Refashioning Race

Refashioning Race

HOW GLOBAL COSMETIC SURGERY CRAFTS NEW BEAUTY STANDARDS

Alka V. Menon

UNIVERSITY OF CALIFORNIA PRESS

University of California Press
Oakland, California

Library of Congress Cataloging-in-Publication Data

Names: Menon, Alka V., 1987- author.
Title: Refashioning race : how global cosmetic surgery crafts new beauty
    standards / Alka V. Menon.
Description: Oakland, California : University of California Press, [2023] |
    Includes bibliographical references and index.
Identifiers: LCCN 2022042496 (print) | LCCN 2022042497 (ebook) |
    ISBN 9780520386709 (cloth) | ISBN 9780520386723 (paperback) |
    ISBN 9780520386730 (ebook)
Subjects: LCSH: Surgery, Plastic—History—21st century. | Race.
Classification: LCC RD119 .M486 2023 (print) | LCC RD119 (ebook) |
    DDC 617.9/52--dc23/eng/20220928
LC record available at https://lccn.loc.gov/2022042496
LC ebook record available at https://lccn.loc.gov/2022042497

Manufactured in the United States of America

32 31 30 29 28 27 26 25 24 23
10 9 8 7 6 5 4 3 2 1

To my grandparents, Krishna Baldev Vaid,
Champa Rani Vaid, and Veliath Rajam Menon

Contents

Figures and Tables

Acknowledgments

This book owes its existence to the support and generosity of people around the world. I am especially grateful to my study participants—plastic surgeons and patients in the U.S., Malaysia, and beyond—for taking the time to assist a graduate student.

This project began as a doctoral dissertation, and I owe a huge debt of gratitude to my dissertation committee—Steve Epstein, Carol Heimer, Carolyn Chen, and Wendy Griswold—for their immensely helpful advice and guidance. Steve's able tutelage has reliably pushed my writing and thinking beyond where I thought it could go. Other faculty members at Northwestern also contributed valuable insight, including Ken Alder, Wendy Espeland, Helen Tilley, Celeste Watkins-Hayes, Héctor Carrillo, Gary Alan Fine, Claudio Benzecry, Tony Chen, and Michael Rodríguez-Muñiz. My graduate cohort was and remains a source of delight and support, especially Anna Hanson, Carlo Felizardo, Hannah Wohl, Kangsan Lee, Iga Kozlowska, and Marcel Knudsen. Northwestern's Science in Human Culture Doctoral

Colloquium and Culture and Society Workshop repeatedly engaged with and strengthened this work.

So many brilliant scholars bent their minds toward improving this research, for which I am profoundly grateful. In selecting me for a Dissertation Development Research Fellowship on the Biotech Body at the Social Science Research Council, Susan Lindee and Karen-Sue Taussig jump-started this project. In addition to my cohort, Jaimie Morse, Jane Pryma, and Gemma Mangione pored over chapter drafts. In graduate school and afterward, I benefited from conversations with many scholars, including Brian Sargent, Mallory Fallin, Robin Bartram, Luciana de Souza Leão, Armando Lara-Millan, Robert Vargas, Dan Hirschman, Joan Robinson, Erica Banks, Omri Tubi, April Hovav, Ashley Mears, Ruha Benjamin, Ann Morning, Alondra Nelson, Dorothy Roberts, Anne Pollock, Tony Hatch, Kimberly Hoang, and Giselinde Kuipers. My writing group—Tess Lanzarotta, Rosanna Dent, and Katie Mas—was instrumental in propelling the manuscript through its final stages. And students in my Race, Medicine, and Technology seminar provided thoughtful comments on portions of the manuscript in fall 2021.

I revised this book as a new faculty member in the Yale sociology department. I thank Rene Almeling for guidance in navigating the transition and for her extensive comments on the book. I received valuable feedback from several Yale colleagues, including Julia Adams, Jeff Alexander, Phil Gorski, Phil Smith, Scott Boorman, Jonathan Wyrtzen, Steve Pitti, and Quan Tran. At Yale, the Comparative Research Workshop, the Council on Southeast Asian Studies, the Center for Race, Indigeneity and Transnational Migration, and the History of Science and History of Medicine Holmes Workshop have been great spaces for testing out ideas.

I am grateful for the financial support I received for data collection and analysis from the National Science Foundation (Grant SES-1556591) and Social Science Research Council. Additional funding was generously provided by the Buffett Institute for Global Affairs, The Graduate School, and the Medical Humanities and Bioethics Program at Northwestern University, and the Department of Sociology, the Council on Southeast Asian Studies, and the Whitney and Betty MacMillan Center for International and Area Studies at Yale University. My findings and conclusions are mine and do not reflect the views of these institutions.

For their administrative support, I thank Murielle Harris, Ryan Sawicki, and Julia Harris-Sacony at Northwestern University and Lisa Camera and Lauren Gonzalez at Yale University. Joanna Friedman helped me keep momentum on the project as a new assistant professor. Chloe Sariego, Uma Dwivedi, Fikir Mekonnen, and Samantha Larkin provided capable and much appreciated research assistance.

I am also indebted to my supportive editor, Naomi Schneider, and her wonderful assistants, Summer Farah and LeKeisha Hughes, at UC Press for their suggestions and patience.

An earlier version of chapter 1 appeared previously as Alka Menon, "Reconstructing Race in American Cosmetic Surgery," *Ethnic and Racial Studies* 40 (2017): 597–616. Portions of the material in chapters 3 and 4 appeared in different form in Alka Menon, "Cultural Gatekeeping in Cosmetic Surgery: Transnational Beauty Ideals in Multicultural Malaysia," *Poetics* 75 (2019): 1–11.

I could not have completed this project without the help of friends and family scattered near and far. Thank you to those who hosted me during my travels for research: J. P., Krishnanjali and Lakshmishree Menon, Rachna Vaid and Ramesh Jagannathan, Urvashi Vaid and Kate Clinton, Vijendra and Amrita Nambiar, and Jyotsna Uppal. Dr. Sulaiman bin Shaari, Vivehanantha P. N. Rajoo, Nandini Menon, and Raghav Menon also helped me find my footing in Malaysia. My extended family (the Vaids, Veliyaths, Menons, and Knudsens) have been incredibly supportive and patient. My parents and sibling (Jyotsna Vaid, Ramdas Menon, and Alok) challenged me early and often, making me a better thinker. They also read drafts and spent hours discussing cosmetic surgery with me. Finally, a shoutout to Renuka, who enlivened the final stages of editing (and every day since). And a special thanks to Marcel, who did so much labor, affective and otherwise, to make this book possible.

Abbreviations

AAFPRS	American Academy of Facial Plastic and Reconstructive Surgery
AMA	American Medical Association
ASAPS	American Society for Aesthetic Plastic Surgery
ASEAN	Association of Southeast Asian Nations
ASPS	American Society of Plastic Surgeons
FDA	Food and Drug Administration
IPRAS	International Confederation of Plastic Reconstructive and Aesthetic Surgery
ISAPS	International Society of Aesthetic Plastic Surgery
JAMA	*Journal of the American Medical Association*
JSAPS	Japan Society of Aesthetic Plastic Surgery
MAPACS	Malaysian Association of Plastic, Aesthetic and Craniomaxillofacial Surgeons
MSPRS	Malaysian Society of Plastic and Reconstructive Surgery
SAPS	Singapore Association of Plastic Surgeons

From Standardization to Customization

RACE IN COSMETIC SURGERY

In 2011, the *New York Times* published an article reporting on ethnic differences in plastic surgery, updating a theme it had first explored twenty years earlier. The report toured New York City clinics, cataloguing the different kinds of ideals and procedures that were requested across ethnic communities. They found surgeons "able to create the cleavage of Thalía, the Mexican singer, or the bright eyes of Lee Hyori, the Korean pop star." Among the many titillating anecdotes, one stood out to me. One of the interviewed plastic surgeons, Dr. Kaveh Alizadeh, remarked: "When a patient comes in from a certain ethnic background and of a certain age, we know what they're going to be looking for. We are sort of amateur sociologists."[1] Arguing that cosmetic surgeons were like sociologists, the analogy suggested that the expertise of cosmetic surgeons was not simply a matter of surgical technique; a core function was being able to generalize about what groups of people want. Dr. Alizadeh singled out ethnicity and age as particular categories of interest, while recognizing that such generalizations were not easy or unproblematic. He acknowledged, "The results can seem less like science than like stereotyping." When I encountered this news story, I was intrigued by the idea that cosmetic surgeons might claim expertise about ethnicity and race—or at least racial legibility on the body.

"Cosmetic surgery" is a term that refers to the constellation of elective, invasive surgical procedures performed by doctors to improve or enhance patients' physical appearance. It is a biomedical specialty that falls under the broader umbrella of plastic surgery, which includes procedures that restore appearance or physical function after illness or injury.[2] It is also a beauty practice, primarily undertaken by women. With the ascendance of "natural looking" ideals of beauty,[3] cosmetic surgeons have shifted from a one-size-fits-all approach that has historically promoted a white look for everyone, regardless of racial membership or nationality, to offering multiple, race-specific standards of beauty.

Those who have studied cosmetic surgery have, justifiably, focused first and foremost on patients. Patient race and gender, and how patients seek to realize these social identities through cosmetic surgery procedures, is an important lens of inquiry.[4] Even those who have been attentive to cosmetic surgeons have generally highlighted professional jurisdictional conflicts.[5] By foregrounding these issues, they have missed the key role that surgeons play in managing cultural associations between race and the body, particularly cross-nationally.

Dr. Alizadeh's remarks can be taken as a provocation to turn our attention to cosmetic surgeons, and more specifically, how they claim expertise in different contexts.[6] How do cosmetic surgeons generate and apply knowledge based on racial categories, and how is this process affected by transnational clinical and economic exchanges? How do they map physical features onto social identities like race, and with what consequences for those identities? And how do they navigate from patients' desires for racially legible appearances to specific surgical interventions? Following racial categories from the clinical encounter to the pages of medical journals, this book furnishes a new perspective on the relationship between bodies and social identities.

To answer these questions, I embarked upon months of fieldwork across the U.S. and Asia. I compared the expert discourse of cosmetic surgeons, aimed at a transnational audience, to the rules of thumb employed by practitioners. To capture expert discourse about race, I analyzed medical journals and international conferences. To understand the use of racial categories in practice, I interviewed cosmetic surgeons and patients in cities across two multiracial countries, the U.S. and Malaysia. Based on this fieldwork, I found that cosmetic surgeons used racial categories to balance between pressures to standardize clinical knowledge and customize looks for patients.[7] Racial categories facilitated communication transnationally with other experts and connections with potential patient-consumers. In addition to delimiting racial difference in the construction of standards of appearance, surgeons traded in the subjective, aesthetic dimensions of racial difference. Ultimately, the *use* of racial categories in cosmetic surgery is standardized, but not their *content*. In their discourse and practice, I argue, cosmetic surgeons refashion racial meaning.

In this book, the term "race" is a sociological concept with specific meaning. I adopt the social constructivist perspective that race is a social invention that changes over time and space, in contrast to the essentialist perspective that conceptualizes race as the sharing of some "inherent, innate, or otherwise fixed" qualities.[8] More specifically, I rely on Michael Omi and Howard Winant's definition of race as "an ordering discourse that systematically subordinates some types of bodies over others." They argue for a "corporeal dimension to the race-concept," calling race "ocular in an irreducible way."[9] Unlike the concept "ethnicity," which can also connote difference, race is closely tied to ranking, hierarchy, and implicit comparisons.[10] According to Omi and Winant's theory of racial formation, the racial structure of a society is the result of compounding and competing, historically situated "racial projects," which are efforts "in which human bodies and social structures are represented and organized."[11] Racial formations are typically thought of as national-level structures that are the result of historical processes. This study uses the case of cosmetic surgery to systematically examine race at one snapshot in time across geographic scales and different sites, situating race in transnational perspective. The malleability of race contributes to both durability and its appeal as an ordering category.[12]

Race has been theorized as multidimensional.[13] I argue that cosmetic surgery can be understood as a racial project that makes race material, identifiable, and coherent as an identity. I analyze cosmetic surgery as a multiscalar racial project, applying Alondra Nelson's insight that racial projects span "macro-, meso-, and micro-level processes." She calls for research "to traverse levels of scale from the microscopic, byte-sized 'molecularization' of 'race,'" to "the individual and collective lived experience of social identity, and to large-scale racialization."[14] This book traces the arc of racial meaning across these scales from the macro level of global expert discourse; to the meso level of collective, national-level understandings of race as a social identity in two sites (the U.S. and Malaysia); to the micro level of how cosmetic surgeons and patients interpersonally interpret and enact race on the body in the clinical encounter. By positing a scalar through line to the concept of racial projects, this book identifies a mechanism linking structural racism, racial stereotypes, interpersonal racial bias, and the body.

Cosmetic surgeons can be understood as a type of "race broker," intermediaries whose professional judgments about race help bridge the gap between structure and interpersonal interaction.[15] At the macro, global level in cosmetic surgery, cosmetic surgeons employ racial categories as expansive yet familiar constructs to coordinate communication of expertise across continents in journal articles and at international plastic surgery conferences. At the meso, national level, in specific countries like the U.S. and Malaysia, cosmetic surgeons describe and justify ideal and appropriate looks for patients using many of the same racial categories. And at the micro, interpersonal level, in the clinical encounter between doctor and patient, surgeons manifest racial categories visually on the body in specific physical features. At each of these levels, surgeons use racial categories to balance competing aims of standardization and customization. In the process of interpreting and enacting racial meaning, surgeons reshape them.

RACE, BEAUTY, AND THE BODY

When scholars write about racial projects, they often highlight undeniably consequential examples of racial inequality like mass incarceration, suppression of the Black vote, discriminatory policing, and vast disparities in health outcomes between Black, Latino/a, Asian, and white Americans. Beauty usually does not make the list. Beauty has a whiff of frivolity, vapidity, self-indulgence, and even hedonism about it. Especially in academia, beauty is seen as "somehow trivial, frivolous, or vulgar."[16] It is no coincidence that women, too, have been stereotyped this way.[17] Ordinary people and scholars alike tend to bracket beauty culture as not serious.

In this book, I make the case that like biomedicine, beauty is a key site where race is made material and embodied. Beauty is a critical part of the architecture of racial meaning, providing insight into the semiotics of race that would be missed with an exclusive focus on disease, crime, housing, or the law. Beauty is an aesthetic evaluation of physical appearance that ranks bodies hierarchically; it is a site in which race and class are manifested.[18] Often associated with and shared by members of a racial group, beauty ideals reflect and reinforce racism: the physical features, hairstyles, and clothing fashions of the racial group in power are often seen as more beautiful than those associated with those at the bottom of the social hierarchy. Many consumers purchase beauty products and services in order to conform to existing racial hierarchies and rise within them. And beauty practices like cosmetic surgery can be gendering as well as racializing: surgical procedures have been employed as a strategy to feminize, masculinize, rejuvenate, and/or whiten patients—as well as to affirm and express racial identity.[19] Racial hierarchies can also be challenged through beauty practices and assertions of local authenticity and distinctiveness. Like race, beauty is relational and changing. Narratives and counternarratives of beauty shed new light on the enduring relevance of race.

Appearance matters. Though even cosmetic surgeons echo the truisms that "beauty is in the eye of the beholder" or that "beauty comes from within," most societies put a premium on physical appearance. In pursuit of beauty, people worldwide underwent 11.3 million invasive surgical procedures in 2018, with Americans comprising about 1.3 million of that total.[20] The American Society of Plastic Surgeons estimates that over $23.7 billion was spent on cosmetic procedures in the U.S.[21] Disfigured or nonnormative appearances are associated with lower social status, leading to discrimination in hiring, lower wages, and even lengthened criminal sentences.[22] Conventionally speaking, cosmetic surgery is a beauty practice, engaged in by patients to enhance their physical appearance. Patients cite a range of motives, including a desire to remove racial markers, feminize (or masculinize) their appearance, or remove identifying features for a more "normal" appearance.[23] Some cosmetic surgery patients modify their physical appearance to better reflect what they envision as their internal self-image;[24] others believe that particular looks can lead to career success.[25]

Underlying many of these changes is a desire to improve social status. Investing in beauty is a form of building body capital, which can translate into potential for romantic relationships, workplace promotions, or other modes of social advancement.[26] Scholars like Debra Gimlin have characterized cosmetic surgery as a form of "body work" that people employ to shape their bodies, akin to exercise and dieting.[27] Investing in the body becomes a mode of self-expression, reflecting taste. By increasing physical attractiveness or approximating a normative appearance, body work helps build the social status, or "body capital," of clients or patients.[28] Body work has often been studied as it relates to gender, age, and class. However, practices like cosmetic surgery can also function as racial projects. Sociologist Sabrina Strings situates the beauty ideal of a slender appearance—so prevalent in the U.S and often portrayed as a universal ideal—in historical perspective as a racial project for white, middle-class American women.[29] As this example highlights, racial projects can be gendered and/or classed. And beauty and body work can intervene on gender, class, and race simultaneously.

In the case of cosmetic surgery specifically, many procedures have the goal of mitigating the effects of aging or enhancing culturally defined markers of femininity, and it is this angle that has received the most attention from scholars.[30] In this book, however, I focus on procedures conducted with aim of creating a new look for a patient, rather than those performed to restore a patient's past appearance. And I am especially attentive to procedures on body parts, including the nose and eyes, that cosmetic surgeons identify as "ethnically sensitive."[31] But in a certain sense, as Cressida Heyes notes, "all cosmetic surgery is ethnic."[32] In the course of my research, it became clear that several other procedures, like liposuction, buttocks augmentation, and breast augmentation, also advanced racial projects, as well as contributed to particular representations of classed femininity.

In addition to constituting a form of body work, cosmetic surgery has become an increasingly accessible and accepted luxury service. Public opinion polls indicate increasing acceptance of cosmetic surgery, particularly among those with greater media or vicarious exposure to the practice through family or friends.[33] Changing attitudes are perhaps both the product of and impetus behind the rise of television shows featuring the practice, such as *Nip/Tuck, Dr. 90210, Extreme Makeover, The Swan, Botched*, and *The Real Housewives*. Such programs popularize procedures while "educating" patients about what is possible to achieve with surgery.[34] Indeed, cosmetic surgery has had a symbiotic relationship with popular culture and traditional and social media, which create and disseminate beauty ideals as well as raise awareness that cosmetic surgery procedures may be necessary to achieve them.[35] While cosmetic surgery is a beauty practice and pop culture phenomenon, it is also a biomedical practice in which clinical knowledge and tools are enlisted in the service of producing conventionally beautiful, racially legible bodies.

RACIAL CATEGORIES, STANDARDIZATION, AND CLINICAL JUDGMENT IN THE CRAFT OF COSMETIC SURGERY

Analyzed as a biomedical specialty, cosmetic surgery illuminates the tension between two modes of reasoning and practice in medicine: science and art. These schemas loosely correspond to evidence-based standards and clinical judgment. Standards are "agreed-upon rules" constructed to achieve "uniformities across time and space."[36] By contrast, clinical judgment, comprised of surgeons' "practical, concrete clinical experience," is "biased by its own particularistic perspective," in Eliot Freidson's classic account.[37] Clinical judgment is often the foil for evidence-based standards, with an assumed gap between the art or customization it represents vis-à-vis the standardizing science of guidelines. At each level of analysis (the macro, meso, and micro) in cosmetic surgery, the tension between medicine as art and as science is on display in efforts to construct race-specific standards for diagnosis, care, and treatment. The craft of cosmetic surgery represents the negotiated outcomes of this tension, encompassing the combination of technical skill at manual manipulation and the judgment and interpretation necessary to apply standards.[38]

To unpack this tension, let us begin with the "science" or "standard" side. The term "biomedicine" emphasizes the standardizing, scientific trends epitomized by evidence-based medicine, which offers "universal, homogeneous, standardized approaches to patient care."[39] Evidence-based medicine codifies expertise in the form of guidelines based on precisely graded studies.[40] Standards, and especially evidence-based guidelines, are a solution that offers best practices to eliminate wide variation in strategies and outcomes.[41] Under a standardizing mindset, once a best or most effective treatment is known, ideally all physicians should adopt it, eliminating practice variation.[42] Rationalizing and grounding treatment decisions in science, standards can be a legitimizing tool for specialties and practices, particularly those at the margins.[43] Even weak, voluntary standards can have big effects, from changing the kinds of research questions pursued to reconfiguring clinical interactions between physicians and patients.[44] Standards and standardization are crystallizations of power structures. Whether or not they are associated with science, their very existence orders the world in particular ways.[45]

The impulse to generate standards using racial categories has a long history in biomedicine. Measuring and identifying physical variation as racial difference is a practice dating to the eighteenth century, done by scientists and governments to tabulate and divide populations. In the nineteenth century, the science of physiognomy matched measurements of individuals' features to character profiles, making claims about groups based on appearance.[46] Anthropometry, or the science of body measurement, catalogued differences in skull sizes and shapes, submitting them as evidence of the superiority of white men over other people. Physical anthropologists started by measuring heads and moved on to other body parts.[47] Though many of these approaches have been discredited, the historical legacies of this way of thinking about race and bodies are still with us in racial categorization schemes.

These longstanding associations between race and the body both constrain and motivate how individuals signal racial identities today, particularly in modern consumer culture. People share common understandings of visual cues for race, invoking hair color and texture, skin color, physical features, and more. Individuals can signal collective identities, including racial group membership, through purchasing decisions that modify these cues, including fashion, hair styling, and (as cosmetic surgery makes possible) physical features. As Alexander Edmonds argues in his study of cosmetic surgery in Brazil, identities, especially racial identities, "are often defined and visualized in consumer culture—a social domain oriented toward 'appearances' and aesthetics."[48] Rather than reflecting ancestry or heritage, identity can be purchased, put on, and repeatedly (ex)changed.

Indeed, associations between physical markers and race appear widely in popular culture. Using caricatures of physical features to mark and stand in for stigmatized groups is a longstanding practice, including such iconic and pernicious stereotypes as large, hooked noses for Jewish people and broad lips for Black people in the U.S. and Europe. From cartoons to minstrel acts and traveling circuses, popular culture has reinforced and perpetuated these associations, as have overtly racist political advertisements.[49] In the U.S., Black people have faced extreme scrutiny of their appearance, even as Black identity is associated with a huge degree of variation in appearance.[50] The characteristics of the body have often been considered as evidence of membership in a racial category. Racial pride and nationalist movements have reclaimed and embraced some physical markers of race as a sign of affiliation and pride, like the Afro hairstyle. These social movements brought about a cultural transformation that critiqued some beauty practices, including surgical procedures, for attempting to make people appear white or whiter.[51]

Amidst a turn to multiculturalism, which explicitly recognized and foregrounded racial and ethnic difference, a space opened up for a reenvisioning of beauty and a coexistence of beauty ideals. In the U.S., this cultural moment was followed by a backlash. Another social norm ascended—colorblindness, an ideology associated with minimization of racism which "explains contemporary racial inequality as the outcome of nonracial dynamics."[52] In response, the watchword for acknowledging social difference in the U.S. has become "diversity," in which racial difference is one of many kinds of social and cultural differences to be recognized. Under the schema of diversity, "ethnic ambiguity," or nonspecific assertions of difference from the white category, also became culturally legible and available as a representation of race.[53]

The niche of racially sensitive cosmetic surgery has come into its own amidst these changes. Operating between poles of multicultural racial pride and colorblindness, "ethnic cosmetic surgery" is one example of the broader emergence and marketing of racially sensitive products and services signaled by and through physical markers on the body. Drawing on these associations, patients and cosmetic surgeons can use the tools of medicine to fashion embodied, modern racial and gendered identities. Cosmetic surgery is one way to realize Donna Haraway's metaphor of the cyborg, "a cybernetic organism, a hybrid of machine and organism . . . who populate[s] worlds ambiguously natural and crafted."[54] Embracing the possibility of self-authorship and hybridity, Haraway paves the way for recognizing prosthetics, implants, and surgical interventions as part of a deliberately fashioned identity.

Industries like media and marketing have capitalized on these associations, creating ideals, representations, and models that set aspirations for how cyborg subjects might modify themselves to appear. Advertisers have used physical archetypes to strategically highlight or at least imply racial diversity. Arlene Davila shows how advertising firms marshal features like skin color and hair texture to evoke notions of Latinidad. She finds that marketing executives share a belief in the existence of a "generic 'Latino look'" that any Hispanic can recognize and identify upon seeing," one that includes "long straight hair . . . [and] just enough oliveness to the skin to make them not ambiguous."[55] Cultural gatekeepers attempt to balance the distinct value of specific "ethnic" features with the possibility of broad transnational appeal.[56] These representations of racial difference are presented as material and naturalized on the body, while the historical and cultural forces that gave them meaning are obscured or erased. Representations of bodies are important; images have the power to shape consumers' and surgeons' desires.

Within biomedicine, racial categories help balance standardization and customization, as Steven Epstein's book *Inclusion* shows. He identifies "niche standardization" as a form of generating knowledge at the level of intermediate-sized groups like race, rather than for all humans or for individuals.[57] Niche standardization leads to the proliferation of several more specific standards rather than one universal standard for everyone. It is a solution devised by experts attempting to impose order and respond to different stakeholder demands, and it reflects the reality that some variation in treatment will persist. Epstein traces how civil rights and grassroots activists lobbied for U.S. clinical research to systematically account for racial and ethnic difference, among other kinds, in biomedical research.[58] Importantly, calls for the standardization of categories of difference in biomedicine have come from the very people about whom knowledge is being generated. That is, the push to generate and apply knowledge in terms of racial categories was at least initially driven by communities of color. In order for a niche category like a racial category to be useful across spheres (e.g., beauty/consumer culture, politics, and biomedicine), categorization schemes must be made to line up and overlap, a process Epstein calls "categorical alignment work."[59] In the case of cosmetic surgery, racial categorization schemes based on physical differences must be reconciled and negotiated with sociopolitical and cultural categorization schemes for race.

Once generated, *applying* biomedical standards, especially race-specific ones, requires another balancing act. In practice, standards start to look a lot less standard. Stefan Timmermans and Marc Berg advance the paradoxical concept of "local universality" to reflect how standards in practice may vary.[60] In deciding when and how to apply race-specific standards to individual patients, physicians use clinical judgment,[61] navigating significant uncertainties about healing and care.[62] Though critics of evidence-based medicine feared it would reduce practice to a rote, cookbook recipe approach to medicine, physicians have shown themselves to be more adept.[63] Clinical judgment has preserved a role for innovation, autonomy, and creativity in medicine, even alongside the development of race-specific guidelines and standards.[64] This has especially been the case in cosmetic surgery, a field which prides itself on its artistry.[65] Tailoring the idiosyncrasies of each patient to the particularities of treatments remains a key clinical function even with the considerable codification and standardization of contemporary medicine. Demands from patients for novelty and new forms of expression spur surgeons to consider racial categories less as binding standard strictures and more as loose, subjective frames that allow them to diversify in order to compete in the market. Promising customization along the lines of racial categories, ambiguously defined, can advance clinical science, shore up medical authority,[66] and establish a clear brand identity for surgeons. Clinical judgment or discretion is thus a central element of the craft of medicine. In cosmetic surgery, techniques, physical features, and expertise are racially labeled not simply for purposes of standardization and objectification, but also to carve out space to maintain subjectivity and variation.

Even as cosmetic surgery demonstrates the mutability and flexibility of the body, it is a permanent change. Surgeons use biomedical knowledge to create physical outcomes that signal socially legible racial and gendered identities. These are certainly not the only relevant social identity categories in cosmetic surgery: age, sex, socioeconomic status, and nationality are also important and intersect with race.[67] However, to show how cosmetic surgery is a scalar racial project that is shaped by factors at the macro, meso, and micro levels, my analysis primarily dwells on moments of tension and contradiction that bring racial dynamics into sharp relief. This book shows how cosmetic surgeons and patients arrive at a surgical look, what they call it, and how they graft bodies onto new or existing social identities.

THE CASE OF COSMETIC SURGERY

At each level of analysis, cosmetic surgery serves as a case for highlighting different phenomena of sociological interest. Most elementally, cosmetic surgery is a good case for examining how bodies become racialized. Social scientists have systematically tracked shifting notions of racial meaning.[68] This book takes the position that racial categories are not pre-given biological entities, reducible to physical features or shared sequences of DNA. Rather, cosmetic surgeons, like some other physicians and biomedical researchers,[69] import and translate racial categories from social life into biomedicine and, sometimes, onto the body. They also incorporate physical features and biological markers into racial definitions and categorization schemes, a phenomenon I have elsewhere called the biological construction of social difference.[70] Racial categories are sociological facts that, when written onto the body, come to be seen as naturalized. This book theorizes about race and bodies in their physicality while continuing to demonstrate that there is nothing immutable, eternal, or bounded by which to delineate race on bodies.

Cosmetic surgery is also a case to explore how medical expertise varies and circulates transnationally. Common procedures originated in different countries and then spread: liposuction as we know it today is credited to French innovation, and body contouring techniques were pioneered in South America. Particular countries have become famous for cosmetic surgery. South Korea has proclaimed expertise in cosmetic surgery in a discourse of "medical nationalism," fusing a style of plastic surgery to national pride.[71] Likewise, Brazil touts the beauty of its citizens and the skills of its plastic surgeons.[72] Rather than examining cosmetic surgery within one national context,[73] this work is inspired by scholarship that follows technological objects across borders.[74] Juxtaposing multiple sites separated by both geographic and cultural distance, this book answers the call for transnational and comparative research to better elucidate the cultural authority of health and medicine.[75] Cross-national comparison allows me to tell a new story about how flows of expertise and beauty ideals in multiple directions can stabilize the ongoing use of racial categories.

Finally, at the highest level of analysis, this book situates cosmetic surgery as a case of biomedicalization, a set of key shifts within medicine identified by Adele Clarke and colleagues. Biomedicalization is characterized by a persistent tension between forces for standardization and customization. Biomedical knowledge, technologies, services, and capital are co-constituted in cosmetic surgery, with trends toward increased commercialization and the production of new identities through and related to biomedical technologies.[76] Biomedicalization theory argues that contemporary biomedicine furnishes a basis for differentiating human kinds, along with customized health solutions to address them—available for a price. This is illustrated by technologies aimed at race-specific markets from genetic ancestry tests to apps to pharmaceutical drugs. Because cosmetic surgery treatment is elective and non-acute, prospective patients can shop around. Surgeons compete to attract patients through word-of-mouth referrals and marketing.[77] Price differentials and regulatory differences have helped cosmetic surgery tourism take off—and made cosmetic surgery more accessible to working- and middle-class patients in wealthier countries.[78]

At the same time, cosmetic surgery differs in important ways from other kinds of biomedical specialties. It lacks some of the institutional oversight by hospitals and insurance companies that governs much of modern medicine: surgeons may operate in standalone clinics, and patients do not necessarily require a referral from another physician to obtain cosmetic surgery. In most countries, cosmetic surgery must be paid for out of pocket by patients, though health insurance schemes in parts of South America and Europe occasionally cover cosmetic surgery as a treatment for low self-esteem.[79] The consumerism of this practice is partially what demarcates cosmetic surgery from the larger field of plastic surgery. To a greater extent than other physicians, cosmetic surgeons are seen by the general public as driven primarily by financial rather than professional motives. And indeed, cosmetic surgeons are well compensated: a 2019 Medscape report estimated the salary of a U.S. cosmetic surgeon to be about $471,000, substantially higher than the salary of $237,000 that a U.S. primary care physician earns on average.[80] Though cosmetic surgery is perhaps further along the continuum of medical consumerism, its unique features help illuminate the potential effects and implications of biomedicalization, especially in medical specialties that also allow patients leeway in their choice of provider.

SITE, SETTING, AND APPROACH

Malaysia and the U.S.

To develop a framework for analyzing cosmetic surgery as a transnational racial project, I focus on two primary sites, the U.S. and Malaysia. Each country has multiple sizeable racial minorities, a robust middle class, and a stated commitment to multiculturalism.[81] And in both countries, locals consider racial groups as discrete, bounded entities, along the lines listed in figure 1, rather than as occurring along a racial continuum. The U.S. is the largest cosmetic surgery market in the world, with the highest number of procedures performed.[82] Malaysia is a small cosmetic surgery market in its own right, but attracts medical tourist patients from around East Asia, the Middle East, and Australia/New Zealand. The Malaysian government has invested in medical tourism as an area for economic growth, with cosmetic surgery as one specialty that benefits. Unlike South Korea or Brazil, which are globally recognized for innovation in cosmetic surgery, neither the U.S. nor Malaysia is seen by surgeons as a most cutting-edge market.[83] The sheer size of the U.S. commands influence, while Malaysia occupies a smaller niche in the global medical tourist marketplace, treating patients from around the world. This niche, I found, afforded Malaysian surgeons a more

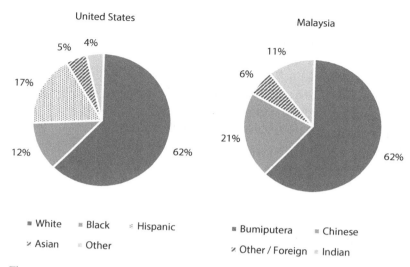

Figure 1. Racial composition of the U.S. and Malaysia, 2016. *Source:* American Community Survey Demographic and Housing Estimates, 5-Year Estimates Data Profiles (Table DP05), U.S. Census Bureau (2016); Office of Chief Statistician Malaysia, "Current Population Estimates, 2014–2016," Department of Statistics Malaysia (2016).

concrete and explicit perspective on white patients compared to their U.S. counterparts.

Malaysia has a population of about 32 million people and portrays itself on its tourism website as "Asia in miniature," elaborating: "There is only one place where all the colours, flavours, sounds, and sights of Asia come together. No other country has Asia's three major races, Malays, Chinese, and Indian as well as various other races." The majority racial group is *bumiputera*, comprised mostly of ethnic Malays and members of indigenous groups, or *orang asli*.[84] Malaysia also has Chinese and Indian minorities and a growing number of foreign workers from all over the world.[85] As Shirley Sun writes of the region, these "categories were significantly generated by historical colonial encounters—that is, they are not biologically coherent categories."[86] Indeed, contemporary Malaysian race relations were shaped by the colonial policies of Great Britain, from which it gained independence in 1957. The British brought in Indian and Chinese laborers to work in some occupations, excluding the prior Malay inhabitants.[87] To redress these imbalances, the Malaysian Constitution granted special privileges for *bumiputera*. Until 2016, when the multiethnic opposition briefly transitioned into power, Malaysia was ruled by a political coalition headed by the United Malays National Organization. Continuing imbalances in the distribution of resources among groups has led to persistent racial tensions, but the country has enjoyed relative stability and has been following on the economic heels of the Asian Tigers. Malaysia has been transitioning toward privatization of its health system in recent years, though it has historically delivered good health outcomes through investment in a public system.[88]

The U.S. is a large, racially diverse country with a population of almost 320 million, wealthier than Malaysia but characterized by significant economic and racial inequality. The U.S. racial structure has historically been divided between Blacks and whites. However, amidst transformations in immigration, the U.S. is increasingly moving toward a tripartite racial structure of Black, brown, and white.[89] For purposes of administration, the official U.S. government identifies the following racial and ethnic categories, which are also in lay, policy, and clinical use: White, Black, or African American; American Indian and Alaska Native; Asian; Native Hawaiian or Other Pacific Islander and Hispanic or Latino.[90] The multiracial composition and racial formation of the U.S. is the outcome of settler colonialism, forced migration and enslavement, and the exclusion of immigrants.[91] The U.S. racial structure has also been shaped by its military and quasi-colonial relationships with a variety of territories beyond the continental landmass of North America, from Hawaii to Puerto Rico, the Philippines to South Korea.[92]

In fact, U.S. plastic surgery developed in conjunction with American military engagements, first in World War II and the ensuing occupation of Japan, and subsequently in the American military interventions in Korea and Vietnam. U.S. plastic surgeons treated battlefield injuries as well as correcting congenital abnormalities and performing cosmetic procedures as a gesture of goodwill. The U.S. healthcare system is vast, fragmented, and heavily dependent on private insurance and private provision of care.

Cosmetic Surgery by the Numbers

The ranks of cosmetic surgeons are less racially diverse than the populations of the U.S. and Malaysia. In the U.S., most cosmetic surgeons are white, though the proportion of some racial minorities, especially Asian Americans, has been increasing.[93] In Malaysia, racial minorities like Malaysian Chinese and Malaysian Indians represent a greater proportion of plastic surgeons (40% and 14%) than their share of the general population (23% and 7%), with *bumiputera* and/or Malay surgeons (46%) comparatively underrepresented.[94] In 2015, more than 75% of practicing cosmetic surgeons in the U.S. and Malaysia were men, resembling trends worldwide. A greater proportion of Malaysian cosmetic surgeons were women (25%) than U.S. cosmetic surgeons (16%).[95] The racial and gender demographics of my respondents are detailed in the methodological appendix. Many of the U.S. plastic surgeons specialized in cosmetic surgery, with some subspecializing further on parts of the body like the face or breast. The Malaysian plastic surgeons were more often generalists, performing both reconstructive and cosmetic procedures all over the body. In both countries, most patients were women.

Reliable statistics in cosmetic surgery are hard to come by, but plastic surgery professional societies offer some orienting insight into the field.[96] These societies distinguish between minimally invasive procedures, which can be performed in an office setting and have a more temporary effect on the body (e.g., the injection of neurotoxins or fillers into the face) and surgical or invasive procedures, which are more permanent interventions requiring more time and

Table 1   Most Popular Cosmetic Surgery Procedures, 2014–2017

Worldwide	U.S.	Malaysia
Breast augmentation	Breast augmentation	Liposuction
Liposuction (fat removal)	Liposuction	Blepharoplasty
Blepharoplasty (eyelid surgery)	Rhinoplasty	Rhinoplasty
Rhinoplasty (nose surgery)	Blepharoplasty	Breast augmentation
Abdominoplasty (tummy tuck)	Abdominoplasty	Abdominoplasty

SOURCE: 2017 statistics released by the International Society of Aesthetic Plastic Surgery, the American Society for Aesthetic Plastic Surgery, and the author's interviews with Malaysian plastic surgeons in 2014–2016.

specialized skill and facilities. Annually, about 30% of all cosmetic surgical procedures occur in Asia, and about 18% occur in the U.S. Asia is the fastest-growing market for cosmetic surgery.[97] The majority of patients worldwide, 85%, are women.[98] In the U.S., women accounted for 90% of surgical procedures, and patients of color accounted for about 32% of procedures in 2017. Patients of color have grown as a share of the broader market over the last twenty years.[99] With the aid of installment payment plans, specialized medical credit vehicles, and falling prices, cosmetic surgery has become more accessible to middle-class patients in both the U.S. and Malaysia. The most popular invasive surgical procedures are listed in table 1.

Cosmetic surgery relies on similar facilities, materials, and knowledge around the world, and the tools for the craft of cosmetic surgery—cameras, scalpels, anesthesia, and, in some cases, implants—are widely available in high- and middle-income settings. Of course, cosmetic surgery is also constrained by the structure and cost of healthcare in specific places. The U.S. is one of the few countries to permit direct-to-consumer advertising of medical services and pharmaceutical products. Bolstered by FDA regulation of medical devices such as implants,[100] U.S. cosmetic surgeons portray their services as fundamentally reliable and safe. Because of its perceived safety and cultural iconicity, the U.S. is a powerful draw for many wealthy prospective cosmetic surgery patients.[101] In fact, medical tourism to the U.S. exceeds the revenues and traveler volumes of any other country.[102] Even so, most of the U.S market for cosmetic surgery is comprised of Americans: only about 5% of cosmetic surgery patients in 2016–2018 were medical travelers from overseas.[103] Seeking specific looks and good value, Americans also travel within the U.S. to obtain cosmetic surgery, undergoing over 18.4 million procedures in 2019.[104] The reputation of U.S. cosmetic surgery and a higher cost of living allow U.S. surgeons to garner premium prices for their services.[105]

As table 2 shows, absolute prices for cosmetic surgery in the U.S. in 2015–2016 were more expensive than the cost of procedures in Malaysia, though the prices were more comparable after adjusting for GDP per capita.[106] The U.S. is widely known to have high healthcare costs,[107] and cosmetic surgery is no exception to this trend.[108] Compared with U.S. cosmetic surgeons, Malaysian cosmetic surgeons are more legally constrained in their efforts to advertise their services directly to consumers. However, boosted by permissive regulatory regimes and active government investment,[109] international medical travel has broadened the potential geographic scope of Malaysian surgeons and their competitors. Malaysia's liberal visa policies have enabled a range of visitors to come for shopping and surgery trips with their families.[110] The cost of procedures in Malaysia is less expensive than the cost in the U.S. and roughly on par with regional competitors like Thailand.[111] Within Asia, which is the fastest growing market for both cosmetic surgery and medical tourism, Malaysia's market niche is providing safe cosmetic surgery at moderate prices. Like prevalence statistics, prices can also be hard to find. Few surgeons post prices on their websites. Many cosmetic surgeons require patients to undergo an initial consultation to receive a customized estimate, and many patients consult with multiple surgeons before committing to one.

Table 2   Total Cost for Cosmetic Surgery Procedures in the U.S. and Malaysia, 2015–2016

	U.S.	% of GDP per capita	Malaysia	% of GDP per capita
Breast augmentation	$11,100	20%	$4,700	38%
Blepharoplasty	$5,800	10%	$1,100	9%
Rhinoplasty	$10,600	19%	$2,500	20%
Abdominoplasty	$10,000	18%	$4,700	38%
Gluteal fat transfer	$10,300	19%	N/A	—

Cost estimates are averages in U.S. dollars from the total cost of procedures reported by surgeons in interviews, including facility/anesthesia fees. GDP per capita figures are constant 2010 U.S. dollars as reported by the World Bank (Malaysia, $12,487; U.S., $55,753). See https://data.worldbank.org/indicator/NY.GDP.PCAP.KD.

Methodological Approach

Between 2012 and 2020, I interviewed cosmetic surgeons and patients in the U.S. and Malaysia, observed their interactions, attended professional medical conferences, and analyzed medical publications. Studying race in cosmetic surgery at the macro, meso, and micro levels of analysis required a multimethod, multisited approach and enabled a variety of comparisons: between expert discourse and everyday generalizations, surgeon-patient discussions in the U.S. versus Malaysia, and formal professional statements versus informal generalizations.

To answer my research question about how cosmetic surgeons generally map physical features onto social identities like race, I conducted sixty semi-structured interviews with board-certified plastic and facial plastic surgeons in the U.S. and Malaysia. Interviews are particularly useful for capturing "representations, classification systems, boundary work, identity, imagined realities and cultural ideals."[112] Interviews allowed me to capture surgeons' narrative accounts of their work. Different interview questions addressed the macro, meso, and micro levels of analysis. I searched for repeated patterns, themes, and rules across respondents to piece together continuities and divergences in the use of racial categories. I recruited respondents by inviting members from national and regional plastic surgery and facial plastic surgery professional societies to participate in a study about social identities and cosmetic surgery. This strategy meant my respondents were the most elite, highly trained licensed practitioners of cosmetic surgery. Almost all interviews were conducted in person in cosmetic surgeons' clinics, allowing me to tour facilities and browse before-and-after photographs of former patients. To supplement surgeons' accounts, I conducted interviews with fourteen cosmetic surgery patients and performed a qualitative content analysis of online reviews written by patients about their own experiences undergoing surgery.

To assess how cosmetic surgeons generated and applied clinical knowledge about race at the macro, global level, I supplemented interview data with content analysis of medical journal articles about rhinoplasty and participant observation of professional plastic surgery conferences. These sites hosted discussions among experts, shedding light on how cosmetic surgeons used racial categories with their peers. Specifically, I collected and analyzed 203 race-specific medical journal articles about rhinoplasty published between 1993 and 2019 by surgeons from the around the world. I also observed the proceedings of plastic surgery conferences in Singapore, Boston, Las Vegas, and Kyoto, where I attended scientific and business sessions and browsed the exhibit hall. Milling about with cosmetic surgeons and staff, I perused sample medical devices like implants, evaluated sales pitches, collected advertisements and informational brochures, and informally interviewed vendors.

Finally, to understand how surgeons navigated from patients' desires for their appearance with respect to race to specific surgical interventions, I gathered additional data from ethnographic observation of cosmetic surgery clinics. I spent one month observing consultations between cosmetic surgeons and individual prospective patients in two different Malaysian clinics. I shadowed one male and one female plastic surgeon through their daily activities, including all consultations with patients for which the patients consented to my presence. In the clinic, I witnessed the embodiment and interpersonal enactment of racial categories. Together, this combination of qualitative research methods offers a snapshot of cosmetic surgery and racial categories across levels of analysis. I include more detail about my fieldwork in the methodological appendix.

In an investigation of the role of race and gender in cosmetic surgery, my own physical appearance, race, gender, nationality, and status as a student were central to how respondents perceived and reacted to me as a researcher. As a woman in my twenties, I was in the prime demographic of a potential rhinoplasty patient. From my accent, I am readily identifiable as American. U.S. cosmetic surgeons read me as a young woman of color based on my appearance, and Malaysian cosmetic surgeons further guessed at my South Asian heritage. Before stepping into cosmetic surgery clinics, I enlisted the help of savvy friends and makeup tutorials to get up to speed on beauty culture and to ensure that I appeared sufficiently professional. Their guidance allowed me to fit in (or at least not stand out) in plastic surgery waiting rooms and increased my awareness of the beauty trends cosmetic surgeons and patients discussed.

Though I had not visited Malaysia before conducting this research, my racial heritage and family ties to the region gave me a legible place in its racial structure. During interviews in both countries, cosmetic surgeons occasionally referred to my physical features or cultural background to illustrate a point—almost always in a way complimentary to me, for instance, emphasizing the ideal spacing of my eyes or the prominence of my nasal bridge. Somewhat to my surprise, most cosmetic surgeons framed participation in my study as a way to give back to the profession while also helping out a student. This introduced a question: did senior, male cosmetic surgeons play up their experiences to impress me? In the end, I do not think so. I heard cosmetic surgeons similarly extol their own capabilities to their peers and to patients, too, in their articles, presentations, websites, consultations with patients, and their interactions with their office staff. Indeed, questions about the interplay between cosmetic surgeons' discourse and practice, narrative and action, served to motivate and enrich the study.

CHAPTER OVERVIEW

This book is divided into two parts. Part 1, covering expert discourse at the global, macro level, discusses cosmetic surgeons' efforts to standardize racial categories, generating a science of racial difference. Part 2 examines how surgeons generalize about and enact race in practice across the U.S. and Malaysia (meso level) and with specific patients in the clinic (micro level).

Chapter 1 presents an analysis of multiple race-specific standards for aesthetic noses in medical journal articles. Written by cosmetic surgeons from around the world for their peers, the articles also included techniques for achieving, for instance, the ideal "Asian American" or "mestizo" nose. Surgeons described the development of racial types as a way of "preserving patients' ethnicity" and explained them as a response to changing racial demographics in the global market for cosmetic surgery. Turning from a comparison of different racial standards for one physical feature, chapter 2 offers an in-depth look at how one racial category, "Asian," is applied to multiple different features. At international conferences, cosmetic surgeons sketched out "Asian cosmetic surgery" as a set of techniques and a style of surgery rooted in particular cultural and historical lineages, distinguishing it from cosmetic surgery in the U.S., South America, and Europe. This chapter situates the construction of expertise about Asian cosmetic surgery within a larger economic, political, legal, and cultural context. While the use of the category "Asian" coordinated communication, its definition was also ambiguous and subjective enough to maximize surgeons' commercial and cultural reach.

In practice, both U.S. and Malaysian cosmetic surgeons used some of the same racial categories that appear in part 1. However, they largely eschewed quantified racial standards when translating them into lay discourse. Instead, they showcased their unique aesthetic sense and clinical judgment by elaborating upon racial differences to customize looks for patients. Chapter 3 highlights similarities between surgeons in the two countries, showing how U.S. and Malaysian cosmetic surgeons both acted as gatekeepers to "natural," racially legible appearances. While U.S. cosmetic surgeons upheld racial boundaries between racial categories like "white," "Latino," "Asian," and "Black" in assessing ideal looks, Malaysian cosmetic surgeons maintained a boundary between "Asian" versus "Western" or "white" looks. Their boundary work also revealed the different standpoints of cosmetic surgeons within each country with respect to global expert discourse: U.S. surgeons were primarily inward looking, focusing on national conversations about racial difference, whereas Malaysian surgeons described looks against the backdrop of the region and even the world. In asserting a preference for a natural "Asian" look, for instance, Malaysian cosmetic surgeons aligned themselves with regional expertise and innovation in cosmetic surgery.

Chapter 4 contrasts how cosmetic surgeons in the U.S. and Malaysia used racial categories and imagery to build brands that set themselves apart from competitors. In both countries, surgeons used racial categories to signal customization. In the U.S., invoking regional stereotypes of places (like the curvy, "international" Miami look), cosmetic surgeons marketed branded looks with racialized undertones. In Malaysia, cosmetic surgeons promised patients culturally sensitive experiences at reasonable prices. Boosted by professional societies and medical tourism advertising by the national government, Malaysian cosmetic surgeons aimed to attract cosmopolitan medical travelers alongside a diverse range of local Malaysians. Finally, chapter 5 takes a closer look at the everyday clinical practice of customizing bodies. With cameras, photographs, and prosthetics, cosmetic surgeons and patients choose whether and how to make racial categories visible in the clinical encounter, subject to the technological affordances and assumptions built in to the tools of their trade.

The conclusion returns to some of the core themes of the book regarding race and the tension between standardization and customization (or, as surgeons might frame it, between science and art). In cosmetic surgery, top-down and bottom-up forces converge to relate racial categories to physical features, surgical techniques, and beauty ideals. By presenting a cross-sectional snapshot of racial meaning at the global, national, and interpersonal levels, this book identifies mechanisms by which racial meaning is stabilized—and, for that matter, changed. The conclusion draws out the larger implications of understanding racial projects as crossing sociological levels of analysis and international boundaries. As biomedicine continues to be changed by globalization, increasing commodification, and diminishing state oversight, cosmetic surgery might be a harbinger of the future of race in medicine.

ON JUDGMENT

Cosmetic surgery is a morally fraught subject. The incidence of cosmetic surgery is on the rise and access to it has expanded in recent decades. Yet the practice remains stigmatized, eliciting both voyeuristic fascination and moral judgment. To be sure, there are many reasons to regard the field with suspicion. Feminist scholarship has critically analyzed cosmetic surgery as a gendered mode of control that promotes adherence to a conventional aesthetic of young, white femininity.[113] Cosmetic surgery changes which kinds of bodies we see as natural or ideal, raising expectations for how people, especially women, should appear.[114] The standards of appearance that cosmetic surgeons promote can be unrealistic, and prey on the insecurities of people—whether that is along the lines of gender, race, or age.

However, the goal of this book is not to condemn or rehabilitate cosmetic surgeons, or argue for or against people undergoing cosmetic surgery. This book uses the case of cosmetic surgery to illustrate how professionals engage in race-making and reshaping, situating these acts within transnational networks of biomedicine, aesthetics, and commerce.[115] By focusing attention on how surgeons themselves make normative judgments about race and gender, I illuminate larger cultural processes of judgment and evaluation by medical professionals. My respondents, who were the most highly trained, elite subset of the field, were more reflexive than past scholarship led me to expect. Counter to the assumptions held by many academics, cosmetic surgeons were not willing to perform just any procedure for the right price. Many cosmetic surgeons acknowledged and, in some cases, adjusted their behavior to address critiques from feminist and racial justice activism. In fact, instead of rigidly adhering to biologized conceptions of identities like race and gender, surgeons considered both social identities and bodies as potentially malleable. It is thus all the more noteworthy that none of the cosmetic surgeons I interviewed was ready to radically depart from norms of appearance.[116] Every surgeon I interviewed reported refusing some requests, though surgeons did not all share the same clear bright lines about when not to operate.

Surgeons' assessments of whether to operate on patients and which racially legible appearances to grant them are professional judgments, with moral and aesthetic as well as clinical overtones. By exercising judgment and refusing requests, surgeons maintained their professional commitment to medicine.[117] Addressing how surgeons make judgments sheds light on the role of professionals within social systems that maintain inequalities. If we take seriously the idea that cosmetic surgeons are part of the cultural apparatus that upholds racial meaning and sets standards of beauty, and see evidence that standards have shifted, what opportunities does this present or foreclose?

PART I   Global Expert Discourse

1 Standardizing Noses in Global Cosmetic Surgery

Cosmetic surgery has long been associated with promoting a single, one-size-fits-all ideal of beauty.[1] From the late 1800s in the U.S. and Europe, physically stigmatized patients and members of racial and ethnic minorities sought cosmetic surgery to mitigate the physical markers of race, in order to "pass" as white.[2] Until the 1970s, American surgeons used the descriptor "ethnic" primarily to describe second-generation Americans of European heritage, including Jews, Italians, Germans, and Russians, who expressed a desire to look whiter or more "American."[3] In the 1990s and early aughts, feminist scholarship raised alarms that cosmetic surgery was fostering a white or whiter looks for patients of color in the U.S., especially women.[4] Cosmetic surgery historically afforded patients the chance to conform to a universal, normative standard of beauty. This beauty standard was consistent with a certain form of feminized whiteness, one exported from the U.S. to other parts of the world through American media and popular culture.[5]

More recently, however, scholars have drawn attention to the proliferation of ideal appearances—especially when it comes to specific
physical features, like the nose. Researchers have described the
desire for thinner, whiter noses in Venezuela; bar hostesses' desires
for a "modern" Asian nose in Vietnam; the emergence of a Korean
look, complete with a more prominent nose, emergent in South
Korea; and observers have highlighted the bandaged displays of conspicuous consumption in Iran, Lebanon, and other parts of the
Middle East.[6] Amidst this broadening of ideals, it makes sense to
expand the focus from what patients request to what cosmetic surgeons are willing to do for patients. In other words, how do surgeons
construct standards of appearance? Shifting the lens of analysis
from the beauty ideals aspired to by patients to standards of appearance generated by cosmetic surgeons, this chapter investigates how
cosmetic surgeons use racial categories to construct standards of
appearance for rhinoplasty by examining medical journal articles.

Colloquially called a nose job, rhinoplasty has existed as a procedure in some form for centuries and remains one of the most popular cosmetic surgery procedures in the world.[7] In the past few
decades, rhinoplasty has grown in popularity and accessibility.
Standards of appearance for noses are simultaneously the product of
changing fashion trends, shifting cultural sensibilities, and longstanding beliefs about the relationship between race and the physical body. Analyzing how surgeons use racial categories to establish
standards for noses reveals how surgeons claim expertise over the
physical body as well as over social and cultural trends.

Consider, for instance, a 2010 special issue of the medical journal
Facial Plastic Surgery, which included the following titles in its
overview of facial plastic surgery: "Asian Cosmetic Facial Surgery,"
"African-American Rhinoplasty," and "Aesthetic Surgery for the
Mestizo/Hispanic Patient." In the preface to the issue, the editors
hailed a new era in cosmetic surgery: "Gone are the pure Caucasian
standards of aesthetic beauty, modified and replaced now by the
mélange of races and ethnic groups with the recognition that various

standards of beauty exist in the minds of our patients rather than in the pages in our textbooks."[8]

This journal was one of several that presented racial-specific standards in cosmetic surgery, including a "Caucasian" or white standard of beauty alongside other options. In medical journal articles about rhinoplasty, cosmetic surgery experts from multiple countries championed race-specific standards of beauty along with the techniques to achieve them.

The fact that cosmetic surgeons have adopted racial terms for describing standards of appearance raises several sociological questions. What does a "pure Caucasian" nose look like, and what does "African-American Rhinoplasty" entail? How do cosmetic surgeons categorize patients and decide what kinds of racial appearances are desirable? And what does this tell us about how medicine shapes notions of human difference like race and gender?

Medical journal articles, like medical textbooks, are a kind of expert discourse, written by experts for other experts and practitioners. They represent a particular type of rarefied and specialized discourse, in which experts instruct and inform one another. They are nonetheless an important site for uncovering the macro, global dimension of the racial project of cosmetic surgery. Though authors were a small subset of the field, textbooks and articles codify the craft of cosmetic surgery for a transnational audience. Writing for a wide audience of clinicians and researchers afforded authors the opportunity to build or burnish a scientific reputation.[9] And indeed, copies of journals like *Plastic and Reconstructive Surgery* and *Aesthetic Surgery Journal* graced surgeons' offices from Kuala Lumpur to Miami and many points in between, testifying to their broad reach among practitioners of cosmetic surgery.

One might expect that cosmetic surgeons would use racial categories as a lingua franca to communicate about physical differences among patients across the world. Standardization of physical types of bodies is perhaps the most obvious and expected way for standardization to show up in cosmetic surgery, as experts note physical differences in physical features or body parts and attempt to organize, categorize, and explain that variation. And indeed, in medical journals, cosmetic surgeons used racial categories to propose a set of gendered standards for different kinds of noses.

However, in these articles, racial categories were not merely a shorthand for physical differences. When defined at all, racial categories in articles were defined using a mix of physical and cultural and sociopolitical criteria. In particular, the connotations of racial categories allowed cosmetic surgeons to inject some ambiguity into standards for nasal appearance, maintaining space for cultural meaning and subjective associations. Moreover, surgeon-authors used racial categories to strike a balance between standardization and customization of noses. Racial labels like "Latin," "Asian," "African-American," or "Oriental" allowed cosmetic surgeons to compare patients and generalize about their experiences while distinguishing their expertise and experience for a broader global audience. Finally, cosmetic surgeons explained racial standards for noses as achieving a goal of "preserving" race or ethnicity, thus framing the goal as a response to changing racial demographics in the market for cosmetic surgery. In contrast to the one-size-fits-all approach, in which physical markers of racial group membership were removed to achieve one universal look, a goal of "ethnic preservation" gave rise to a proliferating number of gendered, racialized looks.

For some experts, racial categories provided a way to delineate their expertise in a way that was also legible to a broader lay market. By doing so, they were also able to facilitate communication across different national contexts. In what follows, I analyze the race-specific standards for noses that appeared in medical journal articles. I outline the norm of "ethnic preservation," which undergirded the emergence of a proliferating number of racial-specific standards for noses. And I consider the consequences of juxtaposing different kinds of racial categories with gender for how we think about organizing and conceptualizing embodied human differences.

RACE AND STANDARDS IN COSMETIC SURGERY

Constructing racial standards for noses can be understood against a historical backdrop of scientific and clinical efforts to locate and fix race as a property of the body.[10] Nose shape, skin color, head size, and blood type have served as potent racial signifiers.[11] Race has been inscribed in sperm and egg cells as well as embryos in assisted reproductive technologies.[12] Using race to standardize the body or outcomes in medicine has often been done to simplify and reduce complexity to a set of biological or physical variables. This garners justifiable alarm from sociologists who recognize the importance of social structure in understanding, for example, racial differences in health outcomes.[13]

But racial categorization schemes do not just do one thing. In addition to being reductive and objectifying, racial standards for noses, for instance, can be also subjective and perhaps even subjectifying. Depending on how (or even whether) they are defined,[14] racial categories can also be ambiguous and generative of cultural meaning and value. Acknowledging and maintaining the subjectivity of racial categories can increase access to new populations as well as aid the production and dissemination of clinical knowledge. Racial and ethnic labeling of data can increase their portability and provide a basis for exchange,[15] conferring value to body parts, samples, products, and tissues. Such labeling also promotes claims of scientific generalizability.[16] I follow the lead of recent studies of biomedicine and race (especially in the field of genetics and genomics) in analyzing how cosmetic surgery as a racial project attaches macro biopolitical concerns about nationhood and racial identity to micro-level objects like physical features of the body.

In writing race-specific standards for noses, surgeons engaged in niche standardization, generating clinical knowledge about racial groups rather than generalizing to a universal human or customizing to a single individual.[17] They dispensed guidance meant to be relevant beyond a single case without generalizing to everyone.

Race-specific standards for noses posited that patients existed in distinct types that can be standardized and then treated in different ways. The logic of exactly what racially differentiated patients varied: it might be rooted in physical appearance, culture, or both. However, standardizing racial categories incorporated specific assumptions about intersecting identities, including gender, socioeconomic status, and nationality. Racial standards for noses often presumed and prescribed gender conformity. The project of definition and standardization of specific racial categories made boundaries between categories sharper and more salient; standardizing a category required specifying how it was different from others.

Racial categories derived meaning and value from the traffic between the sociopolitical arena and biomedicine, but bringing these worlds into alignment required a special kind of work. Steven Epstein has defined "categorical alignment work" as efforts to superimpose classification schemes and allow lay and scientific notions of race to become "treated as functionally equivalent."[18] With categorical alignment work, racial categories advanced by social movements or popular culture could be seen as the same as racial categories based on physical or biological difference.[19]

RACIAL DIFFERENCE IN RHINOPLASTY STANDARDS

To identify articles explicitly addressing race, I conducted keyword searches for "ethnic" and "race" paired with "cosmetic surgery" and "plastic surgery" in the PubMed database. The corpus came to include 203 articles about rhinoplasty published in English between 1993 and 2019. Articles offered technical specifications for conducting invasive, cosmetic facial procedures (e.g., "Asian Rhinoplasty") or normative descriptions (e.g., "Analysis of the African-American Female Nose"). The authors of these articles, which appeared in a variety of journals, hailed from twenty-seven different countries.[20]

More information about the content analysis process and articles can be found in the methodological appendix.

The prescriptive guides for rhinoplasty distinguished between procedures and outcomes for men and women and for patients of different racial groups. Surgeons proposed both the existence of different racial standards and the criteria and evidence to support them. Some articles reported population averages of facial measurements and proposed ideal facial ratios, which, in the abstract, were inspired by neoclassical Renaissance ideals from Western classical art.[21] They also invoked facial canons developed by twentieth-century anthropologists to categorize human types. For instance, a team of Brazilian plastic surgeons cited anthropometric research as a forebear: "Anthropologists measured human skulls in order to categorize and classify them by race. It was discovered then that the nasal index was the best index in order to distinguish the various human races."[22] Citing physical anthropology of the past as an inspiration for contemporary efforts to standardize human difference, they neglected anthropologists' subsequent reevaluation and soul searching about its historical attempts to standardize racial categories.[23] In articles, surgeon-authors adopted a qualified logic of quantification, recognizing systematic statistical variation in population norms based on geography but also the cultural associations of racial categories.

Defining Race

How did cosmetic surgeons define race or racial categories in medical journals? They rarely defined racial groups or explained the basis for racial classification schemes outright. In fact, authors often eschewed the word or idea "race," preferring to discuss "ethnicity" or specific categories. Consistent with prior studies of the use of race in biomedical research,[24] cosmetic surgeons took terms like "African American," "Asian," or "Hispanic" for granted, tacking them on as keywords in the title or abstract and failing to offer definitions.

When classification criteria were made explicit, they most often relied on physical features. Racial hierarchies are perhaps easiest to detect in terms that sound outdated, like "Negroid," "Mongoloid," and "Caucasoid." Even more unsettling is a physical typology of noses that employed a tripartite racial classification of "platyrrhine," "mesorrhine," and "leptorrhine" noses, which roughly corresponded to African, Asian, and white, respectively.[25] This classification scheme appeared infrequently among the articles in my corpus but is evidence of older racial thinking about physical difference. The Merriam-Webster dictionary defines platyrrhine as "broad-nosed, from *platys*: of, relating to, or being any of a division (Platyrrhina) of arboreal New World monkeys characterized by a broad nasal septum, usually 36 teeth, and often a prehensile tail." This definition directly links a form of human nose to a type of monkey, consistent with racist depictions of people of African descent as similar to animals.[26] Though platyrrhine seldom appeared in race-specific standards, this instance underscores how the contemporary racial classification schemes undergirding standards for noses were layered upon past racist iterations. Despite the postwar turn in biology and the social sciences that refuted the idea of racial categories as scientifically valid or rooted,[27] contemporary physical typologies and characterizations of race reinforced ideas locating social and cultural meaning in differences between human bodies. Deploying these typologies to more inclusive ends did not sever the association.

Cosmetic surgeons also used cultural differences as criteria for defining racial categories. When surgeon-authors did offer extended explanations of racial categories, culture and history became part of the story. In articles, some authors offered origin stories for racial categories like "African American" and "mestizo" rooted in past histories of (forced) migration and admixture. For instance, Drs. Patel and Kridel provided an origin story for the category "African American": "African transplantation into the Americas through the African slave trade as well as interracial mixing has resulted in a heterogeneous population that we collectively call black or African American. Diversity within this group is highlighted by vast differences in body habitus, skin pigmentation, and even configurations of the nose. For the most part, African Americans are believed to be a derivative of the Africans, Native Americans, and Caucasians from Northern Europe. Variety is a result of differential expression of features from these ethnicities."[28]

While the focus here was on physical features, the narrative was one of social change and mixture. In fact, the authors described "African American" as a hybrid mixture of pure racial types from the past.[29] If somewhat obliquely, the authors nevertheless raised the long and fraught history of enslavement, displacement, and sexual violence in the U.S. In the passive voice, this particular recounting resembled the popular narrative of the "melting pot" of races taught in American schools. This kind of story contextualized the social and cultural dimensions of a racial category for international audiences less familiar with American racial myths. Authors based in Latin America engaged in a similar project. Take the case of the category "mestizo," a term which some surgeons used interchangeably with "Hispanic" and "Latino/a." Facial plastic surgeon Dr. Cobo wrote, "Initially the term mestizo was defined as the mixture of Indians and Europeans, which began during the 15th and 16th centuries. With the introduction of African slave trade in the 17th and 18th centuries, ethnic variations were introduced, and in our American continent mestizo meant the mixing of three races: Indian, Caucasian, and Negro. Today the mestizo race is characterized by diversity and mixtures and does not have one element, culture, or race predominating over the rest in a persistent pattern."[30] In contrast to the racial origin story for the African American category above, this story foregrounded cultural mixture. These kinds of racial origin stories gestured to centuries of violence and dispossession, tracing the broad historical trajectories that they believed gave rise to present-day racialized communities. Instead of blackboxing physical differences, authors who offered racial origin stories made an argument for the enduring relevance of ancestry and history in understanding their patients' bodies and ideals.

Origin stories for racial categories were complicated, and very few authors included them in medical journal articles. By showcasing the histories of mixture associated with racial categories, origin stories subtly undermined the basis of racial standardization in cosmetic surgery. Though surgeons used racial categories to tame the messy disorder of the past, too honest a reckoning about their origins could challenge the present utility of racial classification for cosmetic surgery. Juxtaposing these histories with techniques to "correct" racialized features[31] could raise questions about power, colonial legacies, and racism that could hamper cosmetic surgery's expansion into new market demographics. So why did surgeons venture these explanations? As most authors did not explain themselves, I can only speculate. Perhaps some surgeons identified with the racial categories and sought to recognize rather than bury the baggage that went along with their use. Others provided these stories as evidence for why surgeons might want to distinguish between racial categories that otherwise shared physical features. Balancing scientific specificity and consumer legibility, the few surgeons who ventured onto this terrain trod lightly.

Goal of Ethnic Preservation

In line with a goal of expanding the field, rather than proposing to eliminate physical markers of race wholesale, surgeons outlined standards that met a different goal: ethnic preservation. Many of the race-specific articles delineated standards that "preserve the patients' ethnicity and achieve facial balance," in the words of one American paper.[32] In that way, patients could better approximate a "natural" look, avoiding detection of surgery and, perhaps, the charge of trying to pass as white. Of the articles in the sample that advocated an ideal look, 61% of articles took the position that cosmetic surgeons should strive to preserve patients' race in their surgical interventions.[33] Indeed, cosmetic surgeons described adherence to a legibly race-specific appearance as a factor that constrained surgical options. For instance, Dr. Cobo urged, "As surgeons we need to give our patients a surgical result that will bring them closer to their aesthetic ideal without changing their ethnic features in a dramatic fashion."[34] Transformations of appearance could be considered a technical and moral failure. Flagship journal *Plastic and Reconstructive Surgery* editor Dr. Rohrich and his colleague Dr. Ghavami made clear that "an imbalance in ethnic facial features . . . signifies an 'operated-appearing nose,'" an undesirable lapse for a cosmetic surgeon, for whom a natural appearance was the preferred ideal.[35] In these examples, ethnic features had a distinct, unique value, as in the fashion industry.[36] Displacing a single white ideal of beauty in favor of a proliferating number of race-specific standards, a goal of ethnic preservation provided space for the exposition of alternate forms of beauty.

In some articles, surgeon-authors explained why they advocated a goal of ethnic preservation. Surgeon-authors anticipated rapid and significant growth in nonwhite, "ethnic" populations in the U.S., asserting the increasing economic importance of U.S. communities of color in cosmetic surgery. For instance, Dr. Wimalawansa and colleagues wrote, "The African American, Latin American, Asian American, and Middle Eastern communities have developed a growing attraction to this field and have the potential to provide an enormous contribution to this industry in the future. . . . [M]inority patients requesting cosmetic procedures are becoming an increasingly important base in aesthetic surgery."[37]

Though these commentators implied that white patients remained the dominant consumer base for cosmetic surgery, they held up people of color as the future of the field. In annual reports and press releases, professional organizations concurred with this anticipated shift. ASPS, AAFPRS, and ASAPS extolled the potential of burgeoning "ethnic" communities in the U.S. to buoy market growth. An ASPS briefing paper highlighted a 243 percent increase in the number of plastic surgery procedures performed on ethnic patients between 2000 and 2013,[38] noting that racial minorities comprised 25% of all U.S. patients. Despite the impressive growth rate, white patients in the U.S. still accounted for 74% of procedures performed in 2015, which was over 10 points higher than the share of whites in the overall U.S. population.[39] Although the projections of growth in cosmetic surgery have not always come to fruition,[40] it was the *potential* of growth into new demographics that generated excitement and undergirded the logic of developing multiple race-specific standards of appearance.[41]

While this narrative and the racial categories mentioned were often U.S. specific, the story of sweeping demographic transformation and increasing access was a broader phenomenon. Perceptions of changing demographics and the possibility of niche standardization animated surgeons' constructions of their audience and of the larger global cosmetic surgery market. Surgeon-authors shared the presumption that pivoting to address the needs of growing U.S. communities of color might also position them to be competitive in the international market for medical tourists. To translate or appeal to new markets, some surgeons argued that they needed to change the looks they offered to patients. For instance, a Taiwan-based team of facial plastic surgeons wrote, "As worldwide wealth accumulates among ethnic Asians and stigma dissipates, there is an increasing demand for aesthetic surgery that emphasizes enhancement of natural beauty rather than Westernization. . . . A new set of aesthetic standards specific to the ethnic Asian nose is emerging."[42] Drawing a line between changing racial demographics and changing beauty standards, the authors advocated for the development of aesthetic options other than "Westernization." Consistent with this logic, some cosmetic surgeons used the term "race" or other more specific racialized labels like African American, mestizo, and so on, to describe standards of appearance. They used racial categories to represent both physical and social difference, delineate distinct standards of appearance, and suggest implicit comparisons.

In adopting a goal of ethnic preservation, surgeons reified the notion of racial difference and, as we will see, gender, advancing the idea that, for example, Black and white women were distinct types of patients with different ideal noses. Though cosmetic surgery could theoretically undermine or challenge some claims of difference between the groups and facilitate passing between racial categories, the stricture of ethnic preservation reinforced claims of racial difference by emphasizing physical (e.g., skin elasticity, hair, and pigmentation) and cultural (e.g., community reaction for ethnic patients) distinctions between groups. To sharpen and expound upon race-specific ideals consistent with the goal of ethnic preservation, surgeon-authors often presented binary contrasts between standards of appearance in an effort to make differences clearly legible.

ETHNIC NOSES, RACIAL REFERENTS, AND THE EMERGENCE OF A WHITE FOIL

To specify a standard, authors often used racial binaries to emphasize contrast. One of the most common was between white and "ethnic" noses, a term which surgeons used to refer to nonwhite or "non-Caucasian" patients interchangeably. The specifics of who was included and the list of characteristics that ethnic patients shared varied, and surgeons used "ethnic" to describe cultural characteristics and/or physical features (such as "ethnic skin"). Surgeons advocated that as a default assumption, a distinguishably "ethnic" appearance should be preserved in a surgical intervention. In offering a standard portrait of the "ethnic" nose, surgeons both constructed the white nose as the unmarked standard and reinforced the boundary between the white and ethnic categories.

Some surgeons offered a description of a generic "ethnic" nose in their articles. A team of facial plastic surgeons gave a typical assessment: ethnic patients, they wrote, "tend to have modest osseo-cartilaginous framework, the skin tends to be thicker, and the cartilaginous structures of the nasal tip can be unsupportive and flimsy, giving the tip a more undefined look."[43] In this blanket characterization, the specific distinguishing features were described in terms of physical traits, such as skin thickness, oiliness, and a

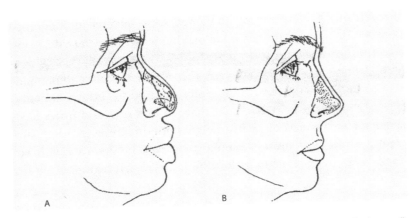

A   B

Figure 2. Facial Plastic Surgery article depiction of "a generalized ethnic nose" (*A*) and "the Caucasian nose" (*B*). *Source:* Thomas Romo III and Manoj T. Abraham (2003), "The Ethnic Nose," *Facial Plastic Surgery* 19 (3):271. © Thieme Publishers, www.thieme.com. Reprinted with permission.

perceived paucity of bone and cartilage in the nasal tip. These were deficiencies to be corrected through cosmetic surgery, but also traits that, in surgeons' minds, put hard limits on the possibilities of transforming patients from ethnic to white. The exposition of an "ethnic" category in articles suggested that all ethnic noses were similar in their difference from white noses. Again, descriptions of a generic "ethnic" nose derived meaning from an implicit or explicit comparison with a typical white nose. The image in figure 2, reproduced from one such article, makes this explicit. In developing the category of "ethnic" noses, surgeons brought into existence an ethnic biomedical object of knowledge, providing a clear example of niche standardization.[44] When the comparison between white and ethnic noses was made explicit, surgeons reported finding that both the ideal and average noses of "Latino," "Asian," and "African American" patients were "distinct from the white standard," recognizing "variability within these populations" as well.[45]

When a referent was explicitly identified, it was usually a white standard. However, some articles about Asian rhinoplasty, published by teams in China and South Korea, centered the racial category "Asian" as a default referent instead. Orienting around the category of "Asian" as opposed to Western or white was made explicit when surgeon-authors used the category "non-Asian" to set it apart. For instance, in an article about the use of a type of rhinoplasty implant, plastic surgeons from the U.S., South Korea, and Taiwan described Asian patients as having "a more tolerant, thicker skin envelope than in the non-Asian."[46] Adopting "Asian" as the default framing for noses, the authors emphasized contrast without gesturing to a white referent. Though mentions of "non-Caucasian" far exceeded "non-Asian" in my sample of articles, the use of the term "non-Asian" reflected the well-developed, extensive expertise in cosmetic surgery within Asia. Indeed, among all of the articles analyzed in this chapter, "Asian" was the only racial category other than white to be used as a referent in this way.

☞ There is a case to be made that "ethnic" features might be the norm globally and that white features are the aberrant ones, statistically speaking. Standards in this case are more than statistical norms, even as they are certainly normative.[47] In rhinoplasty articles, that referent was often, but not necessarily whiteness, which took physical form.[48] A referent, recognized as "normal," was refined, modified, and elaborated upon through the exposition of other racial categories; characterizing (abnormal) "ethnic" noses gave the referent category its boundaries and edges. In such a schema, the referent became visible while its place in the racial hierarchy remained unchallenged.

In the development of racial-specific ideals, the standardization of racial niches also advanced the specification of whiteness as one among other racial categories. Due to its globally hegemonic status and use as a common referent,[49] whiteness was not an equal category. But its physical and social construction revealed the tensions of situating a white ideal in an increasingly globalized medical field. Some cosmetic surgeons wrote about the white nose as one among many racial subtypes, particularly in transnational perspective. In Brazil, a multiracial society which considers many of its citizens to be racially mixed,[50] cosmetic surgeons used the term "Caucasian" to distinguish a subset of patients. Authors based in Europe recognized subtypes among white noses and wrestled with how to classify "Mediterranean" or "Middle Eastern" noses.[51] Writing about "the Middle Eastern nose," some authors described the nose as more on the "ethnic" side of a racial binary,[52] but not as classically "non-Caucasian" either. Whiteness itself could be difficult to pin down in the absence of a racial other or referent.

Though whiteness most often appeared as a relatively amorphous referent, the development of more kinds of racialized standards also spurred whiteness into ever more specific physical configurations. If whiteness, too, came in types, some white noses could be less ideal than others, benefiting from surgical improvement. Drs. Rowe-Jones and van Wyck described a type of white nose as "excessively concave and unnatural with a "ski-jump" appearance in the lateral view and a washed out, flattened appearance."[53] White patients also had deficiencies to be corrected. Cosmetic surgeons could be as unstinting in their descriptions of shortcomings of individual white noses as they were of "ethnic" noses.

Through comparisons of white noses with others, and in contexts where white patients were the exception rather than the norm, cosmetic surgeons fleshed out the white category using physical description. However, physical differences only got authors so far in explaining what was unique or important about a racial category. In several articles laying out standards for, for example, "African American" or "mestizo" noses, surgeons invoked cultural and sociopolitical connotations of racial categories as well.

RESHAPING RACIAL CATEGORIES THROUGH STANDARDIZATION

A goal of ethnic preservation gave rise to several distinct and proliferating standards for "ethnic" appearances, under labels like "Asian,"

"Hispanic," "Latino," "Black," "African American" and "Middle Eastern." When physical characteristics were insufficient to distinguish a racial category or failed to match socially recognized racial categorizations, cosmetic surgeons incorporated cultural criteria into their classification and standardization schemes. In the process, cosmetic surgeons reinscribed race on the body through the application of cultural stereotypes. In articles, then, cosmetic surgeons employed a mix of clinical examples, folk wisdom, and technical physical specifications to define racial categories. The criteria defining each racial standard could be inconsistent and subjective. But the fuzziness of the definitions enabled cosmetic surgeons from around the world to more easily compare notes about their different clinical experiences.

When presenting nasal standards for each racial category, many surgeon-authors began by identifying typical physical characteristics of each group. Take the "Asian" nose, for example. Noting that "the anatomical characteristics of the Asian nose are quite different from those of other races," Dr. Lee and Dr. Song characterized the Asian nose as "including low dorsum height, short columella, a thick soft tissue covering on the tip with flaccid lower lateral cartilage, and a sunken midface with relative protrusion of the mouth due to maxilla or premaxillary retrusion."[54] Several dozen articles written by practitioners based in Asia contained this kind of technical, anatomical description of patients' features.

Articles about the Black or Hispanic nose contained similar kinds of physical characterizations. For instance, Dr. Rohrich and Dr. Muzaffar described the typical "African American nose" as one with "a wide, depressed dorsum, inadequate tip projection, poorly-defined tip, excess alar flaring and/or increased interalar width, a diminished nasal length and height, an acute columellar-labial angle, and a low radix."[55] Similarly, Dr. Patel and Dr. Kridel depicted a typical Hispanic nose as "underprojected and under-rotated."[56] For noses characterized as "depressed," "inadequate," and "underprojected," it was unclear what was the implied comparison group—a "Caucasian" nose, a generic "ethnic" nose, or an ideal African American, Hispanic, or Asian nose? Such depictions not only constructed African American and Hispanic noses as deficient but also suggested the existence of racially specific, ideal noses that could be crafted through surgical intervention. The language surgeons used to characterize typical "African American" and "Hispanic" noses, like the language used to generalize about "ethnic" noses, was largely negative compared with the terms used to describe the "Caucasian" nose. In outlining typical "African American" and "Hispanic" noses as different from (and as "inadequate" and the prefix "under" imply, inferior to) the "Caucasian" norm, cosmetic surgeons were reifying a racial hierarchy that privileged whiteness over other racial categories.

These racialized descriptors had significant limitations for cosmetic surgeons' own purposes. As surgeon-authors noted, "African American," "Asian," or "Hispanic" noses did not absolutely map onto unique physical features. In fact, classification on the basis of physical features themselves could lead to alternate regroupings. Writing about Asian rhinoplasty, several surgeons proposed subclassification schemes and alternate standards based on nose shape and, in particular, the shape and projection of the tip of the nose.[57] Conversely, a shared racial categorization could obscure differences between individual members' actual features. In an article offering subtypes for the "Indian American" nose, Drs. Patel and Daniel depicted "category 1 Indian American rhinoplasty" as "somewhat similar to the type 2 Mexican American nose with their pseudo-dorsal hump and underprojecting tip."[58] In this typology, a category 1 Indian American nose bore more similarity to a Mexican American nose than to a category 3 Indian American nose, which in turn resembled subtypes of African American or Asian noses. The authors did not link the similarities to shared ancestry between Indian Americans and Mexican Americans, as they did for homologies between Hispanic and African American patients. Their description suggested the possibility of an alternate strategy of classification based on physical morphology. Cosmetic surgeons explained differences within racial groups in ways that justified the existence of the larger overarching racial category, even as they also recognized similarities across these groups.

Rather than ignoring the diversity within the resulting broad categories, many authors remarked upon the capaciousness within racial categories. Several authors noted the vast array of nationalities and geography encompassed by the Asian category. Dr. Gruber and coauthors presented the "Asian American" nose as a construct that "incorporates features representative of a variety of Asian countries, including China, Japan, Korea, the Philippines, Thailand, and Vietnam."[59] In their sweeping list, they acknowledged the many parts that comprised the whole. Some authors offered even more specific racial standards to differentiate within racial groups. Authors proposed subclassifying Asian features into "Korean" or "Japanese,"[60] or "North Indian" or "South Indian," referring to parts of the Indian subcontinent.[61] For racial standards like "mestizo" and "African American," some authors offered subclassification schemes that hinted at complex social histories and called into question the existence of separate racial types. For instance, Dr. Ofodile and coauthors offered a widely cited typology of "African," "Afro-Caucasian," and "Afro-Indian" types.[62] Cosmetic surgeons assumed the existence and past relevance of racial types, even as they confronted a different present and anticipated a future of increasing racial mixing. Dr. Lam observed, "Today's globalized marketplace has stressed the beauty of models that are of mixed racial heritage. Also, with rising miscegenation, offspring from these mixed marriages may be striking a new ethnically blended aesthetic."[63] Even as they imagined a mixed-race future, surgeons largely neglected the implications of what it might mean to consider their current patients as already racially mixed and hybrid.

In writing race-specific standards of appearance, cosmetic surgeons also elevated and enshrined cultural differences. Specifying techniques to achieve culturally relevant beauty ideals, surgeons inscribed cultural differences on the bodies of patients. This was especially evident in discussions of Asian rhinoplasty. In their exposition of the "Asian" nose, authors sometimes wedded physical typologies with cultural stereotypes. In one blunt example, Dr. Lam declared, "Asians at times seek rhinoplasty principally or solely for the reason that they will have a greater predilection for wealth or fortune, as a larger proboscis may be thought to gain them that advantage."[64] Here Dr. Lam invoked a "folkloric" belief about nose size to explain both the motivation for the intervention and its form for an Asian patient. In the service of increasing awareness and cultural sensitivity, several authors told of the unfamiliar and even strange beliefs of past Asian patients. Particularly in the U.S. context, attempts to fill in the gaps by explaining Asian cultural difference risked reifying stereotypes about Asian timidity and inscrutability. For instance, encouraging cosmetic surgeons to approach Asian candidates for rhinoplasty with sensitivity, Dr. Ishii wrote, "Many Asians may be reluctant to overtly state their wishes as this may be in conflict with their cultural beliefs. To fully understand the patient's desires, many experienced surgeons ask the patient to bring in photographs of models or refer to their own collection of preoperative and postoperative photographs."[65] Here Dr. Ishii noted experiencing more reticence from some Asian patients and suggested the use of visual imagery as a strategy to aid communication. In the best case scenario, articles also included proactive strategies for how surgeons could educate themselves about different cultures. In the worst case, their perpetuation of cultural stereotypes exoticized Asian patients.

On occasion, authors bandied about the word "culture" with few examples or explanation. This included surgeons practicing on the Asian continent as well as those in the U.S. A team of surgeons based in China and the U.S. observed, "Asian aesthetic goals should be tailored to the ethnicity and culture of the individual patient."[66] In this article, the authors acknowledged the importance of culture and ethnicity without demonstrating how it might matter. Culture here was an empty cipher.

Thus, most cosmetic surgeons would argue that what made, for instance, an Asian rhinoplasty "Asian" was not simply physical char-

acteristics or even geography but also social and cultural expectations. Cosmetic surgeons attributed Asian difference to culture as
well as physical, embodied characteristics. Creating physical standards to represent and address cultural difference also required surgeons to wade into cultural and, as I discuss next, gender stereotypes.
The construction of gender difference occurred alongside the surgical construction of racial difference, and provided another avenue
for conceptualizing or ignoring difference.

GENDERING RACIALIZED NOSES

Particular intersections of race and gender together were instanti-
ated in nasal standards, and attending to race and culture in articles
brought gender difference into focus. The rhinoplasty articles that I
analyzed generally assumed a female patient.[67] Of all the cases presented in the articles in my corpus, about three-quarters featured
women, with the remaining cases referring to men.[68] In proposing
race-specific standards for noses, some surgeon-authors also explicitly incorporated assumptions about gender, describing some nose
shapes and sizes as feminine and others as masculine. Accordingly,
while cosmetic surgery has often been thought of as a process of feminization for women, surgeons also described it as a process of masculinization for men—particularly men of color.[69] Cosmetic surgery
could bring patients into compliance with racial *and* gender norms.

Some authors drew explicit parallels between a desire for conformity to gender norms and racial norms in rhinoplasty procedures.
For instance, Drs. Rohrich and Ghavami commented, "Middle
Eastern patients frequently want to retain specific ethnic traits, such
as a higher dorsum and less obtuse nasolabial and columellar-labial
angles relative to their Caucasian counterparts. This concept is similar to performing rhinoplasty in the male patient, in which masculine
features should be preserved."[70] The authors applied the language
of "preservation," rather than enhancement or transformation, in

describing both gender and racial outcomes in patients.[71] Similarly, for Asian men, surgeons touted nasal augmentation surgery as an explicitly masculinizing intervention: "Asian males may also gain the benefit of increased perceived masculinity associated with a stronger nasal profile. The Asian nose typically already appears feminized with a low nasal dorsum and retruded nasal tip. Augmentation rhinoplasty can reverse some of the feminine characteristics of the typical Asian nose."[72] In this article, the surgeon equated a smaller nose ("low nasal dorsum") with femininity, and explicitly linked augmenting the nose with shoring up masculinity. Indeed, size was a critical dimension of masculinity for the nose. Most surgeons considered larger noses to be more masculine. In justifying rhinoplasty procedures for men, then, the author relied on the American cultural stereotype of the feminine Asian man.[73] While surgeons were warier of performing rhinoplasty on men, they accepted the goal of enhancing masculinity as a motivation for Asian men.[74] This example suggests cosmetic surgery could be a process of masculinization for some men of color. Even as cosmetic surgeons' proposed interventions suggested potential fluidity in racial and gender categories, authors reasserted the durability of the categories along conventional lines.

When reporting desirable looks for a member of a given racial group, some authors illustrated different nasal ideals for men and women. For instance, surgeons described Hispanic women's surgical preferences for "finer, thinner noses with a slightly more concave dorsum." In this case, cosmetic surgery was a feminizing process.[75] By contrast, they characterized Hispanic men as preferring a large, "'macho' nose with a higher, somewhat convex, dorsum," invoking the possibility of surgery as a masculinizing process.[76] By equating larger noses with a bump and "macho" noses for Latino male patients, surgeons were reifying and biologizing racial and gender differences. They further gave physical form to cultural concepts of masculinity in a process of the biological construction of social difference. A large nose with a bump was discursively distinct from the aesthetically ideal white female nose or an Asian male nose, for which a straight nose bridge was prized.[77] A nose with a bump was also perceived as more natural and less obviously altered than a "scooped out" or upturned nose, associated with the surgical excesses of an earlier era. By crafting race and gender onto the physical body, cosmetic surgeons could make these social categories material and legible anew. Ultimately, the construction of race-specific standards for noses also gendered noses.

In addition to characterizing physical features by gender, cosmetic surgeons identified a different set of acceptable and appropriate reasons for why men and women might seek cosmetic surgery. Cosmetic surgeons suggested some psychological screening of all prospective patients for their motivations for surgery. Often they recommended heightened scrutiny for male patients, who were not seen as fit subjects for beauty work.[78] In discussing two male Indian American rhinoplasty cases, Drs. Patel and Daniel reported: "The two aesthetic male cases were 'warranted' but carefully screened as to motivation and SIMON criteria (i.e., single, immature, male, obsessive, and narcissistic)."[79] Cosmetic surgeons applied some of these same criteria, in particular, immaturity and obsessiveness, to women in an attempt to screen out so-called "surgery junkies," people with body dysmorphic disorder and/or those who repeatedly request surgical intervention.[80] For all that the profession of cosmetic surgery heralded the expansion of services to men, these special criteria reflected cosmetic surgeons' continuing hesitance to treat men and suspicion of male patients' motives. In cultures in which men's appearance was not supposed to matter, men interested in modifying their appearance were often seen as less masculine. Cosmetic surgeons were reluctant to operate on men unless they were convinced the men had a good reason for surgery, making it "warranted." The criteria proposed for evaluating men's motives ultimately set a higher bar for intervention than for women.

However, surgeon-authors characterized nasal procedures as potentially masculinizing for men if done within stated, often racially specific, aims. Racial minority status could boost male patients' case for surgery, mitigating the routine red flag for males under the SIMON criteria. Given that many male patients of color expressed their surgical desires in terms of a desire to modify their racial appearance rather than to look beautiful, their case for seeking surgery was relatively bolstered. Concern for one's physical appearance, a trait perceived by surgeons as feminine, could also be explained away as an "ethnic" preference for male patients of color, extending beauty culture to men.[81] At least one author advised readers to anticipate that male patients might fear being feminized by rhinoplasty. Discussing in the case of a young Arab male patient, Dr. Wang reported that the patient "considered a strong nasal profile as a masculine trait and in no way wanted his nose diminished or "feminized.'"[82] To alleviate such fears, cosmetic surgeons outlined how to achieve a distinctly masculine outcome, ensuring, for instance, that the nose was not made too small. Whether cosmetic surgery was perceived as feminizing by surgeons was mediated by the race of male patients.

For surgeons, cosmetic surgery reinforced differentiation by gender, inflected by race. Cosmetic surgeons identified variation in bodies and assigned this variation cultural meaning. Equally important, cultural expectations could become embodied. Cosmetic surgery could shore up gender conformity for men of color who were perceived as having masculinity deficits, like Asian men in the U.S., and for those whose racial identity was tied to a particular performance of masculinity.[83]

DEBATES ABOUT THE USE OF RACIAL STANDARDS IN COSMETIC SURGERY

The ambiguity and fuzziness of racial classification criteria was not lost on surgeons. If noses of, say, Latino men came in different shapes and sizes, and could be found on people from different continents, what gave Latino—or any racial category—coherence? Some surgeons raised this critique in their articles, expressing doubts about the utility of racial categories. Detractors warned their colleagues against relying too heavily on race. Their accounts helped situate the development of racial standards as a niche specialty even within rhinoplasty.

Some surgeon-authors conceded that all racial categories were limited in their ability to describe physical differences. For instance, Dr. Niechajev and Dr. Haraldsson argued, "There is no universal common nose type for any particular race or geographic region. Although for Europeans all African or Chinese noses might look the same, the reverse opinion is expressed by the rural Chinese about Europeans."[84] In their analysis, race need not correspond with nose shape. Rather, emphasizing geographic distance, they pointed to the cultural relativity of perceptions of common or desirable appearances. Other authors suggested that racial categories were context dependent, citing research showing that surgeon background could influence the perception of racial group membership.[85] Authors writing in this vein contended that racial categories were not fixed standards, but sociocultural entities that shifted based on factors like a surgeon's own racial identity.

In the same special issue of *Facial Plastic Surgery* mentioned in this chapter's introduction, Dr. Leong and Dr. Eccles coauthored an essay challenging the usefulness of race and ethnicity in the field. They argued, "When surgeons are describing a particular shape of nose in a scientific or clinical journal, then one should expect some more rigorous and exact way of describing the nose rather than the use of undefined racial/ethnic terms." Their critique acknowledged variation in nasal shapes and characteristics and a need for standardization. But they expressed skepticism about the clinical utility of race, worrying that "standard demographic terms of race and ethnicity" obscured more than they illuminated. They did, however, recognize another potential important function of racial language. They continued, "For purely aesthetic reasons, a patient may aspire to have a nasal shape that they describe as 'Asian' or 'African American,' and in these cases it is not possible to define in scientific terms the shape of nose that the patient wishes the surgeon to model."[86] In outlining their objections and then this caveat, Drs. Leong and Eccles pointed out a key justification for the use of race in cosmetic surgery: its meaning and connection to patients.

Ultimately, race-specific standards for noses represented a relatively small niche. Articles with these kinds of labels in the title numbered in the hundreds over a period in which thousands of rhinoplasty articles were published in medical journals. As the objections above highlighted, it was possible to generalize about patients without reproducing existing social hierarchies and divisions between racial groups or cultural stereotypes. Indeed, alternate existing categorization schemes in cosmetic dermatology and plastic surgery were based on nasal length or size, skin thickness, or nasal tip projection. However, it is instructive that some surgeons nonetheless chose to use racial categories, and even doubled down further by charting variation within racial groups, as with the examples of "Indian American" and "Mexican American" noses above. Racial categorizations have a way of proliferating,[87] particularly in a context in which categories are imported from the sociopolitical arena. Instead of rejecting sociopolitical racial groups as not useful for biomedical purposes, cosmetic surgeons worked within existing racial frameworks to preserve racial categories rather than crafting a new way of doing business.

CONCLUSION

In medical journal articles offering race-specific standards and guidelines, cosmetic surgeons expounded a transnational racial project. Using racial categories to balance standardization with a drive for customization in cosmetic surgery, surgeons fashioned a science of human difference that also left room for art. Undergirded by both physical and cultural criteria, race-specific standards for noses enabled scientific communication between surgeons from

Brazil to Sweden to Taiwan. Emerging out of an attempt to organize considerable variation and complexity and anticipating a larger global market for cosmetic surgery, these standards were also full of contradictions. They were clearly a departure from a one-size-fits-all approach to nose jobs, facilitating a degree of customization for patients who wanted to, in surgeons' words, "preserve [their] ethnicity"—and gender—in their cosmetic surgery outcomes. They were also standards that encompassed both physical characteristics and subjective cultural connotations.

Standards are embedded within existing power relations and engender hierarchies[88]: as Stefan Timmermans and Steven Epstein note, "Every standard necessarily elevates some values, things, or people at the expense of others, and this boundary-setting can be used as a weapon of exclusion."[89] In cosmetic surgery, the development of racial-specific standards of appearance draws attention to the latent assumption of an underlying norm of whiteness in biomedicine,[90] even as it challenges that norm explicitly. In developing racial-specific standards, moreover, surgeons assert authority over racial categorization. The assertion of biomedical authority over race is a longstanding practice, as documented in the literature on scientific racism and sexism. Scholars have traced how the social assumptions of researchers permeate scientific explanations of gender and racial difference.[91] Relatedly, scholars argue for the deconstruction of how experts type bodies by race and gender.[92] But six decades after scientists widely rejected biological explanations for race,[93] there is a reinvestment in the biomedical assertion of authority over race, sometimes mobilized with the goal of redressing racial inequality.[94]

There is some irony in the development, however tenuous, of racial standards in cosmetic surgery, a practice that changes physical features. In characterizing racial types, cosmetic surgeons end up invoking race not as a static, pre-given, biological category, but as an enactment, a process of becoming. This allows biomedicine to become a tool for making patients *more* "ethnic" rather than helping patients efface racial markers. Even with this reframing, and the concomitant rejection of the notion of racial categories as static or scientifically based, cosmetic surgeons reaffirm the continuing importance and relevance of racial difference.

Race-specific standards helped advance a goal of "ethnic preservation" in nose jobs—the notion that cosmetic surgery should not change the perceived racial legibility of a given individual's appearance. The goal of ethnic preservation reinforced and specified notions of racial and gender difference physically, locating them in nose bumps and shapes, as well as in cultural differences between groups. The goal often, but not always, relied on a white norm or referent as a comparison despite the globalization of the field. This project of definition and standardization of specific racial categories had the side effect of making the boundaries between categories more salient and defined as well; standardizing a category required specifying how it was different from others.

Cosmetic surgeons constructed nasal standards for race and gender simultaneously, suggesting that race and gender do not function as wholly analogous as categories in cosmetic surgery expertise. To a significant extent, cosmetic surgeons took sex/gender differences on the physical body for granted, and the project of standardizing racial categories could bring gender or sex to the fore. The journal articles I analyzed described ways to help patients' noses conform to their gender rather than to transform patients across gender lines, much as with racial categories and the norm of ethnic preservation. Articles primarily offered racialized types of masculinity and femininity in the physical looks presented to patients. But it is worth noting that there is a set of plastic surgery procedures that aims to effect gender transformation: facial feminization surgery. Performed by reconstructive plastic surgeons rather than cosmetic surgeons, facial feminization procedures were not mentioned in any of the articles in my corpus, existing in a distinct ambit of expertise.[95] As these procedures become more common, it remains to be seen whether and how they reshape standards for noses more broadly.

These findings have implications for how we think about race and standardization. Cosmetic surgeons effected alignment of racial categories between the biomedical and sociocultural arenas by combining physical standards alongside cultural stereotypes. Most examples of categorical alignment work involve manipulation of abstract ideas. In this case, bringing racial categories from the social world into alignment with a biomedical view involved the manipulation of the physical body. This was necessarily a more permanent and individualized effort to "fix" race on the body even as the identities were recognized to have social origins and consequences. When niche standardization is literally embodied, racial boundaries take on a weight and permanence that seems naturalized.

Differences in physical features have been taken as evidence of inferiority of, for instance, African Americans and Latinos in the U.S. Measurement of physical features has undergirded eugenics efforts in the U.S. Racial category labels and origin stories reflect notions of racial hierarchy, retaining a through line to longer histories of scientific racism.[96] These past efforts shape the present, informing the racial labels used and the lingering connotations that gave racial categories legibility on the body in the first place. This is true even as attempts to create standards and norms of physical appearance for cosmetic surgery patients of color today may also come from a desire to recognize, celebrate, and market differences between people. Though not driven by explicitly antiracist aims, as in other cases,[97] the development of race-specific standards for noses is a complicated engagement with capitalist consumerism and expression.[98]

In this chapter, I focus on expert surgical discourse explicitly addressing race/ethnicity in articles written by surgeons for their peers. Cosmetic surgeons who publish articles were staking out their own specialist clinical expertise and turf as academics. Developing race-specific guidance positioned surgeon-authors as having unique expertise that could build their reputation among both patients and colleagues. I would expect authors of journal articles to be emphasizing differences between patients to distinguish their perspectives and publish their work. The next chapter moves from a discussion of race-specific standards for noses in medical journal articles to professional conferences, which are another form of global expert discourse. Race-specific standards paved the way for the development of race-specific techniques to achieve them. Surgeons showed and shared these techniques at conferences. Turning from a general discussion of multiple race-specific standards of noses, the next chapter examines how surgeons developed a craft to meet the goal of ethnic preservation for one specific racial category—"Asian."

2 Standardizing Techniques

ASIAN COSMETIC SURGERY AND THE ART
AND SCIENCE OF ASIAN DIFFERENCE

On the first day of the 2016 International Society of Aesthetic Plastic Surgery Congress, a plastic surgeon from Japan gave a presentation about Michael Jackson. Drawing heavily on magazine and news articles about the celebrity, Dr. Kobayashi propounded what he called a "fictional story from a medical point of view" about Michael Jackson's history with cosmetic surgery. He began his remarks by displaying a slide with a picture of the pop star's face: "As an aesthetic surgeon who has performed surgery on many nonwhite patients, I am amazed by this patient's psychology and his doctors. I think Michael wants to change from a Black man to a white woman."[1]

Interspersing Jackson's personal and professional highs and lows, Dr. Kobayashi gave a detailed timeline and description of what he estimated were between six and ten different rhinoplasty procedures. He declared 1984, the year of Jackson's fourth rhinoplasty procedure, to be Jackson's high-water mark, when he was "at his best in his work and his face." He ruefully remarked, "The doctor should have stopped here. But over the following years, he underwent another six operations." Dr. Kobayashi outlined a trajectory of decline. By 1988, he surmised, Jackson's nasal "tip may have become fractured and deformed as the implant poked out. These complications are common in Asians where augmentation rhinoplasty with implants is performed." Declaring 2002 to be the "point of no return" for Jackson's nose, he made his key contention: "An Asian doctor [who had experience working] with nasal tip deformity with implants could maybe have helped."

In rapid succession, Dr. Kobayashi displayed several photographs of successfully repaired noses from his clinic in Japan. Hundreds of cosmetic surgeons listened rapt with attention, taking photographs of his slides with their phones. He continued, "If Michael Jackson knew this was available, his life might have changed. In 2009 at the age of fifty, Michael Jackson was in debt, trying to restart his music career. His nose was far too thin. It didn't look natural. . . . [D]espite mental and physical health problems, Michael Jackson brought dreams and happiness to people all over the world and was called to heaven at the young age of fifty-one." In this account, Michael Jackson's cosmetic surgeons in the U.S. lacked the experience necessary to grapple with the challenges posed by Jackson's physiology, failing him. It was striking that an experienced Asian doctor was the shadow protagonist of Dr. Kobayashi's story. For Dr. Kobayashi, Michael Jackson was an exemplar of what he and colleagues termed the "nonwhite" or "ethnic" patient. Dr. Kobayashi suggested that his experience operating on Asian patients would have transferred and provided relief to this famous Black patient (figure 3).

While Dr. Kobayashi's engagement with Michael Jackson was unusual in its degree of detail, the figure of Michael Jackson looms large over the field of global cosmetic surgery. He is a reference and touchstone for cosmetic surgeons from Japan to Brazil as the worst-case patient. Cosmetic surgeons cautioned against operating on patients who had, in Dr. Kobayashi's words, "psychiatric issues" and advised against crossing lines of race and gender and repeated rhinoplasty procedures. Having pushed the limits of what was possible,

Figure 3. Michael Jackson, 1996 HIStory World Tour. *Source:* Phil Dent/ Redferns via Getty Images. Reprinted with permission.

let alone desirable, no cosmetic surgeon wanted to repeat the mistakes made by Michael Jackson's plastic surgeon. But surgeons drew different lessons from his story. Across the board, Jackson indexed the negative potential of cosmetic surgery with respect to race and gender—for scholars and cosmetic surgeons alike, as Kathy

Davis has discussed.[2] U.S. cosmetic surgeons reported that Jackson's cosmetic procedures set back the field from more widely expanding to patients of color for decades. In this view, Michael Jackson's surgically altered appearance was not only an indictment of his plastic surgeon, but also of the entire field for improperly operating on him and neglecting to adapt techniques to his individual physiology and needs. The invocation of an Asian approach to cosmetic surgery as a possible solution to Jackson's problems was an unusual interpretation that sketched out a hypothetical alternate surgical trajectory. Every surgeon sought to define and differentiate their expertise, skill, and craft from competitors. However, promoting Asian cosmetic surgery as an alternative approach to what has become a foundational sin for the field was a bold assertion. The audience was spellbound for the fifteen minutes of Dr. Kobayashi's presentation.

Differences in physical bodies to some extent necessitate different surgical approaches. But cosmetic surgery has also been shaped by different histories, legal environments, and risk tolerances among surgeons.[3] At international medical conferences, cosmetic surgeons accounted for their choice of materials and procedures in presentations to expert audiences who did not share their cultural common sense, nor even necessarily a common set of assumptions about bodies, technologies, patient expectations, risks, and values. This chapter explains one standardizing solution to the problem of global variation: the development of racialized expertise in the form of Asian cosmetic surgery. I conceptualize Asian cosmetic surgery as a racialized body of expertise or "craft." Craft as a concept captures the practical knowledge and cultural and historical contingencies of cosmetic surgery. The craft of Asian cosmetic surgery encompasses technical skill, tacit knowledge, aesthetic judgment, bedside manner, and expertise.[4]

This chapter presents two different stories for the emergence of Asian cosmetic surgery and the genealogy of Asian beauty. It draws from observations of cosmetic surgeons at conferences, which showcase the "state of the art" in the field, to understand the labeling of surgical techniques like blepharoplasty, rhinoplasty, and breast augmentation as "Asian." At conferences, people practicing on different continents exchanged techniques in master classes and presentations of short videos of procedures filmed in the operating theater. In these sessions, the craft of Asian cosmetic surgery coalesced as an aesthetic disposition and set of techniques, incorporating cultural assumptions about the body and responding to specific legal and medical institutions. Moreover, Asian cosmetic surgery took shape within a global market for medical tourism. Asian cosmetic surgery as a body of skills, expertise, and aesthetics aligned some surgeons with regional biopolitical projects in Asia, while also rendering their expertise and niche specialty visible to patients willing and able to travel for care.

RACIAL CATEGORIES AND VALUE IN GLOBAL BIOMEDICINE

The impulse to use racial labels in biomedicine has had political, economic, and scientific drivers. Sometimes the use of race comes from a desire to effect niche standardization. Racial categories can serve as "boundary objects" that circulate through and connect different social worlds.[5] Often racial categories stand in for national or regional populations within global markets. In Aihwa Ong's exposition of Asian genomics, scientists and clinicians use race and ethnicity as affective tools to rally the nation to invest in biosecurity and outrace pharmaceutical companies in developing solutions against infectious disease.[6] Jennifer Liu tells a similar story about Taiwanese DNA, noting that labeling objects in terms of race is not always or necessarily a reductionist move, but can "recuperate[e] a valorized identity."[7] And as racial minorities historically barred from science enter the field, some may be motivated to draw attention to and aid their own racial and ethnic communities, reshaping race-making in clinical knowledge production.[8]

Within globalized fields of "cosmopolitan science," transnational interactions of scientists and clinicians are reshaping biomedical knowledge production and consumption in Asia, South America, and Africa as well as the West.[9] To demarcate their expertise, a subset of genetic and genomic scientists have labeled and branded their research projects, funding structures, and findings with potentially racialized terms. For instance, scientists in Mexico and Colombia tout "mestizo" genomics, while researchers in Singapore call their project "Asian post-genomics."[10] Racialized labels reflect political contestation over assertions of similarity and difference, hybridity and purity, and the entanglement of racial categories in legal regimes of economic value and ownership. While my research is centrally interested in the racialized labels that cosmetic surgeons apply to their knowledge, practices, and patients, these categorization practices may not represent a break with how science has been conducted in the past so much as a deliberate effort to decenter the centrality of the West in science. There is certainly a good reason for scientists outside the West to vociferously assert their difference: to distinguish new problems, new framings, and pride in new networks and alternative centers of knowledge.

CRAFTING ASIAN BEAUTY

The Emergence of Asian Cosmetic Surgery

Asian cosmetic surgery as an effort exhibits similarities to the genomic racial projects advanced by scientists. But that is not how it is typically narrated. The conventional story goes that cosmetic surgeons in the U.S. developed Asian cosmetic surgery to operate on the people of Japan, Korea, and Vietnam, first as the U.S. waged war and subsequently as it occupied each country in succession. Many English-language accounts trace modern Asian aesthetic surgery techniques to Dr. Ralph Millard, the chief plastic surgeon of the U.S. Marine Corps in Korea.[11] As a gesture of goodwill, Dr. Millard performed plastic surgery on Korean men, women, and children as well as American military members. In a 1955 essay titled "Oriental Peregrinations," published in *Plastic and Reconstructive Surgery*, he described his attempts to ascertain an "Oriental" standard of beauty: "With a round-eyed control at a table of slant-eyes the social gathering becomes a veritable laboratory for scientific comparison. Of course there are variations in the Japanese, Chinese and Korean faces but in general there is a similarity—the yellow moon-shaped face topped by bangs of straight black hair, slit-slant dark eyes peeking from behind a mongoloid fold and a curtain of upper lid skin."

Dr. Millard took to "deorientalizing" patients, training a generation of Korean plastic surgeons in his reconstructive and aesthetic methods.[12] This kind of racist language characterized U.S. plastic surgeons' descriptions of procedures and Asian patients in this era. With time, women from Asia came to the U.S. as war brides, creating a market within the U.S. for a different kind of cosmetic surgery: accounts from plastic surgeons and women themselves suggested a desire to blend in to keep the interest of their husbands and to remove racial markers.[13] Plastic surgery set to the task of repairing and smoothing out the collateral impact of American foreign policy and wars.[14]

This is one important narrative shaping contemporary plastic surgery in Asia. But other origin stories for Asian cosmetic surgery have been relatively neglected in the U.S. An alternative narrative of the discipline would foreground Dr. Khoo Boo Chai, a cosmetic surgeon trained in Japan who began practice in the British colony of Malaya. From 1961 to 2003, Dr. Khoo was based in Singapore, where he outlined a precursor to Asian cosmetic surgery based on his experience with what he called "Oriental" patients. Over the course of a long career, Dr. Khoo presented his surgical techniques throughout the world. He specified a standard of "Oriental beauty" that encompassed everything from the removal of physical markers associated with Asian identity to the addition of features such as dimples.

Cosmetic surgical procedures have been documented in Asia, especially Korea and Japan, since the nineteenth century. Articles describing a technique to modify eyelids to give the appearance of a more visible crease and rounder fold had been published in Japanese as early as 1896, and a significant literature in Japanese emerged in the interwar period.[15] Its reach beyond Japan's borders was limited in part by the bitterness engendered by Japan's occupation of neighboring Asian countries during World War II. By dint of his Japanese training, Dr. Khoo was steeped in a longer historical trajectory of practitioners performing eyelid procedures within Asia.[16] Knowing "a little bit of Chinese" and fluent in English, Dr. Khoo was uniquely positioned to leverage his training and experience operating on Chinese and Malay patients into a larger exposition of Asian techniques for Western audiences in the pages of plastic surgery journals.[17] Dr. Khoo became a well-known and frequently sought after expert on Asian cosmetic surgery.[18] Unlike U.S. surgeons operating on Asians in the same period, Dr. Khoo primarily promulgated "Oriental" rather than "Western" standards of beauty. He opined on the nature of Asian beauty in several textbooks and anthologies. Like Western plastic surgeons citing historical Renaissance ideals as inspiration for their aesthetic sense, Dr. Khoo drew on beauty as discussed by Confucius. Nonetheless, he recognized that these exact ideals were often not what his patients came in requesting. Some, he noted, wanted "to be Westernized."[19]

Dr. Khoo's story affords a different perspective on cosmetic surgery in Asia, one that also affected the trajectory and distribution of global cosmetic surgery expertise. Building upon the techniques developed by military doctors and experimenting to create new ideals and methods, South Korea has become a world-renowned center of cosmetic surgery, propelled to a global role by governmental support and overseas promotions.[20] There is a well-established beauty circuit in East Asia, with clinics (especially in South Korea) recruiting patients from China, Japan, and a larger Asian diaspora in the U.S., Canada, and Australia.[21] Drawing from these influences, Asian cosmetic surgery encompasses the diversity of beauty ideals and techniques developed within the continent while also distinguishing itself in substance and style from general and "Western" cosmetic surgery. "Asian aesthetic surgery," as it was called by ISAPS, refers to differences in substance and style from "the West" while retaining significant diversity within its ranks. Indeed, comparisons with the West, and with approaches designed to work on "Caucasian" patients, helped stabilize the idea of Asian cosmetic surgery as an object.

Genealogies of Asian Beauty

Today, cosmetic surgeons identify surgical styles and techniques as regionally, nationally, or racially linked. For instance, the 2016 ISAPS meeting in Kyoto listed a special theme of "Asian aesthetic surgery," featuring sessions on eyelids, noses, and other facial features. English-language textbooks in this vein (such as *Asian Blepharoplasty and the Eyelid Crease, Asian Rhinoplasty,* or *Atlas of Asian Rhinoplasty*) as well as numerous journal articles delineating specific "Asian" techniques were written by plastic surgeons in Taiwan and South Korea, as well as the U.S. At national and international meetings of cosmetic surgeons, Asian cosmetic surgery referred to many things: a specific patient population, unique cultural attitudes, and a kind of distinct surgical approach practiced primarily, but not exclusively, by cosmetic surgeons in Asia. The 2016 ISAPS Congress on "Asian aesthetic surgery" in Kyoto was not the first conference to showcase Asian aesthetic surgery. However, it was an unusually large and prominent international platform for the practice, representing an attempt to bring the world up to date on the state of cosmetic surgery in Asia.[22] For this iteration of Asian aesthetic surgery, cosmetic surgeon presenters traced a historical lineage for aesthetics entirely within Asia, constructing a separate area of homegrown, marketable expertise akin to "Asian genomics" or "Asian biotechnology."[23] These claims, rooted in the notion of a distinct patient body, paved the way for the development of unique techniques, styles, and expertise.

Around Asia, cosmetic surgeons and patients have gestured to Chinese, Japanese, and Korean traditions of physiognomy to explain preferences for certain face shapes and the prominence of eyes and noses. At conferences, surgeons sought to reframe and make explicit their international audiences' assumptions and expectations. Calling upon alternate genealogies of beauty—an assertion of Asian difference—was one way to do so. Cosmetic surgeons have used Chinese, Japanese, and Korean traditions of physiognomy and depictions of women in classical art to explain preferences for certain face shapes and the prominence of eyes and noses.[24] For instance, at a presentation at the 2016 Congress of the International Society of Aesthetic Plastic Surgery in Kyoto, more than one cosmetic surgeon included an image of a painted scroll featuring a beautiful woman with large, round eyes in their PowerPoint presentations. Asian presenters at conferences built up the notion of an Asian aesthetic surgery by asserting a unique Asian aesthetic sensibility that stemmed from physical and cultural difference. A Korean cosmetic surgeon started his presentation by emphasizing differences between white and Asian patients. Calling eyes the "windows to the soul," he continued, "The concept of the beautiful eye is different for Orientals and Caucasians." As audience members took notes, he advised where to make incisions, how much muscle and fat to remove if necessary, and when to consider "revision" procedures. In this framing, a "Caucasian" or white eye was not so much a goal or a referent as it was an alternate trajectory, falling outside the sphere of Asian cosmetic surgery.

An Asian genealogy of beauty was not simply a discursive strategy for cosmetic surgeons at international conferences. In the clinic, I observed Malaysian cosmetic surgeons invoke Chinese traditions of face reading, or physiognomy, when suggesting an "Asian" look for their patients. In a gleaming clinic ensconced within a shopping mall, a middle-aged Malaysian Chinese woman complained of sunken temples and close-set eyes to her younger Malaysian Chinese surgeon, Dr. Huang. I watched as Dr. Huang googled to find a black-and-white *mien shiang* face-reading map. On the screen, Dr. Huang zeroed in with her mouse on the side of the forehead. Paraphrasing the pop-up message, Dr. Huang explained to the patient that hollowed-out temples could signify poor relations with one's husband—at least, she noted, according to this website. The patient glanced at her supportive husband, who was seated in a chair a few feet away. Concerned, the patient directed Dr. Huang to ensure an even brow and the appearance of greater fullness at the margins. Dr. Huang injected a neuromodulator (more popularly known by the brand name Botox) to relax muscles near her temples.

Mien shiang, a Chinese face-reading tradition, imbued physical features, such as moles, indentations, and/or face shape with meaning. These became targets for change by Chinese patients, even as some of these features were ignored by other patients. Mien shiang was a traditional practice, a way of interpreting the body. Dr. Huang told me that many of her young patients dismissed it as old superstition. Botox is a comparatively new cosmetic material used worldwide to mitigate age-related wrinkles. By pairing mien shiang with Botox, Malaysian cosmetic surgeons forged a distinct, historically and regionally specific genealogy for beauty.[25] Mien shiang constituted a distinct aesthetic vision and way of seeing beauty for Asian cosmetic surgery, and cosmetic surgery offered a remedy for perceived bodily imbalances. Mien shiang provided an alternative aesthetic explanation and justification for cosmetic surgical intervention, one that Dr. Huang believed resonated with this patient, and perhaps others like her. By invoking mien shiang to describe and identify physical impairments, cosmetic surgeons also implicitly highlighted continuities in patients' requests for improvement and change. At the same time, mien shiang turned the attention away from global ideals of beauty and toward a distinct standard of beauty historically associated with China. Asian cosmetic surgery combined problems and solutions in novel combinations.

Cosmetic surgeons deliberately crafted historical narratives about the origins of Asian cosmetic surgery and for the phenomenon of Asian beauty more broadly. These genealogies supported and gave context to the very idea of a unique craft called Asian cosmetic surgery, with specific traditions and referents behind it. Of course, in different countries, one might expect the details to vary: *mien shiang* might have had resonance in Malaysia as a Chinese face-reading tradition but was not the way of thinking about beauty and appearance that I would expect to find, for example, in a South Korean clinic. There were many possible narrative constructions of Asian beauty. Cosmetic surgeons participated in and contributed to the craft of Asian cosmetic surgery by writing themselves and their historical and cultural constructions of beauty into a broader narrative.

ASIAN TECHNIQUES IN COSMETIC SURGERY

To realize a distinct form of beauty, practitioners of Asian cosmetic surgery proposed specific techniques. In interviews and at conferences, cosmetic surgeons shared techniques for modifying several physical features, including the eyes, nose, cheeks, lips, breasts, and abdomen. But cosmetic surgeons most often applied the label "Asian" to procedures that altered the appearance of the eyes (like blepharoplasty) or the nose (like rhinoplasty). Cosmetic surgeons offered innovative techniques under the banner of Asian blepharoplasty and Asian rhinoplasty, sometimes purporting to achieve a different kind of beauty. Though these procedures were the only ones to be explicitly called "Asian," the craft of Asian aesthetic surgery also presented a slightly different approach and orientation toward other procedures and implants that addressed particular economic, political, and cultural factors in Asia.

Asian Blepharoplasty

Blepharoplasty refers to modification of the upper or lower eyelids and is used worldwide by surgeons to adjust eyelids that droop as a result of weakening or aging muscles. Asian blepharoplasty, more specifically, denotes a modification of the upper eyelid to create the appearance of a pronounced eyelid fold and is associated with a rounder and/or bigger eye. This procedure is also sometimes called double eyelid surgery.[26] About half of the people in East Asia are born with a double eyelid fold. Those born without it sometimes seek to create the appearance of the double eyelid with cosmetics, tape, or surgical modification. Cosmetic surgeons have proposed different ideal heights for the placement of the fold. Another eyelid modification procedure, epicanthoplasty, alters the shape of the upper lid fold by excising skin at the interior corners of the eyes. This provides a lengthening effect. Again, about half of people in East Asia are born with a tapered nasal crease shape. The precise techniques for performing each step of epicanthoplasty or blepharoplasty can vary, giving cosmetic surgeons plenty to discuss and debate at conferences.

U.S. cosmetic surgeons framed these procedures as leading to multiple possible racialized outcomes. Dr. Millard cited this procedure in his exposition of Asian-specific surgeries, proposing techniques to, in his words, "deorientalize" patients. Dr. Millard dismissed the techniques of surgeons from Seoul, Hong Kong, and Tokyo as rendering eyelids "slightly more attractive but still retain[ing] their oriental character," which led to results that, "in [his] opinion do not warrant the short-cut." For Dr. Millard, "oriental character" was something that patients should mitigate or abandon in favor of a "Caucasian" appearance.[27] By contrast, contemporary U.S. surgeons were more wary of sweeping interventions. For instance, Dr. Jefferson, a white U.S. surgeon practicing in the U.S., told me, "Asian eyes have a very characteristic ethnic beauty to them." Dr. Jefferson echoed Dr. Millard in identifying a distinct "character" to the eye, but argued for its value and preservation rather than elimination.

Asian cosmetic surgeons not only differentiated potential racialized outcomes, but also argued for different racialized techniques. Cosmetic surgeons in Singapore and Malaysia expected U.S. cosmetic surgeons to approach eyelid procedures on Asian American patients differently. I asked a Singaporean plastic surgeon, Dr. Chin, whether there would be differences in the outcome for the same patient if they were operated on in Singapore versus the U.S. He responded, "It does depend. . . . It's a bit different because the Asians will in general operate on them in the same way he would operate on an Asian patient. And the reverse, if an Asian patient is done in Singapore, it will be different than if she has done the surgery in the United States. Then, of course, the American surgeon will approach his Asian patient the way he approaches Caucasian patients." Here Dr. Chin makes clear that he expected the same patient to undergo different surgical techniques in the U.S. and Malaysia. In other words, holding the body constant, the craft of cosmetic surgery itself differed across the U.S. and Asia. Dr. Chin argued that surgeons' clinical experiences, shaped by the patients they most frequently treated, honed their aesthetic sense and ability to discern and enact subtle changes for patients and to properly predict healing and scarring. Elaborating, Dr. Chin emphasized, "To foreigners, all Asians look the same, but Asians do not look the same." Dr. Chin suggested that U.S. surgeons might lack sustained, frequent clinical experience with Asian patients (and vice versa, that Singaporean surgeons saw fewer white patients). This could lead to real differences in technique.

Even beyond any one procedure, technical innovations and the growth of new beauty ideals kept shifting and tweaking the state of the art about how to operate and with what aim. While cosmetic surgeons had their preferences and tried-and-true techniques based on their experience, they did not necessarily consider colleagues with different approaches to be wrong. Rather, by highlighting the differences in their approach relative to the U.S. counterparts, practitioners of Asian cosmetic surgery were asserting their mastery and development of a distinct craft.

Asian Rhinoplasty

Though Asian blepharoplasty has historically received the most attention, cosmetic surgeons also often characterized rhinoplasty techniques in racialized terms as well. Asian rhinoplasty most often refers to augmentation rhinoplasty, a modification of the nose that makes the nose bridge more prominent by adding material.[28] Asian rhinoplasty was the subject of multiple sessions at the ISAPS Congress; it also appeared in several textbook chapters and medical journal articles. This description of "Asian rhinoplasty techniques" for English-speaking audiences was typical: "For Western patients, reduction rhinoplasty with dorsal hump rasping and lower cartilage resection is classic. In contrast, silicone implant augmentation rhinoplasty is the most commonly used technique in Orientals."[29] In this review article on Asian rhinoplasty techniques, the authors described Asian rhinoplasty as the opposite of rhinoplasty performed in "Western" patients: Asian rhinoplasty makes the nose bigger via the use of synthetic implants, whereas Western rhinoplasty reduces the size of noses by removing material. Of course, there were many other possibilities. In addition to varying which aspect of the nose to modify (bridge, nasal root, nasal dorsum, tip, nostril shape), cosmetic surgeons differed in the specifics of the materials and techniques used. Even just within augmentation rhinoplasty, cosmetic surgeons could choose from different materials for implants. To build up the nose bridge, many preferred to use autogenous materials, often cartilage and/or rib taken from the patient's own ear, rib, or elsewhere in the nose. Others preferred alloplastic implants, comprised of synthetic materials such as MEDPOR, Gore-Tex, and other varieties of rigid, medical-grade silicone, which could be carved and inserted to make a more pronounced nasal bridge or tip.[30]

Though similar implants and tools for rhinoplasty were available to cosmetic surgeons in the U.S. and Asia, cosmetic surgeons on both sides of the Pacific warned me that they had a difference of opinion. Cosmetic surgeons from Asia preferred to use synthetic, alloplastic materials as nasal implants, which were typically made of medical-grade silicone.[31] U.S. cosmetic surgeons—like their colleagues in Europe—advocated the use of autogenous material from the patients themselves, particularly cartilage from the nose and ear. The use of cartilage from the rib was more controversial and typically advised primarily for revision and/or reconstructive rhinoplasty procedures. In the U.S., only board-certified plastic surgeons or ear, nose, and throat surgeons were willing to attempt performing the invasive operation of rib harvesting, which could require a surgical suite and increased the length and expense of the procedure.

Preferences for techniques and materials reflected underlying differences in attitudes toward the body and risk, though this was not always obvious to surgeons. They sometimes talked past one another while debating the relative merits of one technique over another. An exchange at an ISAPS "Asian Rhinoplasty" panel brought these differences to the surface. Presenters from Taiwan, Korea, the Philippines, China, and Japan all shared their preferred techniques for implanting synthetic nasal implants made of silicone and Gore-Tex. A cosmetic surgeon based in the Philippines, Dr. Felizardo, outlined his preferred "hybrid" rhinoplasty technique combining "synthetic and natural" materials, claiming a distinct knowledge base. With pride, he remarked, "Our experience using biomaterials using Gore-Tex, silicone, etc., is more extensive than the use of these materials by Caucasians." He explained how he used a variety of hardened silicone (ePTFE) in combination with material from a patient's cartilage or rib to make patients' noses bigger and more pronounced.

Dr. Felizardo then made a pitch for the superiority of synthetic materials in rhinoplasty: "You can use cartilage from the ear or rib to augment the dorsum. But in my twenty-five years of experience, I've seen a lot of warped cartilage. I am partial to synthetic materials because the shape holds." Again leaning on his clinical experience of complications, he argued that synthetic materials better addressed his patients' needs. Acknowledging that discretion and clinical judgment had to be applied, he concluded his short presentation with exceptional cases in which he had used autogenous materials, like cartilage grafts for the augmentation of the tip of the nose. Copanelists from China and Singapore seconded Dr. Felizardo's preference for synthetic materials rather than the use of autogenous material from the rib. This seemed to settle the matter: Asian rhinoplasty should not hesitate to use synthetic materials.

However, the question-and-answer session following the panel immediately called this consensus into question. A Belgian cosmetic surgeon, Dr. Lambert, stood up in the audience and challenged the very premise of the panel—that synthetics could or should be used. The midafternoon panel had been a quiet, routine affair, but now some audience members were shifting in their seats and whispering to one another. Prefacing his remarks that he must be missing something, the questioner continued, asking why Dr. Felizardo used synthetic silicone rather than natural cartilage for nasal augmentation. Initially, the panelists looked at each other, puzzled. Assuming the question had been misheard or misunderstood, Dr. Felizardo first attempted a clarification, explaining that surgeons needed a lot of material; there simply was not enough cartilage in the patient's nose or ear to go the distance. Dr. Lambert defiantly countered that there was plenty of material in the rib. While back-and-forth exchanges occasionally enlivened Q&A sessions, this was especially spirited. An undercurrent of tension suffused the room.

In response, Dr. Felizardo mounted a robust defense of synthetic implants, laying out in the process the distinct logics undergirding Asian rhinoplasty. He slowly reeled off his reasons: synthetic implants were cheaper to insert (hundreds rather than thousands of dollars), safer (not requiring an additional surgical site in the chest for removal of a piece of rib cartilage), and preferred by patients (whom he described as reluctant to modify their bodies). Who wanted to risk an infection in a second site on their bodies simply to add to their nose, when synthetic materials provided a cheaper alternative? Dr. Lambert was not ready to let the matter rest, interjecting with another question: "What about the potential risk of infection posed by synthetic implants?" Bristling at the implication that he was less concerned with patient safety, Dr. Felizardo doubled down on his patients' preference for synthetic implants. Whatever Dr. Lambert's experience in the West, it was a tough sell to get his patients to consider a second harvesting site for natural material.

After several minutes and with no reconciliation in sight, Dr. Felizardo and Dr. Lambert agreed to disagree, noting that cultural common sense varied across locations. For Dr. Lambert, synthetic nasal implants were a nonstarter. His questions opened the black box of the panelists' ready acceptance of them. By contrast, for the presenters from Asia on the "Asian rhinoplasty" panel, rib grafts were simply not part of their regular tool kit of surgical techniques. Many thought they were unnecessarily complicated and risky for a facial cosmetic procedure. Despite a risk of infection, synthetic implants seemed safer to Asian cosmetic surgeons. Asian rhinoplasty had adapted to respond to the perceived riskiness of cartilage harvesting. Seeing synthetic materials as comparatively effective, Asian surgeons took their use for granted, and moved on to showcase different techniques to insert them. While the ISAPS exchange was a tempest in a teapot, it revealed real differences in Asian and Western surgeons' clinical experiences, judgment, and ultimately, craft.

Certainly, assessments of the relative risk of the use of natural versus synthetic implants was not as clearly settled as either Dr. Felizardo or Dr. Lambert believed. Dr. Lee, a U.S.-based surgeon who identified with an Asian approach, later gave me an extended and wide-ranging disquisition about the things that could go wrong with natural implants in rhinoplasty. He pointed out that rib grafts, in particular, entailed significant risk and time:

> For the rib, you gotta make a huge cut in women that's probably like two inches long right in the chest area and that operation carries a risk of collapsed lung and other stuff. It takes I think about an hour, hour and a half just to get the cartilage. I certainly can't do it in an office setting. So there are high risks with that. And then you put that whole thing, you can't carve it that well. And then when you finally stick it in, you don't know what it's gonna do in six months. It could move, it could warp, it could resorb, it could do all kinds of stuff.

Pivoting, Dr. Lee then argued, "[Synthetic] implants are simple, safe, takes really fifteen minutes to put in, and they're really safe using the proper technique and people just don't know how to use proper technique." He attributed "anecdotal" stories of complications with synthetic implants to those inserted out of the clinics by people other than doctors. Paradoxically, he asserted that the insertion method for synthetic implants was so "easy" that many nondoctors did it on their own outside of sterilized settings. The resulting higher rate of complications gave what he called a "bad rap" to the whole procedure. In this depiction, the use of synthetic implants in rhinoplasty was too easy or basic to be prestigious; by contrast, "taking out a rib" asserted surgical authority and expertise, consistent with the more interventionist and even macho reputation of U.S. cosmetic surgery.[32]

The use of silicone implants remained an open debate in the global discipline. Authors of a 2011 review article in the widely read journal *Plastic and Reconstructive Surgery* summarizing the results of several rhinoplasty studies wrote: "The use of silicone in rhinoplasty is a point of worldwide contention among plastic surgeons. Perhaps the difference in opinion on whether or not this is a valid option stems from what some surgeons deem acceptable risk and others do not."[33] The authors declared the complication rate for the use of synthetic implants in rhinoplasty to be "higher" but "acceptable" compared with autogenous cartilage. While the article concluded that autogenous cartilage was "the preferred method," the U.S.-based authors offered a more qualified assessment than anyone I observed or interviewed. With few rigorous studies of the relative risk of infection of different implants, there was ultimately not a clear enough consensus to close out the debate. Scientific findings informed cosmetic surgeons' thinking about risk and safety, but surgeons interpreted the evidence in line with prevailing cultural norms and expectations, which were further inflected by different institutional and legal contexts.

Breast Augmentation

Cosmetic surgeons' attitudes toward implants differed based on the body part under discussion. Debates about the relative merits of synthetic versus natural implants for nasal and breast procedures exposed underlying differences in the cultural, economic, and institutional situation of cosmetic surgery across contexts. Breast augmentation is perhaps the most familiar breast procedure, in which surgeons make breasts larger through the insertion of synthetic implants of differing sizes and shapes or by adding fat. Synthetic breast implants came in different volumes and shapes, and were filled with saline, silicone, or specialized gels, each offering slightly distinct appearances, motility, and feel. In contrast to rhinoplasty and blepharoplasty, cosmetic surgeons did not tout techniques under the label "Asian breast augmentation" at conferences or in medical journals. In fact, cosmetic surgeons often described breast augmentation as "universal," saying the procedure was conducted using much the same technique for women across racial backgrounds.[34] At the same time, they acknowledged that ideal breast appearance varied according to cultural and national differences. In contrast to their suspicion of synthetic implants for rhinoplasty, U.S. cosmetic surgeons had a reputation for preferring rounder and larger volume silicone implants than their counterparts everywhere else, including Asia. And at conferences, medical device vendors confirmed that breast implants sold to surgeons practicing in Asia were smaller and "anatomic" in shape, resulting in a more "natural" profile.

At least one U.S. cosmetic surgeon argued that an Asian style of cosmetic surgery might affirm a more general preference for synthetic implants over the use of natural materials. Dr. Lee, the American proponent of synthetic nasal implants, was an advocate for the use of synthetic implants in the breast as well. He was irked by the discrepancy between U.S. surgeons' preference for "natural" materials like fat, cartilage, and bone for nasal procedures and for "artificial," synthetic materials for breast augmentation. In light of U.S. surgeons' enthusiasm for synthetic implants in breast augmentation procedures, he interpreted their hesitation to use synthetic implants for nasal augmentation as hypocrisy. He told me, "When I tell my fellow plastic surgery colleagues who are Caucasian about the nose implant, they freak out. 'Oh, you can't use it because it's unsafe. You get an extrusion, you get infection.' Listen, they use implants on the cheek, on the chin, and on the breast. But somehow you can't use it on the nose. I don't know what happened there." Dr. Lee framed his use of synthetic breast implants as a bid for consistency, seeing a contradiction in blanket advocacy for synthetic implants in some kinds of procedures but not others. He attributed U.S. cosmetic surgeons' implant preferences to pride and a desire to perform difficult techniques rather than to a principled stand for patient safety. In fact, Dr. Lee further argued for the relative safety of synthetic implants and the dangers of fat: "Fat is not bone. It's soft and it resorbs and they say, 'OK, then we'll go and put more fat and more fat.'" Dr. Lee was concerned that using a person's own tissue from elsewhere in the body to add volume to her nose, breast, or face would fail. By noting that fat tissue transplanted from the waist might result in a lumpy appearance or that fat might not stay put, he emphasized the fallibility of the natural body.

For proponents of "natural" implants, the ability of the body to resorb natural materials was a feature rather than a bug, one that reduced the risk inherent in the cosmetic procedures. But for Dr. Lee, "natural" material was more fickle and unpredictable than "artificial" synthetic implants. There is certainly a gendered undercurrent to describing the bodies of breast augmentation patients, who were all women, as unpredictable and not fully under the (male) surgeon's control. Dr. Lee exhibited a form of "surgical anxiety," a term that sociologist So Yeon Leem has used to describe the stress that Korean cosmetic surgeons feel about the intransigence and uncertainties associated with the natural body and the healing process.[35] For Dr. Lee and, he argued, other practitioners of Asian cosmetic surgery, synthetic implants could be one strategy to mitigate such uncertainty and reassert control while delivering a final result to patients more quickly.

In fact, silicone breast implants have had a checkered track record for safety. Regulatory bodies like the U.S. FDA repeatedly expressed concerns about them, and in the early 1990s, reports of ruptured silicone implants and complications gained widespread media attention. In 1992, after repeated reports and industry inaction, the FDA removed silicone gel–filled implants from the market altogether. It was not until 2006 that the FDA next approved a new silicone gel–filled implant, alongside increased scrutiny and restrictions.[36] With subsequent long-term follow-up monitoring, silicone breast implants have been found to be associated with a slightly higher risk of anaplastic large-cell lymphoma cancer.[37] Almost thirty years after silicone implants were initially banned from the market, breast implants have again come under scrutiny: in July 2019 major manufacturer Allergan issued a worldwide voluntary withdrawal of one of its implants after reported complications in patients.[38] These scandals and controversies in the U.S. pushed surgeons in the direction of different kinds of breast implants, including fat grafts and saline implants, while perhaps dissuading some in Asia from conducting breast augmentation procedures.

Given the existence of Asian rhinoplasty and Asian blepharoplasty, why, then, was there no "Asian breast augmentation" in articles or conferences? The craft of Asian cosmetic surgery was shaped by past scandals, different regulatory apparatuses, and different risk tolerances. It is possible that U.S. cosmetic surgeons were so strongly associated with breast augmentation procedures and a large-breasted aesthetic that breast augmentation itself seemed to be an implicitly American procedure. Doing less dramatic or fewer breast augmentation procedures was what comparatively distinguished Asian cosmetic surgery. In addition, practitioners of Asian cosmetic surgery were navigating a distinct set of attitudes toward the gendered body, constructions of "natural" materials, and degrees of tolerance toward medical invasiveness. Despite clear differences in implant preferences, U.S. cosmetic surgeons were not anti–synthetic implant while Asian cosmetic surgeons were pro–synthetic implant, or vice versa. Rather, cosmetic surgeons in the U.S and Europe expressed a preference for using synthetic implants for breasts and natural materials for the nose. Asian cosmetic surgeons made a name for themselves in employing synthetic implants for noses and limited or no augmentation for breasts.

In short, differences in craft could not simply be explained by embodied differences in the average patient confronting surgeons in the U.S. versus Asia. Asian cosmetic surgeons' and patients' preferences for less invasive procedures required the use of synthetic material and were also predicated on a different cultural valence toward the "natural," unmediated body. U.S. cosmetic surgeons preferred more invasive procedures that showcased their talents and expertise. Recognition of these differences and their contingency staved off attempts at more universal standardization, but also contributed to the racialization of techniques.

Institutional and Regulatory Influences on Asian Techniques

Certainly, the craft of Asian cosmetic surgery incorporated a historically and legally contingent analysis of risk based on surgeons' different clinical experiences. At transnational meetings, cosmetic surgeons linked their own preferences for some kinds of materials and procedures to cultural and stylistic responses to different legal structures and expectations of risk. Cultural attitudes toward the body and different sociolegal arrangements further set the stage for what distinguished some techniques as "Asian." Larger institutional structures in health insurance and the legal system also informed the commonsense assumptions of the craft of Asian cosmetic surgery.

For instance, health insurers in the U.S., Europe, and South America classified some nose and breast procedures as reconstructive, rendering them eligible for insurance subsidies. This was especially clear for breast reduction procedures, which reduced the size, profile, or weight of breasts by removing fat tissue.[39] Though almost all breast procedures not related to breast cancer were classified as cosmetic or aesthetic and not eligible for insurance reimbursement or coverage in Malaysia and other parts of Asia, breast reduction procedures were covered as a reconstructive intervention by some U.S. health insurance plans. Similarly, rhinoplasty in the U.S. could receive some insurance coverage if surgeons identified a functional deficit. This opened up opportunities for plastic surgeons to offer patients more expensive techniques. Dr. Silber made this connection explicit. "People are using rib grafts like you wouldn't believe. Why? They're billing insurance like $30,000." In his opinion, the use of rib material was "not for better rhinoplasty, it's for better income." Requiring more time and specialized labor, rib grafts cost more and garnered higher potential insurance reimbursements. While rhinoplasty absent injury or accident was nominally an aesthetic procedure paid for out of pocket by patients, it could be covered by insurance in the U.S. as a reconstructive procedure under some circumstances.[40] Insurance coverage made the procedure more accessible and affordable for patients with health insurance, allowing surgeons to perform more invasive and expensive procedures at the same cost to patients.

Moreover, lawsuits and redress in court were less readily available as a remedy for bad cosmetic surgical outcomes and surgical complications in Asian countries compared to the U.S. In fact, cosmetic surgeons in both the U.S. and Malaysia identified the weaker malpractice suit system in Asian countries like Thailand, Malaysia, and South Korea as an advantage for Asian cosmetic surgery, driving some of the price differentials that in turn spurred medical tourism. By contrast, U.S. cosmetic surgeons worried that unhappy patients with complications would sue them for medical malpractice and win high payouts. Though few cases were ultimately decided against cosmetic surgeons, the mere prospect governed how cosmetic surgeons in the U.S. practiced. Many surgeons described their actions and preferences in technique as geared toward avoiding the unlikely but devastating event of a malpractice lawsuit. Surgeons in the U.S. and Asia attributed American reluctance to use synthetic implants for rhinoplasty procedures to fears of liability in the event of complications. Independent of the scientific evidence about whether synthetic nasal implants led to more complications, U.S. rhinoplasty expert Dr. Bennett claimed that the failure of a synthetic nasal implant was more likely to count as evidence of harm in a court of law. While the scientific verdict was out on whether complications were significantly higher with synthetic implants, it was seen as less compelling for a patient to criticize the use of material from their own body.

THE COMPARATIVE ADVANTAGES
OF ASIAN COSMETIC SURGERY

Asian Markets for Asian Expertise

Asian aesthetic surgery was further supported by the construction of a burgeoning Asian market for consumer goods and services. Marketing research firms lauded Asia as the fastest-growing market for cosmetic surgery—as well as for medical tourism. Due to lower labor costs, government investment in higher education, well-developed physical infrastructures (in some locations, if not country-wide), established legal institutions, relative political stability, and "a liberalized market economy," some Asian countries were well positioned to offer safe, affordable plastic surgery that might attract medical travelers as well as middle-class citizens.[41] The project of "Asian cosmetic surgery" has been accompanied by the regional development of cosmetic surgery tourism networks. Cosmetic surgeons emphasized differences in types of patients and in techniques to attract patients and build regional networks.

Ascertaining the exact number of patients traveling or amount of money changing hands for cosmetic surgery tourism has proven difficult. The range of industry estimates is huge; the market for international medical travel has been pegged as low as $11 billion and as high as $100 billion.[42] The 1998 Asian financial crisis has been cited as a turning point for medical tourism, especially for Southeast Asia. In its aftermath, Thailand and Malaysia pivoted toward medical tourism to recoup their investments in advanced private medical facilities. As the U.S. tightened its borders and visa requirements following 9/11, they welcomed patients from the Middle East.[43] Buoyed by its potential to promote economic development, medical tourism has grown.[44] While South Korea boasted the most cosmetic surgeons and the highest volume of medical tourist procedures in the early 2010s, Malaysia and Thailand also competed to attract lower middle class patients from wealthier countries where cosmetic surgery was more expensive, like Singapore, Australia, and New Zealand. Supported by the intersection of state agencies and private corporations, medical travel facilities in Asia have become "global," international spaces that depend on national investments in workforces and infrastructures.[45]

Expertise in cosmetic surgery is also itself a symbol of what Ruth Holliday and her coauthors call "medical nationalism."[46] Medical and scientific capabilities, shown through displays of technical prowess and advanced medical interventions, can also be a source of national pride and participation in global biomedicine and science.[47] Plastic surgeons in Brazil, South Korea, and Thailand have become world renowned for their aesthetic sense and technical expertise, benefiting from institutionalization and investment by their respective governments.[48] In historian John DiMoia's account, cosmetic surgery in the Republic of Korea emerged from several converging factors, including emergent professional norms, consolidation of power and expertise in the medical community, and "the acceptance of and confidence associated with medical intervention as a means to realize and achieve one's desired self-image."[49] Nationalizing scientific and clinical expertise also garners cultural authority and regional soft power. As political and cultural elites, cosmetic surgeons shaped and displayed modified, beautiful bodies to, in the words of Oluwakemi Balogun and Kimberly Hoang, "project a new image of their countries as eager and ready to compete in the global economy."[50] Developing the craft of Asian cosmetic surgery supported economic and biopolitical projects as well as a clinical, scientific one.

Competitors and Alternatives to Asian Expertise

Asian cosmetic surgery was one type of racialized expertise that groups of surgeons had shaped into a craft. One might expect there to be other parallel racialized or nationality-based categories, such as European, Middle Eastern, Mediterranean, Korean, or Brazilian. Certainly, these kinds of nationalized and racialized labels were also applied to physical features, beauty ideals, techniques, and even institutional medical, economic, or legal systems. However, the craft of Asian cosmetic surgery largely stood alone as an entity; no other racial category had quite the same level of institutionalization as a craft at transnational conferences or in the academic cosmetic literature. "Latin" was the only similar racialized category that came close. The uniqueness of Asian aesthetic surgery highlighted how tenuous it could be to use racialized labels to link medical services and prospective markets. To make the linkage work depended on a series of contingencies with several important implications.

First, physical difference alone did not bring a racial category into being; the mere fact of difference was not automatically accorded recognition. The story of Blackness makes this especially clear. Despite being present in medical journals and beauty standards, and despite its salience in the American imagination and global relevance, Blackness almost never appeared at the conferences I observed. In particular, clinical cases involving Black patients were largely absent from conference proceedings in the U.S. and in Asia. The exceptions proved the rule of Black otherness. At the ISAPS Congress in Kyoto, a surgeon from France presented a case of a Black woman who requested a breast reduction and breast lift procedure. Photographs of her large breasts projected onto two enormous screens caused a stir in the sleepy lecture hall. Once again, several cosmetic surgeons around me simultaneously raised their phones to take photographs of the screen.[51] This single patient attracted more attention than any other case presented at the session. Dr. Shanmugam, a Malaysian surgeon attending the conference, commented with awe that her breasts were the largest he had ever seen in over fifteen years of practice. Aside from the African American celebrity Michael Jackson, this was the only case presentation of a Black patient that I witnessed over the course of the ISAPS meeting in Japan. In both cases, cosmetic surgeons presented and reacted to the patients as extreme foils, signifying grotesque spectacle. The absence of Black patients and surgeons from sub-Saharan Africa is telling. At conferences, cosmetic surgeons sought to showcase their best work, of which they were proudest: the absence of Black patients suggests an implicit belief that Black patients were not general exemplars of beauty. Surgeons did not want to distinguish their brand or craft as associated with Black patients. Instead, they gestured to Black patients as a foil to other kinds of beauty, with Blackness continuing to serve as a negative reference point. Racial categories required champions to make a case for their relevance, importance, and value relative to one another.[52] Without that kind of action and attention, the use of racial categories perpetuated and upheld existing racial hierarchies.

Second, labeling a body of expertise in racialized terms required a clear contrast. Cosmetic surgeons from Latin America distinguished their patients culturally and in embodied terms in their conference presentations, sometimes using the label "Latin" to set apart their patients and cultural expectations. For instance, a Colombian surgeon told an ISAPS audience that "Latin women are very comfortable with their bodies and their sexuality, not afraid to show it off." She showed a picture of a beautiful young woman in micro, cut-off shorts to illustrate Latinas' preference for what she called "natural curves." Expertise and innovations from Latin America were recognized and lauded on the global stage. Cosmetic surgeons from Mexico, Colombia, and Brazil presented at each of the large conferences that I attended. Yet surgeons in Latin America did not themselves fully organize or coalesce around categories such as "Latin" or "mestizo" except for purposes of contrast. It was not an identity that surgeons affirmed in the absence of comparison. And the nuances of these and other possible racial categories salient within specific

Latin American countries were not discussed at the transnational conferences that I attended.[53]

Practitioners of Asian cosmetic surgery emphasized contrast based on price, culture, geography, and history, and worked hard to maintain an alternate genealogy of beauty and anticipate a distinct, hypermodern future. "Asian cosmetic surgery" was a style supported by cosmetic surgeons in multiple countries, including the U.S. A range of actors contributed to the enterprise and sought to build it out transnationally, an effort without a regional parallel. It is also not a coincidence that proponents of an "Asian cosmetic surgery," no matter their geographic location, considered there to be racial differences, rooted in culture and biology, between "Asian" and other patients. Surgeons practicing in Latin America, Europe, and the U.S. did not mount a similar public relations effort. They were comparatively ambivalent about emphasizing how their expertise was different.

Cosmetic surgery in Latin America, North America, and Europe was more intertwined and less easily distinguished as separate, standardized types due to ongoing cross-border flows of surgical trainees and patients. Plastic surgery was historically connected in these countries, with U.S. surgeons training in Germany, France, and the United Kingdom, and vice versa. Today, this transnational loop includes several European countries (including Belgium and the Netherlands), Brazil and other countries in South America, and the U.S. and Canada. The greater historical interconnectedness between plastic surgery in these countries made the craft of surgery in these contexts less easily disentangled, compared with more philosophical and technical variation that characterized the contemporary Asian approach. It is important to note that in Europe, Latin America, and North America, surgical trainees circulated as well as patients. While some patients did travel regionally within these areas, as well as intercontinentally, governments in Europe, North America, and Latin America had done less to encourage cosmetic surgery tourism flows in the current era of more affordable air travel than their Asian counterparts. This firsthand exchange of clinical information would be more likely to inspire cross talk and dissemination of techniques across the U.S., Latin America, and Europe such that expertise would not be so easily separable. The movement of cosmetic surgeons helped standardize knowledge and minimized clinical differentiation based on region or race, whereas the movement of patients for medical tourism may have contributed to the opposite tendency.

CONCLUSION

I argue that the craft of Asian cosmetic surgery is a set of expertise, techniques, and values that simultaneously assert Asian racial difference as a matter of science and art. Physical differences in patients' bodies were not enough to bring this practice into being; building and elucidating the art of Asian cosmetic surgery required surgeons to emphasize contrasts. Asian cosmetic surgery developed in relation to alternative referents, like U.S. cosmetic surgery, and as the result of combined efforts of cosmetic surgeons in different cultural, economic, and political contexts. Asian cosmetic surgery reflects specialization and surgical dispositions rooted in regimes of training, expertise, law, and experimentation that are distinct from the practice of cosmetic surgery in the U.S., South America, and Europe. My exposition of this craft shows how history, attitudes toward the body, aesthetics, and institutional contexts inform where and how cosmetic surgeons perform nips and tucks on the body.

Craft encapsulates the practical and technical work that cosmetic surgeons do alongside the more formalized and codified forms of expertise. The techniques discussed here were developed by cosmetic surgeons circa 2016, shown off to an audience of peers. But I do not expect that these procedures or techniques to remain static. Rather than evaluating the novelty or the distinctiveness of these techniques, this chapter discusses what it means to apply the label "Asian" to a body of knowledge and suite of skills.

In conferences, as in medical journal articles, the racial category "Asian" functioned as a standard—but a fuzzier one. Cosmetic surgeons enhanced their reach not by rigidly standardizing "Asian" or "Latin," but by leaving the definition of such categories loose, incorporating both physical and cultural factors. While standardization in medicine has been portrayed as clarifying, reducing, or simplifying difference,[54] the value of the Asian category derives from its multiplicity and ambiguity, which also advances clinical understanding.

A close look at Asian cosmetic surgery illuminates the effects of transnational and economic exchange on the development of one biomedical craft. Labeling expertise with racial categories allows for a shared brand identity and coordination around expertise that nonetheless builds in room for surgeons' individual clinical judgment and aesthetic sense. It enables cosmetic surgeons to more easily compare notes across vast gulfs of both geographic and experiential distance. Similarly, it makes cosmetic surgeons from distant locales legible to patients considering traveling to receive care. Furthermore, a racial category like "Asian" has enough ambiguity and possible linkages to different cultural and historical genealogies that it can be used to tell multiple narratives of beauty. While "Asian" means one thing at an international conference compared with "Western" or "American," it may mean something else in a Malaysian or Korean cosmetic surgery clinic. In this way, developing "Asian cosmetic surgery" as a craft extends cosmetic surgeons' authority and expertise transnationally. The big tent of Asian cosmetic surgery is productive for the field of cosmetic surgery.[55]

The salience of Asian cosmetic surgery stems from its economic and political resonances as well as clinical factors. Just as research has found for the national level, at the global level, racial categories are also part of transnational racial projects, shaped by political, historical, cultural, and scientific currents. Asian cosmetic surgery is bolstered by regional efforts to promote transnational science and biotechnology initiatives, as well as cultural products such as K-pop. In the absence of constituencies and mobilizations around racial categories, whether due to the perception of less purchasing power or lower aesthetic value, they do not necessarily appear on the global stage, as in the case of Blackness. A racialized craft is ultimately valued and visible insofar as it can be marketized and/or aligned with the interests of states.

The story of "Asian cosmetic surgery" as told here challenges the idea of Western dominance in this field of biomedicine. However, it also shows how difficult it is for racial categories to shed their political and historical baggage, even when deployed transnationally and/or for inclusionary purposes by experts. Shifting focus to how surgeons discuss racial categories in the context of clinical practice in the U.S. and Malaysia, part 2 illuminates the meso and micro layers of the racial project of cosmetic surgery.

PART II

Discussing Clinical Practice
in the U.S. and Malaysia

3 "Looking Right"

CRAFTING NATURAL LOOKS IN
COSMETIC SURGERY

In medical journal articles and conference presentations, cosmetic surgeons dealt in the abstract, generalizing from their experience and from systematic study to sketch out discrete, ideal racialized types.[1] The realm of clinical practice was considerably messier. Dr. Parlato (Latino, Chicago) explained the leap from textbook to clinical practice:

> I tell patients, "I want you to look natural." I want faces to look beautiful, but I don't want people to necessarily know they've had plastic surgery. . . . You develop an aesthetic sense, but it's like fashion. It's a very personal thing. You can't canonize fashion and you can't canonize metrics of facial proportions of beauty, but we try. Look at any textbook that formally looks at rhinoplasty. It'll tell you that the dimensions from the tip to the bridge should be this amount and the distance, from here to here, your nostrils should be from the borders of your eyelids down. That's an idea. But I don't necessarily utilize numbers and statistics in my practice. I simply visualize things and so I'm less analytic than I form an impression and that's what I go for.[2]

Though he had worked at an academic medical center, coauthored several medical journal articles, and participated in basic science research, he also argued for cosmetic surgery as an art depending on an aesthetic sense. He took a "I know it when I see it" approach to recognizing beautiful, natural looks. Dr. Parlato's reliance on his intuition and his hesitance to objectify or standardize beauty was typical of surgeons I interviewed in the U.S. and Malaysia. They relied on their clinical judgment and intuition in contending with the symbolic and social meanings of looks.

Like Dr. Parlato, most of my respondents valued "natural" looks, which referred to appearances that made it seem as though no cosmetic surgery had been done. Surgical procedures that transformed the perceived racial group membership of patients violated this aesthetic norm. Creating natural looks required surgeons to reinscribe and elaborate upon racial difference. This chapter focuses on how cosmetic surgeons in the U.S. and Malaysia styled themselves as gatekeepers to natural looks. In both countries, natural looks maintained the lines of existing racial group membership: U.S. cosmetic surgeons rejected looks that they perceived as crossing racial lines, calling them "artificial" or "unnatural." Malaysian surgeons delineated a natural, "Asian" look. Though surgeons in both countries entertained and granted some requests for artificial looks, they made it clear that these were "weird," "wrong," implying they were inferior. Cosmetic surgeons judged these procedures to be technically possible but morally and culturally inadvisable.

While surgeons in both countries trained their judgment on natural appearances, they operated in different symbolic and scalar registers when it came to race. In the U.S., I found that cosmetic surgeons sought to preserve racial distinctions and prevent the crossing of racial boundaries between U.S. racial groups. By contrast, in Malaysia, I found that cosmetic surgeons advocated for a natural "Asian" look as opposed to an artificial "Caucasian" look. In maintaining a racial boundary between "Asian" and "Caucasian" looks, Malaysian cosmetic surgeons primarily acted as gatekeepers between the local and global spheres. And, whereas U.S. cosmetic surgeons focused on U.S. specific racial meanings, Malaysian cosmetic surgeons situated beauty ideals within a regional context.

CLINICAL JUDGMENT AS A FORM OF EVALUATION

Physicians use their clinical judgment to tailor medical interventions to each patient's physical body. Clinical judgment is implicated as an element of craft in cosmetic surgery, encompassing the idea of knowing which standards to apply when. Translating expert discourses on race from medical journals into practice required a certain degree of expertise in everyday conceptions of race. Clinical judgment incorporated cosmetic surgeons' unique experiences as well as commonsense ideas about race into their decisions about when and how to consider race in shaping a look. Touting their own judgment and discretion allowed cosmetic surgeons to distinguish themselves from competitors and incorporate racial specificity and variability into their practices.

Unlike in many medical specialties, there is no formal designation of illness in cosmetic surgery. In cosmetic surgery, the underlying illnesses and pathologies that warrant and justify medical intervention are actively contested.[3] Cosmetic surgeons have to decide whether a patient has a reasonable and realistic request for enhancement. Cosmetic surgeons broadly agree on what people do not want: "No one likes bulges. No one likes lines," as Dr. Kozlowski (white, Chicago) put it. Other surgeons added crooked noses, bumps, or deformities to the list. Surgeons offered to "correct these deformities" and help patients "blend in" and achieve a normal or neutral appearance. Surgeons gestured to general aesthetic principles like symmetry, harmony, and balance.[4] But there remained considerable and extensive gray areas about when and whether cosmetic surgeons should operate. This chapter dwells on those uncertain gray areas, especially those linked to race and gender.

To successfully operate on patients, surgeons needed to do more than deliver a technically proficient outcome. They had to exercise judgment about whether and how they could satisfy the expectations of patients who sought to change aspects of their appearance that signaled social identities like race, gender, or class. This required social discretion, symbolic interpretation, and even aesthetic taste. In fact, these were the very characteristics that drew some surgeons to the field. Dr. Mannheim (multiracial, Chicago) told me, "I like the psychosocial aspect of it. I see myself as one-third artist, one-third scientist, and one-third psychologist. The fulfillment of my life's work is making people happy." For all that surgeons valued the opportunity to exercise discretion and engage directly with psychosocial meaning, they recognized this as a challenge. Dr. Carras (white, L.A.) succinctly noted, "Operating on happiness is not an easy thing to do."

The decision surgeons often faced, then, was whether to operate and how, in a field in which the correct course of action was nebulous. Scientific reasoning was important, but could only get surgeons so far. In the end, as Charles Bosk argues, "clinical results, not scientific reasoning, determine how correct judgement is."[5] Choosing *not* to operate on a patient is one of the most common errors of judgment among surgeons, whereas the most common error of judgment in cosmetic surgery is choosing *to* operate, according to Bosk. As a result, the additional layers in clinical judgment—especially aesthetic and moral elements—become both clearer as part of the diagnostic analysis and also more consequential. Cosmetic surgery turns aesthetic, moral, and social concerns about racialized bodies into physical or technical challenges that can be solved with surgical solutions.[6] Conversely, surgeons characterize some procedures or outcomes that they consider to be socially questionable as technically impossible to achieve. In my research, the narratives guiding transformation were particularly important. What surgeons thought they were doing—how cosmetic surgeons conceptualized the goals and symbolic meaning of requests for a "natural" or "ethnic" look—mattered.

NATURAL LOOKS IN THE U.S.

Cosmetic surgeons were gatekeepers to ideal, racialized appearances. Dr. Ackerman (white, NYC) outlined his preferred aesthetic as "natural-appearing, rejuvenating surgery that looks good and doesn't look obvious." He gave several examples of racialized rhinoplasty outcomes that violated this aesthetic sense: "If I have an African American patient who wants a very thin and petite nose, A, it's not technically that feasible, and B, it's not going to look right. If you see an African American with a very petite, very thin nose, you will immediately think rhinoplasty, especially if they have classic African features. It doesn't match correctly."

"Looking right" was a judgment call reflecting racial commonsense notions with an aesthetic component. Dr. Ackerman linked racial group membership to particular constellations of physical features, and he offered a moral and aesthetic evaluation of mismatches between features and racial identities. Here, he identified the racial marker as the clearly surgically altered nose: The "petite, very thin nose" on a face with "classic African features." To bolster his case, he argued that changing racial features was also a technically difficult problem. Indeed, Dr. Ackerman first refused the nasal procedure on technical grounds ("it's not technically that feasible") and then on aesthetic and cultural ones ("it's not going to look right"). He went on, "We will see a lot of people of Jewish, Italian, or Middle Eastern heritage who also want a little, petite nose with a very defined tip, more typical of northern Europe. The thickness of their skin alone doesn't really allow for that. We will get them as close as we can to what we think looks good, but there is a limit, and that's a limit that we can't control." Describing physical characteristics as recalcitrant took them out of a surgeon's hands and beyond their "control." Invoking several different racial groups, he indicated this was not only a Black/white matter. The language of mismatch suggested a social disjuncture as well as a technical limitation—though no doubt, physical tissue, cartilage, and skin thickness could also present obstacles to creating a "very defined" nasal tip. Dr. Ackerman rejected such requests on the grounds that it was too risky for both clinical and social reasons.

As with Dr. Ackerman, many U.S. surgeons associated race with physical features and implied that racialized physical characteristics posed technical or physical challenges for cosmetic surgery. Like many ordinary Americans, U.S. cosmetic surgeons understood race as a physical, visual phenomenon, rooted in the body. Cosmetic surgeons were in agreement in recognizing specific features of the body—from skin pigmentation, skin thickness, to cartilage and bone structure and beyond—as hard limits with technical ramifications for surgical outcomes. When cosmetic surgeons reported being unable to comply with some patients' requests for racial transformation, they often pointed to the limits of the physical body.

Surgeons described bodies in terms of how their physical features and properties made them more or less amenable to change. Bodies could present hard constraints and limitations to intervention, including the very features that cosmetic surgeons associated with race in medical journal articles, like eye and nose size and shape, fat placement, quantity and location of cartilage, skin thickness, and skin pigmentation. Dr. Bronfman (white, NYC) bracketed some physical differences as impossible to alter through surgery: "You can only achieve what the patient gives you in their tissues. I can't just turn someone into anyone they want to be. There are limitations based on the quality of their tissues, how tight it is, how much excess there is, how much fat there is. It's important to me to be able to look at the patient, see what the patient wants, know what I can deliver, and bring their expectations in line with what I can deliver." U.S. surgeons were reluctant to risk injury or complication in the pursuit of aesthetic improvement. Dr. Bronfman refused to operate when he thought the risk-to-benefit ratio was too high, a personal judgment call on the value of a procedure for a patient. In other words, cosmetic surgeons' reluctance to grant procedures that crossed racial lines was also undergirded with clinical caution. But as this quote also suggests, even physical "limitations" were a moving target, subject to an implicit risk calculus and assumptions about healing and patient satisfaction. Technical and social analyses were difficult to disentangle: the limitations of the body and the limitations presented by race were often elided by surgeons on purpose.

Natural and Artificial Looks

In practice, as in medical journal articles, cosmetic surgeons considered natural looks to be those that were "racially congruent," that is, consistent with a patient's racial group membership. This helped to maintain the illusion that no cosmetic surgery had been performed. Evaluating racial propriety was an important element of U.S. cosmetic surgeons' aesthetic sense. U.S. cosmetic surgeons encouraged patients of color to improve their appearance without changing their perceived racial group membership, calling this "ethnic preservation." The goal of ethnic preservation encompassed efforts to modify patients' appearances to meet racial-specific ideals of beauty. Dr. Mannheim (multiracial, Chicago) characterized it as "not putting a white skinny girl's nose on every patient that you see." Clarifying with celebrity examples, he added, "I'm not changing you into a white person. I am giving you a handsome Black nose, not Keira Knightley's nose on Michael Jackson's face." At the extremes, like the nose of a white British actress on a Black entertainer's face, surgeons did rule out some racialized looks. Here, Dr. Mannheim rejects the idea of racial transformation by evoking an image of a more natural, subtle transformation. These distinctions required aesthetic discernment and clinical judgment. To achieve a surgical outcome while maintaining a person's ascribed racial appearance required a honed aesthetic sense as well as an awareness of current beauty trends across communities. This was not simply about correctly tailoring physical features to racial boundaries: as the hypothetical image of a young white woman's nose on Michael Jackson's face illustrates, cosmetic surgeons also considered gender conformity as an important component of a natural look. By tailoring looks by race and gender, cosmetic surgeons could showcase their ability to artfully realize human differences.

While cosmetic surgeons across the U.S. also continued to offer patients procedures that resulted in a white or whiter appearance, many leaned toward ethnic preservation as their preferred aesthetic for its natural connotations. Cosmetic surgeons presented ethnic preservation as a more common request from patients. For instance, a cosmetic surgeon who was only a few years out of residency, Dr. Johnson (Black, Chicago), weighed different racialized goals: "[Patients] either want to be more Western or you just have a patient who wants to have some general rejuvenation and look more similar to their one attractive cousin or something. . . . It's more so the latter, that patients are wanting to just look like a very attractive African American person or Asian American person. They don't want to necessarily look like the ideal attractive American." Leaning back in his chair, he distinguished between patients of color who wanted to look like a "very attractive" member of their racial group and people who wanted to look like the "ideal attractive American," here explicitly coded "Western." Dr. Johnson's matter-of-fact portrayal suggested that some patients continued to request procedures to look "more Western." But he reported seeing more patients seeking ethnic preservation, acknowledging that his identification as a person of color may have played a role. He elaborated, "They're just looking for subtle improvements; that's what we mean by a natural look." The foil to the natural African American or Asian American look was the artificial "Western" look. "Subtle" or incremental improvements did not change others' perceptions of a patient's race, sometimes escaping detection altogether. Dr. Johnson directed patients to ethnic preservation: "If, for example, an African American woman comes in and says, 'I want a rhinoplasty,' I say, 'I want you to find me some pictures of your family member or a magazine with a Black person who has the nose you want.'" By suggesting that patients select models of the same race, he gently guided patients along that path. In interactions with patients, U.S. cosmetic surgeons assessed the racialized implications of patient requests for surgical procedures and nudged patients toward their preferred aesthetic.

While multiple physical features served as racial markers, surgeons did not see all of them as worthy of preservation or emulation. For instance, surgeons expected Asian American patients to ask for some modifications to the size and shape of the eye; they did not necessarily expect their patients to ask for a single eyelid or for an "Asian" nose. A specialist in what he termed "Asian cosmetic surgery," Dr. Lee clarified, "You can't really make the nose flatter. If they have a big bump, you can take it down, but it's not truly gonna make them look Asian, you know? So it has to do more with the eye and tilt it up." Dr. Lee (Asian, NYC) pointed out that a "flatter" nose was also associated with Asian patients but was not a feature that people sought. According to Dr. Lee, a patient's request for almond-shaped eyes to look Asian was reasonable, but the same patient's request for a flat nose would be strange. Surgeons made similar characterizations for Black patients seeking rhinoplasty. To surgeons, it was not that any physical marker associated with race was fair game. They clearly preferred some racially legible looks over others.

In addition to evaluating what patients asked for, surgeons evaluated how they asked. In consultation with patients, cosmetic surgeons crafted a narrative of change about the purpose and aims of the surgical intervention: that, for instance, patients were trying to look more refreshed, or wanted bigger breasts or a thinner nose. When presented with a photograph of a patient who appeared racially ambiguous and asked to evaluate whether their result was pleasing, surgeons would not say outright; they wanted to know what the patient had requested. How the patient narrated their request was a critical part of their evaluation. Dr. Kozlowski (white, Chicago) reasoned: "If an African American wants something with their nose—they don't say it, but they're looking for something a little more Caucasian. Not as wide, a little more projection, but . . . if they're hinting too much, I'd have to say, 'Look. This is the shape of your face. This is your ethnic background. If I give you, actually this would apply to anybody, if you have a very round face and you want a pinched thin nose, it's not going to look right.'" Dr. Kozlowski indicated that holding the physical appearance of the patient constant, he would be uncomfortable if an African American patient asked outright for a white nose. He was more inclined to operate if the same patient couched their request in race-neutral language, asking, for instance, for a nose "with a little more projection." This echoed Dr. Ackerman's rejection of mismatches while making clear that the phrasing of patient requests mattered. Dr. Kozlowski initially suggested that the changes that most African Americans requested could be interpreted as whitening. But if an African American patient were to make this desire explicit, they became a questionable candidate for surgery. Surgeons did not believe that any single procedure could turn a Black patient into a white one, nor did they think the goal itself was feasible.

Historically, cosmetic surgeons were deeply concerned by the prospect that Black people could "pass" as white, aided by surgery.[7] Lingering traces of this concern met an impulse of multicultural celebration of difference in surgeons' contemporary preference for ethnic preservation. Cosmetic surgeons worried that patients requesting racial transformation had deeper psychological issues that could not be satisfied by surgery. As he continued speaking, Dr. Kozlowski stepped back from the language of racial transformation into more incremental interventions such as "not as wide, a little more projection." The goal of ethnic preservation was to avoid an aesthetic and social mismatch between certain shapes such as a round face and pinched thin nose. It was also to avoid a mismatch between narratives of change and appearances. Like other American surgeons, Dr. Kozlowski took a socially questionable desire (wanting to switch between racial groups/to look whiter) and rendered its difficulties in aesthetic and technical terms. But this characterization also revealed that how patients framed requests factored into surgeons' evaluations of acceptable appearances.

Cosmetic surgeons sometimes read racial meanings into ostensibly neutral terminology. Dr. Bennett (white, Chicago) quipped that patients rarely came in with requests to "'keep my beak-like nose'— they won't say that. They'll say, 'Oh, straighten this part.'" Cosmetic surgeons interpreted descriptors such as "refined" or "straight" as requests for whiter features when made by patients of color. Dr. Solomon (Persian, U.S.) marked the word "refine" as code for making patients appear whiter: "In the field of plastic surgery, we use the word 'refine' as a way of expressing a desire to look more Caucasian. But that's a semantic term. I don't necessarily agree with it. . . . There are certain features like larger nostrils, less defined nasal features. Those are things that society and media over time have defined as less ideal or less refined or sophisticated." Even after acknowledging the implicit request as one for racial boundary crossing, Dr. Solomon considered "refining" the nose to be acceptable and achievable for patients of color as a more delineated, limited request. Identifying media and society as influences that shaped patient desires, he suggested that some racial implications were almost subconscious. They were only detectable by stepping back and reflecting on the larger picture of surgery in the U.S.

Patients of color often used racially neutral language in their requests for surgery. For instance, a twenty-two-year-old Latina woman described her motivation for seeking a rhinoplasty as achieving a "straight," unremarkable, refined nose that did not stand out, in preparation for her goal of becoming a news anchor. The framing of desires in such race-neutral ways despite clear racial implications allowed both surgeons and patients to side-step potentially uncomfortable conversations about race.[8] Whitening had not disappeared as a racialized goal of cosmetic surgery. But many U.S. surgeons reported discomfort with requests for whitening, consistent with a shift toward a multicultural sensibility. Accordingly, patients and cosmetic surgeons read between the lines to assess the racial implications of even facially neutral requests, as for "refining" the nose. Interpreting the racialized undertones of a request for surgery was part of their clinical judgment. The right phrasing was one way for cosmetic surgeons to construct a multicultural-sensitive narrative of change.

Why did U.S. cosmetic surgeons, who prided themselves on their bluntness, bother with such careful parsing of language? U.S. cosmetic surgeons also prided themselves on not simply saying yes to anyone who walked in the door, differentiating themselves from beauticians and other kinds of aesthetic laborers. Cosmetic surgeons balanced customer whims with asserting their authority and expertise. Judgment was a key function of their role as surgeons. Race was one important social terrain where they could distinguish themselves. Because the daily practice of cosmetic surgery challenged the notion that racial categories were stable, discrete, or immutable in the first place, there was a need for racial boundary policing and careful storytelling about narratives of racial change. In translating abstract ideals onto concrete bodies, cosmetic surgeons were redrawing boundaries as they literally wrote race on the body. Cosmetic surgeons knew how racialized bodies *could* be changed; the question became whether and how they *should* be changed.

Moreover, cosmetic surgeons' attention to the symbolic and aesthetic interpretations of looks was also prompted by an important material consideration. Surgeons feared that patients who requested to cross racial boundaries could never be made happy by cosmetic surgery procedures. And they associated unhappy patients with protracted, expensive follow-up procedures—even lawsuits. Senior cosmetic surgeons, in particular, identified lawsuits from unhappy or unsatisfied patients as a fate they wished to avoid. For instance, Dr. Bennett (white, Chicago) gestured to "lawyers out there making their living on malpractice cases. So we tend not to take on anything that doesn't seem like a pretty sure thing." There was some grounding for these fears; U.S. plastic surgeons were more than twice as likely to face at least one malpractice claim annually compared with other physicians.[9] Surgeons characterized facial procedures with racial connotations, like rhinoplasty and blepharoplasty, as especially prone to misunderstanding. Surgeons' judgments about what was appropriate with respect to race also incorporated what they perceived as a heightened risk of unhappy patients.

Defining Racial Boundaries

In advocating for a natural look, U.S. cosmetic surgeons actively policed the crossing of racial boundaries between several U.S. racial groups. And to be clear, cosmetic surgeons considered requests to cross any racial boundary as potentially leading to an "artificial" look. Though some white or Black patients requested an "Asian" eye, Dr. Parlato (Latino, Chicago) refused requests for a slanted or almond-shaped eye unless they were made by Asian patients. He told me that "although I could technically do that," he refused to because "they don't look Asian, they look just weird." Positioning his refusal on moral and aesthetic grounds, he called the requested appearance "weird," rather than objecting on grounds of patient safety or healing. He added, "I feel that those patients . . . sometimes they border around having psychiatric problems to be honest with you and it's better not to operate on them." Invoking the red flag of "psychiatric problems," Dr. Parlato thought that these patients were better left alone. In his clinical judgment, shaped by experience and aesthetic sense rather than expert discourse, crossing racial boundaries was possible but wrong. Unlike most of his peers, he admitted that there was not necessarily a technical or physical obstacle to doing so. Many surgeons judged requests for procedures that crossed racial boundaries to be unreasonable, unrealistic, and even pathological, long given as reasons not to operate.[10]

However, surgeons recognized that there was at least some market for artificial looks that played with racial boundaries— particularly among white patients. Procedures for white patients to take on physical markers associated with other racial groups could generate racially ambiguous outcomes, if not outright artificial ones. Surgeons thus used their discretion in granting white patients a very limited set of "ethnic options."[11] For instance, Dr. Lee deemed requests from white patients for a more "Asian" appearance as acceptable, interpreting it as an actionable request for "almond-shaped eyes" rather than for an eyelid with a single fold. Some surgeons also considered performing procedures on white patients to give them a curvier silhouette or bigger derriere.

Similarly, mixed-race patients could pose a challenge to cosmetic surgeons' preference for adapting patients' appearances without crossing racial lines. On the one hand, some U.S. cosmetic surgeons extolled the aesthetic value of racial hybridity and ambiguity, which they described as popularized by celebrities like the Kardashians. For example, Dr. Boutros (white, Chicago) explained, "Now with interracial marriage, there's less true ethnicity of one type. . . . [T]he mixing is absolutely beautiful. It's been a lot of fun navigating through the features because of that mixing. Its results have been some incredibly magnificent faces." In her view, the process of racial mixing was leading to striking and aesthetically pleasing new combinations. Cosmetic surgeons in this camp admired the unique amalgamations of features that Mother Nature could generate through interracial couplings. Echoing public discourse, some cosmetic surgeons praised the beauty and inevitability of a mixed-race future for the country.[12]

The children of interracial couples challenged the idea of the existence of pure racial types. However, most cosmetic surgeons simply ignored the possibility of racial hybridity. In the best-case scenario, "mismatched" racial features could cause mild confusion. In the worst case, they were blamed for causing psychological distress. Dr. Ghorbani (Persian, U.S.) described the curiosity that other people had in assessing people with racially mixed or hybrid appearances who they could not readily type: "When you have a Caucasian looking nose on an Asian person or African American person, it confuses the observer. They're like, 'Oh, is this person mixed? Where are they from?'" In contrast to the surgeons who celebrated racial ambiguity or hybridity, he described it as "confusing." To avoid friction, he avoided these patients. In this analysis, racially mixed people were already illegible to surgeons and the general public, resisting racial typing. One of the few cosmetic surgeons to describe the case of a mixed-race patient had a more alarming tale. Dr. Reiter (white, Chicago) recalled his experience with a mixed-race child: "The youngest cosmetic procedure I ever did was on a five-year-old who had a Japanese mother and an Irish father. He looked Asian, he had Asian eyes, but he had like reddish, blonde hair and fair skin. So he was actually referred to me by a child psychiatrist who said that he would like to have his eyes converted into more Caucasian looking eyes instead of Asian eyes. I did that and it was a successful operation. I never saw him back."

Since that case in the mid-1990s, he had never seen another like it. On the advice of the child psychiatrist, Dr. Reiter was willing to perform this double eyelid surgery, a procedure that he claimed to otherwise avoid. For this distressed patient, a trait perceived as racialized was a pathology that could be treated through surgery. However, it was telling that this was the only case of a mixed-race patient he could remember in twenty-plus years of practice. For Dr. Reiter, racial hybridity or ambiguity was not simply a matter of being racially illegible to others; being racially mixed could pose challenges to individuals who identified with one part of their racial heritage but had physical markers associated with another. Racial mixing could obscure the racial heritage of a person, which could be psychologically unmooring for individuals and for those trying to place them. By clarifying racial group membership by using surgical procedures, cosmetic surgeons could help redirect the racial perceptions of others and change first impressions of a person's race.

There were contradictions in how cosmetic surgeons discussed the relationship between naturalness, racial mixing, and race-specific standards of beauty. The features of mixed-race and/or racially ambiguous people suggested a potential continuum of looks, rather than the existence of beauty in types. In abstract terms, surgeons recognized mixed-race people as unique, and sometimes, as strikingly beautiful. They credited nature with producing new, beautiful looks through increased mixing of populations over time. Racially mixed people provided inspiration for alternative imaginaries of beauty. However, cosmetic surgeons also discussed racially mixed patients as boundary-crossing aberrations.[13] While nature could be inventive and bold, it could also produce aesthetically undesirable and perhaps even "unnatural" looks. Cosmetic surgeons were not confident in their ability to technically deliver or to socially justify racially mixed looks for patients. None of my respondents expressed willingness to try their own hand at aesthetic experimentation in unconventional directions for mixed-race patients. They left it to nature to generate novel combinations through racial mixing. Instead, for mixed-race patients on a case-by-case basis, surgeons were willing to "correct" patients who appeared racially in-between to make them more clearly racially legible as one type. Surgeons naturalized and prized racial categories as epitomizing beauty in a generally finite number of types—and tended to stick to these types in the interventions they conducted for mixed-race patients, too.

NATURAL LOOKS IN MALAYSIA

Like their U.S. counterparts, Malaysian cosmetic surgeons recognized race as a factor in evaluating beauty ideals and looks. And like U.S. surgeons, Malaysian cosmetic surgeons claimed aesthetic sense as a critical feature of their clinical judgment. However, they focused on maintaining a different set of racial boundaries in their beauty interventions: between natural Asian and artificial white looks. They too reported disinterest in and reluctance to change appearances between the racial categories most common in the country—Chinese, Indian, Malay, and Other. In an interview with Dr. Sankrithi (Malaysian Indian), I discussed the example of a U.S. patient who identified as half white, half Latina who asked a surgeon to make her look more Latina. I asked him whether Malaysian patients ever made similar requests. Dr. Sankrithi responded: "We don't have that problem. Each one is having his own identity and they want to maintain that identity. An Indian wants to be an Indian. He doesn't want to be a Chinese. A Chinese, the same thing. . . . [W]e may change other things. We may change religion. Change your beliefs. Because it is advantageous to do this, or disadvantageous to do that. But that [changing race] would be difficult." Citing Indians and Chinese, the two Malaysian racial groups he most often saw in his practice, he separated out practices and beliefs from appearance. To many Malaysian surgeons, it was self-evident that surgical procedures would improve a patient's appearance within the bounds of a given racial identity, rather than changing from one to another. As Dr. Sankrithi put it, patients "want[ed] to maintain" their racial identity. Taking racial identities as pre-given categories that bounded ideal appearances, Malaysian surgeons like Dr. Sankrithi thought it unlikely or impossible that patients in Malaysia would undertake cosmetic surgery to appear as a member of another *local* racial group.

After talking to more Malaysian surgeons, I realized I was asking the wrong question. I had been focusing on Malaysian racial groups, when regional and global ideals and racial categories supplied additional options, including a white or "Western" look. In acting as gatekeepers to and producers of racialized appearances, Malaysian cosmetic surgeons encouraged patients to opt for a natural "Asian" look. Instead of maintaining boundaries between Malaysian categories, they primarily policed the boundary between "Asian" and "Caucasian" looks. The clinical judgment of Malaysian cosmetic surgeons was shaped by different cultural assumptions and concerns about race, stemming from Malaysia's position within Asia and the world. Malaysia stands metaphorically and geographically between Asia and the Middle East, with a growing consumer-driven economy modeled along the lines of East Asia and increasing Islamic identification among Malays. Its large domestic Indian and Chinese populations further link the country to a broader Asian economy and have helped shape Malaysian beauty ideals. As a result, Malaysian cosmetic surgeons negotiated racial formations at different scales, navigating inter-Asian racial hierarchies and the multiple hegemonies of the U.S. and global whiteness. As part of a comparatively small but thoroughly transnationally networked cultural industry, cosmetic surgeons could facilitate—or impede—the spread of cultural forms from transnational sources.[14] Malaysian cosmetic surgeons governed access to desired and appropriate appearances, deciding which transnational beauty ideals to draw from and how to fashion aesthetically and socially appealing cosmetic surgery looks.

Developing a Natural "Asian" Look

Malaysian cosmetic surgeons encouraged their patients to pursue a natural "Asian" appearance. No procedure better epitomized this look than blepharoplasty. Scholars and surgeons alike have debated whether the ideal outcome of Asian blepharoplasty, a procedure in which the appearance of an eyelid fold is created or heightened, results in a white appearance. This kind of blepharoplasty was common in Malaysia, and Malaysian cosmetic surgeons characterized the result of this procedure as either "Caucasian" or "Asian." In Kuala Lumpur, I spent a few weeks shadowing a Malaysian Chinese cosmetic surgeon, Dr. Huang. A stylishly dressed, carefully made-up plastic surgeon who was only a few years out of training, she indicated her preference for giving Malaysian patients looks that reflected an "Asian" ideal of beauty. Explaining the difference between eyelid ideals, she started out confidently, "If you want the crease to be like 10 millimeters, that's more Caucasian, and fine, I will do it for you. But I will warn you first that you will look a little bit different, a little bit odd. For in terms of the lid crease height for Asian, very natural is about 6 millimeter. Just the distance between the lash and lid that you want to create, I think about 7, 6 to 7." She began to slow down. Musing aloud, her tone became a little more uncertain and more tentative as she went on: "If you want a little bit thicker, I think 8. 8 would be the highest for any Asian girl who wants a double lid. If they want to be natural, I would do about 6 to 7. Eight would probably be the highest, the thickest that I would do."

Dr. Huang indicated a clear preference for giving Malaysian patients an "Asian" rather than "Caucasian" look. She also employed the familiar discursive frame of "looking right" to describe a "natural" look that maintained the illusion that no surgery had been performed. She told me, "It just doesn't look right when you have very Asian features and you have a Caucasian eye. . . . For an Asian, you should remain to look Asian. Enhance it a bit here and there, but don't overdo it." Echoing the logic of ethnic preservation, she sketched out an aesthetic philosophy prizing an Asian appearance, which could be improved upon and perfected even as it was maintained. She wanted her patients to still be recognized by sight as Asian after the procedure.

Indeed, most Malaysian cosmetic surgeons described a smaller eyelid height, such as 6 millimeters, as "natural" for Asian patients. Though millimeter distinctions may sound minuscule, they were readily apparent to my untrained eye. Like Dr. Huang, most Malaysian cosmetic surgeons characterized larger eyelid heights as "more Caucasian." The descriptors applied to a "Caucasian" or white ideal, such as "different" or "odd," imparted a negative aesthetic and even moral connotation. She made an aesthetic argument in favor of a natural Asian look that enhanced patients' appearance while maintaining their perceived racial identity.

Patients echoed the language of naturalness, describing an Asian beauty ideal as "natural," "small," and "conservative." For instance, Andrea, a thirty-six-year-old middle-aged Malaysian Chinese patient, told me, "I'd still like to maintain Oriental features, so I told the surgeon that I prefer to have a low crease. . . . I would like something more natural." Andrea then recognized the ambiguity in these terms, adding, "The definition of natural can be different for each person. Again, it's because I trust [the surgeon] to do something which I can accept." A strong trust relationship with the right surgeon helped anchor the abstraction of "Asian" and "Caucasian" beauty ideals into a concrete reality for patients. Having made her request, Andrea delegated the specifics of aesthetic and racial boundary drawing on her own body to her surgeon. Ultimately, most patients deferred to cosmetic surgeons' judgment of what was possible as well as desirable in a look.

In her attempt to draw clear lines above, Dr. Huang began to falter when she got to the potential of a racially in-between hybrid look. While she recognized an Asian look (at approximately 6 millimeters) and a white look (at about 10 millimeters) as discrete, she was uncertain about where exactly to draw the line in the potentially hybrid zone between them: what did 8 millimeters signify? While surgeons like Dr. Huang were uncertain about where to draw the line in their own practice, patients were more willing to embrace the potential ambiguity. Lydia, a young Malaysian Chinese patient, asserted that patients like her wanted to "look not pure white but a mixed racial look." The request for a "mixed" or in-between look belied the natural ideal of pure, discrete racialized types. But again, the narrative of change mattered. Gender scholar Kathleen Zane calls for consideration of hybridity or mixture as an alternative to a white look, one that also incorporates a desire for authenticity and that reflects "ethnic pride politics or aesthetics of morality."[15] A hybrid look implied a different trajectory than an embrace of a white look, one potentially associated with alternative notions of modernity, technological self-authorship, and investment in the self. Rather than bracketing the in-between as racially neither here nor there, a consideration of a racially hybrid look helps expose the situated socioeconomic and political meanings of beauty within Asia.[16] Hybrid looks associated with an Asian appearance could be signs of belonging or distinction. Under some circumstances, single eyelids and a more slanted eye shape have been marks of distinction: Zane points to a wealthy ethnic Chinese community in the Philippines in which a slanted eye shape connoted difference from other Filipinos. She also argues that the lack of a double eyelid was advantageous for Peruvian emigrants to Japan seeking to assert Asian heritage. Though these cases were undoubtedly the exception rather than the rule, they also hint at more complicated meanings and dynamics of physical appearance within Asia.

Some Malaysian cosmetic surgeons claimed that the very category of "Malaysian" was a potentially racially hybrid entity that encompassed differences across Asia. Dr. Shanmugam (Malaysian Indian) explained to me, "'Malaysian' is a combination of Chinese and Indonesians and Indians. That's how Malaysia formed. There is no true 'Malaysian' face, there isn't anything like that." In this description, Dr. Shanmugam argued for seeing Malaysian society as ethnically and racially mixed—but a mixture that could be separated into clear racial types. These were racial types, not simply differences reflecting cultural heritage; Malaysian cosmetic surgeons employed a racial logic of comparison and hierarchy. By shifting the referent "other," Malaysian cosmetic surgeons shifted back and forth between racial structures unique to Malaysia and a global racial structure including whiteness.

As Malaysian cosmetic surgeons reflected on their unique experiences and expertise relative to others, they called on multiple racial formations simultaneously. For example, Malaysian cosmetic surgeons described different physical characteristics as racially constitutive compared with U.S. surgeons. Dr. Huang (Malaysian Chinese) mused:

If you compare an Indian girl to a Chinese girl, they are completely different. It's almost as good as comparing a Chinese girl with a Caucasian girl, like that. The unique features are Asian Chinese or Oriental ethnic because they are the most difficult people to treat in terms of eyelid surgery recovery and bruising and all that. Ugh. They are horrible. I know because when I was operating on Caucasian patients in the [United] States. Oh my God. Their skin was so thin, and it's just so easy to do. . . . [T]hey heal so fast! But the Asians, they bruise like crazy.

The racial "other" to "Asian" is variously "Indian" or "Caucasians" in Malaysia. In describing "Indian girls" as closer to "a Caucasian girl" than "a Chinese girl," Dr. Huang asserted a view typical around Malaysia, and in Asia more broadly. She described the bodies, and particularly the skin, of Asian patients as a challenge: "They are the most difficult people to treat" because of the bruising that results, and concerns about discoloration and scarring. She contrasted "Asians" with "Caucasians," who were comparatively "so easy to do." Partially this indicated the intransigence of Asian bodies and the difficulty they engendered. But it also suggested that greater and different skills were necessary to successfully operate on Asian patients. Having completed training in Malaysia, South Korea, and the U.S., she was confident that her expertise encompassed the difference and diversity of Asian bodies. Malaysian cosmetic surgeons did not transcend or elide physical and cultural differences among their patients. In fact, they recognized and continued to highlight them, especially in marketing materials (see figure 4). At the same time, their ability to shift to a register distinguishing Asian and white simultaneously opened up the possibility of appealing to a larger transnational market.

In juxtaposing a distinct "Asian" ideal against a "Western," "Caucasian," and/or "American" ideal, Malaysian cosmetic surgeons grouped their Malay, Indian, and Chinese patients under the broader rubric of "Asian." The assertion of a distinct natural Asian ideal, linked to Asian values and opposed to the West, closely resembled what Aihwa Ong has identified as the modus operandi of Southeast Asian countries: "By claiming to be 'Asian,' especially in their particular mix of rapid development and selective political repression, they break discursively with Western ideals of the modern and are thus able to claim a distinctive modernity rooted in the Asian race/nation/culture."[17] A white ideal as an artificial foil in physical and cultural terms helped shape the Asian ideal in Malaysia. Propounding an Asian ideal also linked Malaysian surgeons to a regional biopolitical and cultural trajectory of rising Asia.

Figure 4. Advertisements at an aesthetics clinic, Kuala Lumpur, Malaysia. Photo credit: Alka Menon.

In their discussions of the relationship between the body and race, Malaysian cosmetic surgeons also made visible racialized stereotypes about white patients. In particular, Malaysian surgeons considered procedures like facelifts and breast augmentation, which U.S. surgeons largely deemed to be desired across racial groups, to be coded as white. Casting facelifts as a racialized request spurred by physical and cultural differences between white people and "local" Malaysian patients, Malaysian surgeons mostly performed facelifts for white medical tourists. When I asked why, Dr. Fang (Malaysian Chinese) answered, "Caucasians tend to age much earlier than Asians, so you find a 50-year-old Caucasian will probably look like a 55- to 60-year-old Asian." All of my Malaysian respondents asserted that white patients experienced more significant wrinkling at a younger age than their Asian patients, which they attributed to differences in skin pigmentation and thickness. They argued that these physical differences created earlier and more frequent opportunities for aesthetic intervention.

In addition, Malaysian cosmetic surgeons described a cultural difference between white and Asian women. Surgeons like Dr. Bala (Malaysian Indian) generalized that older white women were more invested in looking young than Malaysian women: "At 60, we are different. At 60, a white lady, she's a socialite. She still wants to look good so she says, 'Pull it down one more time' so they can look good for their cocktail parties. Whereas the Asian culture is at 60, you don't flaunt yourself so much." In contrast to Dr. Fang's explanation, Dr. Bala invoked culture and norms of behavior to explain why white patients requested more facelifts than Asian patients. Dr. Bala argued that age imparted increased social status in Malaysian society, such that it was not necessarily desirable to eliminate physical markers of aging right away. I do not present these generalizations from cosmetic surgeons as general truths about Malaysian society. Rather, these examples expose some of taken-for-granted assumptions about the culturally bound meaning of physical features like wrinkles. They also emphasize the intersectionality of social identities like race, gender, age, and nationality. I had initially bracketed discussion of procedures like facelifts, thinking that they would not reveal much about how surgeons thought about race. Associated with older white women in the U.S., too, facelifts are the quintessential example of older patients trying to look like a younger, "refreshed" version of themselves. However, Dr. Bala's comment turned this assumption on its head for me. The desire to appear younger was a gendered and racialized phenomenon as much as an age-related one. Some of the procedures that U.S. cosmetic surgeons interpreted as "universal," or lacking racialized inflections, were taken by Malaysian cosmetic surgeons to be racialized as white. Their characterizations offered an explicit perspective on whiteness and whites, who were a minority in their practice.

The Meaning of a White Look in Malaysia

Cosmetic surgery has, justifiably, been criticized for promulgating U.S. beauty ideals and Western hegemony.[18] Malaysian cosmetic surgeons were aware of this dynamic, and some pushed back. Dr. Bala (Malaysian Indian) emphatically insisted: "We are not a boob society. The Americans, they have a 34, they want to make it a 36. Or they have a 36, and they want to make it a 38. Or even a 40! ... Americans say bigger is better, their cars are bigger, better, you know. So stupid, I'm sorry to say. Malaysia is not a boobs society. In fact, sometimes they say, 'Doctor, make it a bit smaller.' And I'm telling them, 'If I make it smaller, no result will be seen, there's nothing there!'" Identifying large breasts as the quintessentially "American" look, Dr. Bala launched into a discussion of the differences between American and Malaysian beauty ideals. He distinguished his practice by insisting that Malaysian patients preferred smaller breasts. Without prompting, Dr. Bala characterized Malaysian cosmetic surgery patients as uninterested in and even hostile to a large-breasted aesthetic, in contrast to the "Americans." Like many of his colleagues, Dr. Bala interpreted requests for breast augmentation through a racialized, global lens. And indeed, Malaysian patients reported preferring smaller breasts and breast reductions. In Malaysian surgeons' eyes, requests for big breasts could be, as Dr. Rajan put it, a "white lady thing."

Following an aesthetic logic of ethnic preservation, Malaysian cosmetic surgeons characterized a white look as artificial and inappropriate for Asian patients. In fact, multiple Malaysian surgeons cited the amply bosomed U.S. celebrity Dolly Parton as the opposite of Malaysian ideals of conservative feminine beauty. Malaysian surgeons cast Dolly Parton as representing an ideal of artificial, hypersexualized, feminized white beauty. Using her example, Dr. Shanmugam (Malaysian Indian) dissuaded a Malaysian Indian breast augmentation seeker from large implants: "'You don't want to look like Dolly Parton. You're a married lady, you got a job. You don't want men talking to your breasts. You want them talking to your face." Signifying the clear pursuit of what Debra Gimlin has called an "obviously augmented appearance" and an overt display of sexuality,[19] Dolly Parton represented a crossed line for Malaysian cosmetic surgeons. Large breasts have been interpreted as a "visual cipher for the independent sexualized self," and no doubt some Malaysian women requested them in order to express their sexuality.[20] A sign of conspicuous consumption, obvious surgical looks could connote meanings from independent womanhood to a savvy economic investment in one's own earning potential.[21] We do not know the underlying motives in this case. But we know that Dr. Shanmugam wanted to change the patient's mind. First he raised the specter of a sexualized and racialized stereotype. Then he floated other potentially salient identities, like mother or professional. He argued these identities could be contradicted or subsumed by a large-breasted appearance. Dr. Shanmugam mapped different identities onto different breast aesthetics. Alongside race, gender and class were also important in his construction of why large breasts would be inappropriate. Implying that avoiding the "artificial" (and Western) connotations of large breasts was best, Dr. Shanmugam claimed success in ultimately steering his patient to smaller implants.

All Malaysian respondents preferred that their Malaysian patients select a natural "Asian" look for breast procedures. Dr. Pang (Malaysian Chinese) associated larger breasts in Asian women with immorality and disreputability: "For patients who come in and ask for gigantic oversize [breasts], I turn them away. . . . I don't want them to have an appearance to look too cheap or too much like special professions." Dr. Pang invoked sex workers under the code "special professions" to discredit large breast implants, implying only they had a motive for such an artificial look. With a "natural" look, cosmetic surgery procedures were barely detectable, with the use of technology erased. Smaller breast implants allowed Asian patients to pass as never having had work done at all.[22] Large, obvious breast augmentations dispelled that illusion, and for surgeons, signaled "cheap," low-class patients trying to show off. Compared with U.S. surgeons, Malaysian surgeons recommended smaller, "anatomic" implants to their patients.[23] Malaysian cosmetic surgeons defined "small," "reasonable" implants as 100 cubic centimeters (cc) or less, which was considerably smaller than the 300 cc U.S. average.[24] Smaller, natural breast implants could represent an alternative to American ideals of big-breasted beauty. Surgeons' preferred narratives of change favored incremental, natural Asian looks, signifying respectability, regional pride, and independence from the West.

In light of this, it is worth revisiting what a white look might have meant in this moment in Malaysia. Labeling aesthetic ideals "Caucasian" in Malaysia implicitly discredited them. Based on many Malaysian cosmetic surgeons' distaste for a "Caucasian" ideal, one might infer a negative judgment rather than a neutral or positive valence. Malaysian cosmetic surgeons associated a request for white looks with middle-class and wealthy Malaysian Chinese women. In electing an "obviously augmented" appearance,[25] Malaysian Chinese women were displaying their status and wealth in a form of conspicuous consumption—in addition to emulating a Western beauty ideal. Requesting a white look set these Chinese patients on a different trajectory, a global trajectory in which they were "flexible elites" who traveled in a global circuit rather than a Malaysian or even exclusively Asian one. Malaysian cosmetic surgeons understood why some patients might benefit from a white look, even as they disparaged its aesthetic merit. Accordingly, to characterize breast augmentation and eyelid procedures as effacing an Asian identity in favor of a Western one may be missing the point. Naming the beauty preferences of Chinese women as "Western" was an othering move that depicted Chinese patients as part of a global elite, set apart from Malaysian norms. Like cosmetic surgery patients from around Asia, women in Malaysia navigated complex social dynamics in which their choice of cosmetic surgery looks would be interpreted differently by different audiences[26]—and sometimes by their own surgeons. Thus, calling a look "white" or "Western" could be a form of aesthetic and moral judgment in itself.

There is one more physical characteristic frequently associated with a white or Western look in Asia. Throughout Southeast Asia, and in parts of South Asia, scholars have documented a preference for light or fair skin tones, which Evelyn Nakano Glenn has called a "yearning for lightness."[27] Colorist hierarchies rank fairer skin tones as more beautiful, often associated with higher class status. To what extent was a preference for fair skin in Malaysia a desire for a white ideal? It is tough for me to say. Skin tone came up less often than I expected in my interviews with surgeons, with many declaring it beyond their remit. For instance, calling himself a "pure cutting aesthetic surgeon," Dr. Fang (Malaysian Chinese) explained, "In my practice, I confine myself to assignments that I feel the dermatologists and the general practitioners cannot get into, which is pure cutting." Many respondents reported receiving requests for skin bleaching or lightening but did not offer such procedures. In the larger competitive market for aesthetic services, avoiding these procedures distinguished them from beauticians and other practitioners with nonmedical training. It also imposed some distance from this beauty ideal.

Certainly, light and fair beauty was a prominent feature of the Malaysian landscape: most models in Malaysian advertisements were fair skinned, including and especially models for Korean and Japanese beauty products. In every pharmacy, cosmetics and personal care products promised to lighten and brighten the skin, and malls were dotted with medical spas offering laser treatments, acne cures, and other skin-resurfacing services. However, one Malaysian aesthetic physician characterized the preference for light or fair skin tones as an Asian trend rather than an emulation of a white look. Dr. Burhan (Malay) explained: "In Malaysia, the phase of whitening was maybe seven, eight years ago where it was all the rage. But it kind of died down. And then a local celebrity does something, one day she looks tan. Then three weeks later she looks fair, and then people are all seeking out that." He described the trend as shifting within Malaysia. But I also want to highlight his focus on the "local celebrity," who, in his account, drew new attention to an aesthetic possibility and gave it legitimacy, helping raise the profile of the look. His remarks suggested that a fairer or lighter look was especially legible when translated through "local" celebrities and trends. "Whitening" was an aesthetic goal the surgeon had seen before and anticipated encountering again—but mediated through local beauty culture.

The Meaning of a Korean Look in Malaysia

As translators of abstract ideals onto concrete bodies in a medical tourist market, Malaysian cosmetic surgeons offered a distinct perspective on globally circulating artificial looks. Dr. Huang (Malaysian Chinese) went so far as to declare a white look passé, commenting, "The Westernized look is very much in the past. Maybe ten or twenty years ago. It's all the Korean wave now." Whereas a "Caucasian" ideal was the unnatural ideal of the past in Malaysia, a "Korean" ideal was the artificial ideal of the future, the product of another globalizing cultural industry. The nationally specific label reflected the South Korean government's investment in and export of cultural products, known as the "Korean wave," or *Hallyu*.[28] Models from K-pop, K-dramas, and films inspired requests for a Korean look.[29] Amidst a backdrop of quickly changing beauty ideals, cosmopolitan whiteness was giving way to the Korean look, a newly packaged global beauty ideal.

Accordingly, instead of describing a large eyelid as "Caucasian," some Malaysian plastic surgeons interpreted patient requests for a larger eyelid height or obviously surgically altered eyelid appearance as "Korean." A Korean look allowed Malaysian patients and surgeons to tell a different story about the type of beauty work being done. When I asked whether all Malaysian patients wanted to look natural, Dr. Rajan (Malaysian Indian) shook his head and responded, "No, they want to look like a Korean pop star. That's a Malaysian thing now. . . . [I]t's a fad." Noting that patients brought in photographs of Korean pop stars and looked to Korean dramas for inspiration, several Malaysian surgeons reported that patients requested an obviously altered beauty ideal—pronounced eyelid height, augmented nasal bridge, narrowed jawlines—to match images from Korean culture that were circulating in Malaysia. The Korean look was an obvious, artificial look that was distinct from a natural Asian look and has been described as an imitation of a white look. But after crossing oceans back and forth multiple times and with the rising soft power of South Korea, the Korean look has acquired its own racialized meaning and narratives. Cosmetic surgeons from L.A. to Kuala Lumpur received requests from patients for a Korean look.

Despite being obviously technologically modified and surgically enhanced, the Korean look was recognized as desirable and acceptable by Malaysian surgeons for young patients. Malaysian cosmetic surgeons offered patients a semblance of the world from Korean pop, film, and TV dramas with less of the conformity. Dr. Huang complained that "[Korean patients] all look the same! It's like, all Barbie dolls lining up on the street." Promising her patients that they would not "lose their identity," she committed to giving patients a toned-down version of the Korean look. The aesthetic, and the cheaper cost, was a comparative advantage of cosmetic surgery in Malaysia. Korean competitors countered by enticing Malaysian customers with cosmetic surgery tourism package deals.

For Malaysians, the Korean Wave offered a new and different narrative about culture, beauty, and technology and an appealing, technologized alternative to the West. Malaysian surgeons credited several surgical innovations to South Korean surgeons, including specific eyelid techniques, skin rejuvenation, and jawbone-contouring procedures. But they did not perform these procedures themselves, considering them to be "radical," potentially unsafe, and aesthetically dubious. A Korean look was within the realm of the imaginable and desirable as an alternative modernity in Malaysian surgeons' clinical judgment, reflecting Malaysia's Asian possibilities. Korean and white looks adhered to an alternate order of globalized beauty, and Malaysian surgeons capitalized on demand for them. These looks also served as foils against which Malaysian cosmetic surgeons could define their own aesthetic sense and taste.

Based on their clinical experience and judgment, Malaysian cosmetic surgeons guided patients preferentially toward a natural Asian look. For patients inclined toward more obvious surgical looks, Malaysian surgeons considered requests in regional and global context. Even if aesthetically questionable according to local norms, a white look could make sense for a wealthy jetsetter. Similarly, a Korean look might increase the legibility of a Malaysian model in the beauty blogger scene. The impact of global norms, ideals, trends, and categories on Malaysian surgeons' judgment and translation efforts was easier to see than the impact of the same on U.S. surgeons. But in both countries, global trends of beauty shaped surgeons' judgment and work. Malaysian surgeons navigated expert and lay discourses about race and beauty while also asserting their own unique contribution as practitioners within Asia.

CONCLUSION

The racial-specific standards that appeared in expert discourse were largely eschewed by surgeons in practice. In the cosmetic surgery clinic, the social lives of racial categories became more complicated, and the standards in medical journals remained on the shelf. Instead, U.S. and Malaysian cosmetic surgeons recognized and elaborated upon racial difference as a category of aesthetic and symbolic importance. Cosmetic surgeons exercised judgment, shaped by their specific cultural contexts, in adjudicating desirable, ideal racialized appearance. Their evaluations of racialized looks simultaneously included clinical, cultural, and moral dimensions.

In practice, cosmetic surgeons went about the business of crafting "natural" looks. They encouraged their patients to pursue looks that did not appear to be the result of cosmetic surgical intervention. Such looks involved incremental improvement and were not obvious: procedures that dramatically altered or confused the perception of a patient's racial group membership could not, by definition, be natural. Cosmetic surgeons touted their individual discretion in determining "natural" and "artificial" looks. And they all drew slightly different lines about what they would do with respect to racialized appearances. This led to a proliferation of looks that conformed to different racial and gender ideals, which were also inflected by nationality and socioeconomic status.

In the clinic, cosmetic surgeons in both countries engaged in a racial project of maintaining boundaries between racial groups. Surgeons in the U.S. and Malaysia used similar racial categories to interpret and construct cosmetic surgery looks. And in both countries, surgeons preferred procedures that left patients clearly legible as a member of the same racial group. However, U.S. and Malaysian cosmetic surgeons drew on different scales of racial meaning. U.S. cosmetic surgeons primarily upheld and adjudicated boundaries between nationally recognized racial groups. By contrast, Malaysian cosmetic surgeons were primarily engaged with gatekeeping a boundary between a natural "Asian" look on the one hand and artificial "Caucasian" looks on the other. Malaysian surgeons' interpretations and translations of looks were informed by the racial formation of Malaysian society and the transnational biopolitics of Malaysia's position within the Asian region.[30] An Asian look in Malaysia drew from different genealogies and materialized in different forms than it did in the U.S. The case of Malaysia helps make clear how constructions of race and gender in beauty ideals "may thus be negotiated simultaneously as act of resistance against foreign influence (*nationalism*), means to safeguard 'indigenous' elements of culture (*own cultural tradition*), and as claims of memberships in global geopolitics (*innovative global standards*)."[31] As cultural intermediaries between the global and national and between medical and beauty industries, Malaysian surgeons toggled between racial referents in explaining the aesthetic and social merits of different looks.

In addition to evaluating looks for their symbolic implications about race, cosmetic surgeons gauged the appropriateness and desirability of surgical *requests* from patients for their racial implications. With patients, cosmetic surgeons fashioned narratives of change that also emphasized natural transitions. These co-constructed narratives of change were provisional and instrumental, temporarily uniting surgeons and patients for purposes of the procedure. When patients wanted something noticeably different (that is, obvious or artificial), their chances of receiving the look depended on whether a surgeon and patient could come together to develop a shared narrative of change. If patients were too blunt in requesting modifications that could be associated with racial transformation, they could jeopardize their chances of getting what they wanted. Given their active role in shaping narratives of racial change, cosmetic surgeons served as arbiters of racial meaning. At the same time, they rewrote and challenged racial meanings.

While part 1 illustrated the proliferation of standards of appearance by race in expert discourse, this chapter introduces the complex social and cultural meanings that went into their proliferation in specific national contexts. By zooming in, we can see how surgeons weighed competing motives and structures of racial meaning—most obviously through the analysis of what a white look meant for patients of color in the U.S. and for Malaysian patients. As this chapter suggests, white looks had not disappeared; surgeons in both countries discussed a white look as a request and an option for patients. But their moral and symbolic meaning had shifted in both countries. In Malaysia, calling a look or patient request "white" or "Caucasian" could be read as a dismissal of patients by surgeons, highlighting the complex intersections of race and nationality with gender and wealth. Similarly, within the U.S., surgeons and some patients characterized a white look as "artificial" for people of color. Despite its historical legibility as a beauty ideal, delivering a white look for Black, Asian, and/or Latino/a patients opened U.S. cosmetic surgeons to charges of racial insensitivity and even technical incompetence.

The fact that different narratives for racial change and transformation are circulating, with some preferred by surgeons over others, shows how racial mores and commonsense notions can coexist and change. Cosmetic surgeons are intermediaries who link structural and symbolic racial meanings and norms into beauty ideals in specific times and places. Cosmetic surgeons take narratives of racial meaning and elevate or reject them. This is a mechanism by which structural racism and longstanding racist notions can manifest in cosmetic surgery. It is also a mechanism for broadening or reconfiguring racial meanings for expressions of racial pride on the part of surgeon or patient. Cosmetic surgeons in both the U.S. and Malaysia sculpted and contoured bodies in line with the prevailing expectations and aspirations of their respective societies. Individual cosmetic surgeons acted as gatekeepers who decided whether a given patient should have access to surgical transformation—or not. In translating expert discourses using racial categories into lay discourse about what could or should be done in particular societies, surgeons paved the way for particular enactments of race. The next chapter adds an additional dimension to this racial project, examining how surgeons discussed racial categories in the context of a competitive market.

4 Race and Customization in the Market for Cosmetic Surgery

Cosmetic surgeons acted as gatekeepers to natural, racially legible looks. But in addition to being clinicians, cosmetic surgeons were businesspeople who sought to make themselves legible to potential consumers. Racial categories could ease or hamper this outreach. Zooming in more closely into the business of cosmetic surgery in the U.S. and Malaysia reveals two different approaches to how surgeons deployed racial categories to craft coherent, recognizable brands.

On the one hand, in the U.S., some surgeons marketed racialized or "ethnic" looks in the service of building a brand. In addition to evaluating whether and how to apply racial and other scientific standards, surgeons used racial categories to convey their ability to customize looks and tailor experiences to different kinds of patients. Dr. Allison (white, NYC) reflected on what she wanted her work to signal: "If somebody came and said, 'I want to look like a Bengali tiger, fix my eyes,' I'm not sure I could do that. I'm not sure I would feel confident in my own abilities to deliver on what that person wants because it's so different from what I would think is attractive.

When you do surgery, it's like a little piece of artwork that you are doing and you have to be able to, figuratively, sign your name at the end and be like, I'm proud of what I did, or this is an expression of who I am." Asserting a form of aesthetic integrity and artisan identity, Dr. Allison considered surgical results to evince her personal brand. By way of illustration, she invented an outlandish request for Bengali tiger eyes, based on an exaggeration of a cat-shaped eye, to emphasize its status as an aesthetically inadvisable transformation of the patient. She then contrasted this request with the more familiar and accepted request for modification of the Asian eyelid: "The Asian eyelids where they will have the crease put in—I think that you're not necessarily changing the identity." Dr. Allison juxtaposed the deliberately artificial request for tiger eyes with a request for Asian eyelids to emphasize her commitment to looks that maintained patient identity rather than transformed it.

By contrast, in Malaysia, cosmetic surgeons constructed brand identities based on the delivery of racially and culturally sensitive care. When I asked Dr. Christine (Malaysian Indian) what she wanted to signal to prospective patients, she made no mention of aesthetics. Instead, she put herself and her expertise on display: "I have my own columns in newspapers, I have my own segments in TV shows. So they know the brand." Dr. Christine was careful to emphasize that her media appearances were "not advertising, just giving information." Comparing cosmetic surgery in Malaysia to the U.S., she explained, "Here there's a lot of mixtures in ethnicity, so it's a bit tricky to know how to treat. . . . We learn to be a bit different in our management." Her brand conveyed competent responsiveness to the different needs of diverse Malaysians, signaling her efforts to customize experiences in a culturally sensitive way.

This chapter examines how cosmetic surgeons in the U.S. and Malaysia used racially resonant looks and experiences, respectively, to build brand identities and appeal to specific market demographics. In subdividing the market using racial categories, both U.S. and Malaysian cosmetic surgeons followed in the footsteps of pharmaceutical companies, which have advertised drugs to members of some racial groups.[1] Uniting ethnic marketing with biomedicine, some surgeons parlayed niche standardization of expertise by racial categories into niche marketing. Above and beyond their association with specific looks and a kind of aesthetic judgment, racial categories could also denote a style or experience of care delivery to different demographics of patients. In turn, brands helped consolidate and shape the contours of the racial project of cosmetic surgery.

In both the U.S. and Malaysia, guidelines govern advertising for medical services, including cosmetic surgery. The U.S. is one of the only jurisdictions in the world in which it is legal for medical providers and pharmaceutical companies to market directly to consumers. However, U.S. professional societies like ASPS and ASAPS prohibit "false, fraudulent, deceptive or misleading" communications in advertisements.[2] Malaysia has legal protections regulating acceptable speech in advertising containing almost identical language.[3] But in both countries, information about cosmetic surgery and cosmetic surgeons appears in health and beauty magazines, reality television shows, tabloids, and on social media. Surgeons' use of racial categories to fashion brands thus reflects and reproduces broader cultural dynamics while remaining subject to each country's professional norms and legal strictures.

This chapter begins by discussing how some U.S. cosmetic surgeons used racialized looks to construct brand identities, sometimes expanding beyond "natural" looks to "artificial" looks in the process. Under the logic of colorblindness,[4] simply talking explicitly about racial categories in the U.S. seemed racist. Wary of the charge, and aiming primarily to attract patients within the country, U.S. surgeons relied on racially resonant stereotypes and associations with iconic American places to connote racialized looks and brands. I then turn to Malaysia, a context in which multicultural norms did not preclude the explicit discussion of race to the same extent. Rather than emphasizing distinct aesthetics or looks, Malaysian surgeons promised racially sensitive experiences of care. Reflecting a different orientation to what race could connote and mean, they touted their ability to accommodate differences in language, religious beliefs, and attitudes toward the body. Unlike most U.S. surgeons, for whom white patients were a de facto default referent, Malaysian cosmetic surgeons articulated an explicit perspective on white patients as a demographic with specific cultural preferences and needs.

THE U.S.

Ethnic Marketing

In the U.S., cosmetic surgeons curated brand identities that promised customization, emphasizing the uniqueness of their aesthetic judgment. U.S. cosmetic surgeons carefully considered where they wanted to fit into the market and how they wanted to portray their offerings. Likening cosmetic surgery to the quintessential commodity, Dr. Ackerman (white, NYC) explained, "You can sell as much Coke as people want to buy." He continued, comparing his own skill and price point as a board-certified facial plastic surgeon to potential competitors: "If there is a family practice doctor who's doing Botox, he might out-price me. But I'm offering a superior product in terms of my sense of aesthetics and my knowledge of anatomy. It's like a Mercedes and Honda." To break through the noise, some U.S. surgeons constructed brand identities using racial categories.

This often took the form of ethnic marketing targeting people of color. On their websites and in publications, some U.S. cosmetic surgeons billed themselves as specializing in "ethnic plastic surgery" or an "ethnic" look. Dr. Rajavi's practice provided a vivid example of what this entailed. In the waiting room of his clinic, a flatscreen television played short video clips illustrating and explaining different procedures. One clip featured a patient who had undergone ethnic rhinoplasty. Cutting from the patient to Dr. Rajavi (Persian, U.S.), the camera zoomed in as Dr. Rajavi defined what he meant by the term "ethnic": "It's tailored to your face, natural rather than cookie cutter." When I interviewed Dr. Rajavi, I asked him if he specialized in ethnic plastic surgery. I was surprised when he responded: "I wouldn't say ethnic's my niche. . . . When I first started out, I saw the paucity and lack of ethnic noses being done well. And I have good training in it so I marketed that because I knew it was in demand and I knew I was pretty good at it. Then every Tom, Dick, and Harry started advertising ethnic nose jobs. The young guys come out, they look at things and they copy/paste it."

Dr. Rajavi had written articles and given talks on ethnic rhino-plasty. He identified as a member of an ethnic minority. He had links to ethnic rhinoplasty on his website and videos in his clinic. But he made no pronouncements about the uniqueness of "ethnic noses." Instead, "ethnic" was his brand, a marketing strategy that set him apart. Though he grumbled about the competition, his perception that the strategy had taken off so broadly contributed to its aura of success. Promising to enhance physical markers associated with race, like the nose, or elaborating upon racial types afforded surgeons the opportunity to establish their brand.

Dr. Rajavi was not the only surgeon to toe this line. Many surgeons who identified as people of color or racial minorities followed suit. Dr. Delshad (L.A.) also called herself an "ethnic specialist" on her website and promotional materials. In addition, she conducted outreach in her community and at plastic surgery conference meetings about her efforts to build a brand that incorporated her identity as a woman of color. She too highlighted the effectiveness of the racial or ethnic tie-in primarily for marketing purposes, explaining, "This whole 'I do ethnic rhinoplasty' is a marketing tool. It just means I'm sensitive to you. . . . I'm not going to try to make your face fit into my mold, I'm going to try to make a nose that's custom made for you, which is what all plastic surgery is anyway." Like Dr. Rajavi, Dr. Delshad described her expertise as "ethnic" in marketing materials as an instrumental strategy to increase traffic from patients and capitalize on her own ethnic network. Characterizing "ethnic cosmetic surgery" as a promise to patients of color to customize looks to their bodies, she made it clear that specializing in "ethnic" looks was a signal rather than a field of knowledge. Calling oneself an "ethnic specialist" signaled an aesthetic orientation that departed from the past norm of a one-size-fits-all look for patients. Ultimately, both white surgeons and surgeons of color employed ethnic marketing as a strategy to appeal to different U.S. racial niches in the market.

The Brand of Ethnic Enhancement

Some cosmetic surgeons went a step further in building brands revolving around different types of beauty, promising patients "ethnic enhancement," or procedures that would enhance expression of their race or ethnicity. Many surgeons associated a full, curvy figure with pride in a Black or Latina identity. They offered procedures such as buttocks augmentation, buttocks lifts, liposuction, and body contouring to emphasize these features. The "Brazilian butt lift," a procedure which increased the size and modified the shape of the buttocks by adding fat, was the quintessential realization of ethnic enhancement. Dr. Reiter (white, NYC) reported that the Brazilian butt lift was more popular "among Hispanic and Black populations than others. That's because that's what their preference is, what they view as more beautiful, or more important to beauty." Similarly, Dr. Galonnier (white, Chicago) reported a "huge wave of African Americans want liposuction with fat transfer to the buttocks . . . Latinas sometimes." Surgeons attributed the popularity and visibility of "ethnic" looks to changes in media attention. Dr. Hanson (white, NYC) identified "certain celebrities like Jennifer Lopez, Beyoncé, and the Kardashians that have gotten a lot of publicity based upon their buttocks and it's gotten more accepted." Celebrities illustrated as well as popularized the ideals. For example, Beyoncé was cited by surgeons and patients as epitomizing a full-figured, curvy ideal of appearance (figure 5). Highlighting differences in the preferences of Black and

Figure 5. Beyoncé, 2016 Costume Institute Gala. *Source:* Larry Busacca/Getty Images Entertainment via Getty Images. Reprinted with permission.

Latina women in particular, surgeons promoted their ability to deliver procedures that could meet this ideal.

A handful of surgeons interpreted and framed race-specific beauty ideals and the rise of cosmetic surgery procedures to achieve them as an affirmation of historically marginalized racial identities. For instance, Dr. June (Black, U.S.) described a preference for "ethnic features" as "extremely healthy because that reflects self-love. Yes, I want to have something improved, but I still want to fit within my ethnic group. To me, that's a positive thing." This surgeon positioned ethnic enhancement as part of a larger cultural project of reclaiming and asserting racial identities, promoting new forms of racial expression.

On the medical aesthetics review site RealSelf, patients echoed the language of "ethnic enhancement." Black and Latina patients writing reviews about Brazilian butt lifts and buttocks augmentation procedures also described their desires as racially and ethnically affirming, suggesting that there was indeed a receptive audience for such appeals. Some posters articulated a decisive preference for an "ethnic," "Black," or "Latina" look in their requests for cosmetic surgery. On online discussion boards, patients rehearsed and formulated such requests, comparing notes. On RealSelf, a typical exposition came from a poster, alias "BronxGurl," who introduced herself as a twenty-seven-year-old "Black woman of Caribbean descent" living in a "predominantly Latino" neighborhood. She indicated she was having "major, major, major issues with both my weight and my perceived lack of curves." By way of indicating her preferred community and aesthetic, BronxGurl explained she was "surrounded by beautiful curvy women every time I step out of the door." She made it clear that she wanted to look like the "beautiful curvy women" around her rather than conform to a white appearance. Another poster, Becca, made it clear that she sought a recognizably "ethnic" look: "I'm African American so I definitely don't want to end up with the 'Jackson' nose." She added that she was "a 19 year old girl that wanted to be transformed on like a Kim K level." Becca claimed Kim Kardashian, a reality TV star associated with an ambiguously "ethnic" look, as a model for how she wanted to appear. In the same post, she distanced herself from the artificial, white-appearing ideal represented by Michael Jackson, another iconic celebrity. Prospective patients claimed to seek racialized looks in language that resembled how surgeons marketed them.

Some surgeons and patients lauded the emergence of brand identities showcasing ethnic enhancement, capitalizing on the market potential of this larger cultural transformation. For instance, Dr. Milstein (white, L.A.) characterized "the Latina market" as "being a little bit more out there, willing to push [the envelope]," with requests for "lip augmentation being a little bigger, breast augmentation a little bit larger." Using the language of "market," Dr. Milstein oriented his brand to meet these requests. But like many surgeons, he did not dwell on how he knew that Latina patients wanted such procedures nor what it meant for him to contribute this look to the market. Surgeons often described "ethnic enhancement" as procedures that were "out there," or obvious, showy, and artificial; such procedures often highlighted, rather than disguised, that cosmetic surgery had been performed. To create a brand identity around ethnic enhancement meant acknowledging displays of conspicuous consumption while also showcasing Black, Latina, or other beauty ideals. Building a brand around ethnic enhancement thus meant building a brand around artificial looks.

Surgeons' discussions of larger buttocks highlighted the tradeoffs in using racialized looks as a brand identity. Dr. Solomon (Persian, U.S.) waffled as to the perception of the aesthetic value of augmenting buttocks, remarking: "Many people stereotype African Americans as having bigger rear ends. Some find that attractive or sexy, some find it tasteful or not tasteful. Whatever." Dr. Solomon gestured to different opinions about the aesthetic merits of large buttocks before clarifying they were "not tasteful if you're Caucasian." Relegating a request for bigger buttocks to a racial market niche reinforced the cultural otherness of Black and Latina women. It is certainly the case that surgeons continued to associate bigger butts with a racialized niche rather than a broad-based branding strategy. Dr. Galonnier (white, Chicago) said, "White people will never ask for bigger butts, Indian people will never ask." Few respondents had fielded requests from white patients for bigger buttocks. This is in keeping with statistics from plastic surgery organizations that estimate a far lower prevalence of buttocks procedures compared with breast augmentation, nose jobs, and tummy tucks.[5] While ethnic enhancement was generally a celebratory expression of race, it could reinforce the notion of essentialized racial difference, linking it to gender, class, and sexual stereotypes.

Cosmetic surgeons described their patients as "walking billboards" for their brand identities, aware that every patient they treated could be seen as a representation of their aesthetic sense. But while, as chapter 3 discusses, surgeons prized "natural" ideals of beauty, "artificial" looks—including some of the outcomes associated with ethnic enhancement—were the most visible as products of cosmetic surgery. The dilemma for surgeons was that if patients opted for a "natural" look, others might not know they had undergone cosmetic surgery, which was a missed opportunity for advertising surgeons' abilities. Dr. Stone (white, L.A.) ruefully reflected, "When you see these enormous breasts—it may not be beautiful, it may not even be sexy, but it certainly gets a lot of looks. And that's what they want maybe. Look at my stuff. Those are the ones you notice. And this is also my kind of mantra, you never really notice the good work. You only notice the bad work." Surgeons like Dr. Stone lamented that "good" or natural cosmetic surgery was comparatively invisible. Like many surgeons, he implied that artificial looks were "bad," but gained recognition—even if through notoriety. For all that surgeons emphasized natural looks, surgeons were also cognizant that some patients wanted an artificial "plastic look,"[6] and there was money to be made in catering to their requests. Though there were fewer ways to appear "natural," especially as laid out in race-specific standards, the number of "artificial," "obvious," or "fake" looks were subject to the limits of the imagination and to patients' bodies.

RACE AND CUSTOMIZATION IN THE MARKET 139

Maintaining a balance was even more complicated for procedures, like buttocks augmentation, associated with ethnic enhancement. The racial connotations of the looks and procedures factored
into surgeons' calculations of whether they wanted to be associated
with them. Dr. Allison (white, NYC) explained:

> Butt augmentations, I would say, are more ethnically oriented. It's
> much more of a Hispanic, Black sought-after aesthetic ideal. I don't
> really see too many white patients who come in specifically for that
> procedure. Some of them have very legitimate desires and some of
> them just want to have massive rear ends. You have to weed that out.
> Because there are just too many issues. There is also the whole illegiti-
> mate side of the hotels and whatnot which are a real problem because
> somehow those tend to become very widespread. . . . When complica-
> tions do happen, they are fatal.

Here, she sidelined buttocks augmentation as a racialized practice that contrasted with her preferred brand identity. Within one
sentence, Dr. Allison went from discussing butt augmentations as a
potentially "legitimate" desire for some Black and Latina women
to echoing tabloid horror stories of women obtaining non-medical-
grade silicone injections to their buttocks from illegal practitioners.
To be clear, buttocks augmentations have had a higher rate of complications and risk than other cosmetic surgical procedures, and this
danger is heightened for procedures performed by unlicensed or
inexperienced practitioners.[7] However, compared with the drier,
cautionary tone of professional society reports about buttocks augmentation, Dr. Allison's telling was more *New York Post*.[8] By asserting judgment against buttocks augmentations and associating them
with "Black" and "Hispanic" patients, she implicitly differentiated
her own brand as white(r) and more legitimate.

When surgeons raised the specter of large buttocks as racialized
and, to quote Dr. Solomon above, "less tasteful," they were calling
upon an old trope that associated Black women with exaggerated
features and hypersexuality.[9] While some surgeons entertained

buttocks augmentation under a rubric of ethnic enhancement for Black and Latina women, they were less sure of its value as an "ethnic option" for white women. Surgeons' opposition to such procedures for white patients was not fully attributable to adhering to the goal of ethnic preservation. Nor was it a critique of cultural appropriation; in fact, none of the surgeons I interviewed raised this concern.[10] Rather, their hesitation to perform procedures like the Brazilian butt lift was tinged by continuing racialized stigma associated with Blackness. Skeptical surgeons like Dr. Allison construed brands that too explicitly traded on race as attracting the wrong kind of patient: for instance, whites looking for racial boundary-crossing procedures, or Black and Latina patients who wanted very different procedures from white or Asian patients. Big buttocks derived not only value but also potentially stigma from their relation to Black and Latina identities.

To expand to new markets by attracting more patients of color, surgeons felt they needed to showcase new beauty standards. However, they confronted the challenge that at least for the time being, the majority of U.S. cosmetic surgery patients were white. Thus, some cosmetic surgeons weighed ethnic marketing to Black, Latina, and Asian patients against the potential loss of white women as customers in their practice. They worried that too close an association with looks racialized as Black, Latina, or Asian could taint the brand for white patients. Dr. Lee (Asian, NYC), who billed himself as a specialist in "Asian plastic surgery," reasoned, "Being in New York City, I just feel like I have to specialize in something." Dr. Lee was one of several surgeons in the U.S. who cultivated a niche market among Asians and Asian Americans. He described specializing in Asian cosmetic surgery as a way to ensure better care for patients while taking advantage of his surgical abilities, his own identity as an Asian American, and its distinctiveness in a crowded market. He wondered whether by marketing "more toward the Asian population" on his website, "maybe [he] scare[d] off some of the Caucasian patients." Conveying a sense of the fraught limitations of ethnic marketing, Dr. Lee nevertheless concluded that ethnic marketing was worth it for him. U.S. surgeons framed marketing to people of color as in tension with maintaining a base of white patients.

For surgeons who embraced ethnic marketing and "ethnic enhancement," developing brands around racial looks represented a break with the past in U.S. cosmetic surgery. The development and recognition of multiple racial-specific alternate beauty ideals was generally a celebratory expression of the art of racial difference, particularly for patients. It also gave surgeons the opportunity to be creative in expanding their business. However, resultant brand identities tended to work within rather transform racial hierarchies. Even as procedures like buttocks augmentation arguably celebrated Black beauty and challenged thin, white norms of beauty, they reinforced racial otherness and racialized stigma. In other words, while they constituted real alternatives to a white ideal for patients of color, they did not altogether displace racialized and classed hierarchies of beauty.

Ultimately, however, the majority of my U.S. respondents were hesitant to engage in ethnic marketing of any sort. Dr. Ghorbani (Persian, U.S.) decided against using racial labels, noting, "On my current website, I have an Asian rhinoplasty page, an African American rhinoplasty page. My new website, I'm taking it out because I don't know if it's slightly racist or not, you know?" Only a few years out of training, Dr. Ghorbani was still building his practice, and he was concerned about limiting his potential market. In the U.S., cosmetic surgeons feared that talking about race itself was racist, consistent with a colorblind logic; if racial discourse was absent, then racism and racial animus was assumed also to be kept at bay.[11] Accordingly, surgeons like Dr. Ghorbani were not confident that racial categories were a durable form of appeal to patients, deciding that the time for ethnic marketing may have passed. To play it safe, many U.S. surgeons chose not to engage.

In setting out brands, then, cosmetic surgeons could either embrace racialized "artificial" looks, like those associated with ethnic enhancement, or use them as foils against which to position their own "natural" brand aesthetic. Physical features associated with ethnic enhancement, such as buttocks, lips, and curvy figures, also expressed idealized configurations of sexualized femininity.[12] In conveying a brand, surgeons chose whether to narrate these looks as a matter of enhancing patients' race or ethnicity, emphasizing their femininity, or both, depending on their target audience. As the next section shows, in crafting racially meaningful looks for sale, surgeons also incorporated stereotypes and generalizations about socioeconomic status, sexuality, and gender.

Implicitly Racialized Looks in the U.S.

When fashioning brands, some U.S. cosmetic surgeons dispensed with overtly racial labels and instead evoked racialized aesthetics with regional, place-based names. For instance, Dr. Solomon (Persian, U.S.) invoked the *Real Housewives* franchise, a popular reality television program, to illustrate regional cultures of plastic surgery. He juxtaposed the example of the *Real Housewives of Orange County*, in which the featured stars were "blonde with big lips and big breasts and very skinny waistline, not a big ass" to the *Real Housewives of Atlanta*, characterized by "big lips, big breasts, big ass, you don't have to be skinny, exaggerated facial features." Other television shows and celebrities popularized an ambiguously ethnic look, exemplified by Kim Kardashian or models like Gigi and Bella Hadid. Some cosmetic surgeons signaled implicitly racialized brand identities by gesturing to such iconic figures, with widely familiar, artificial surgical looks. By narrating these looks as expressing intersecting kinds of identities, including ones based on region, gender, and class, surgeons could leave the racial connotations implicit.

Echoing the language and branding patterns of many other hair, fashion, and beauty products, U.S. cosmetic surgeons developed Miami and L.A. looks for people from all over the world.[13] Neither look was known for its subtlety. Both appeared in very similar forms to the obvious, "artificial" looks associated with ethnic enhancement above—though the two had slightly distinct racialized connotations. The Miami look offered proximity to Latinidad. By contrast, the L.A. look presented an ambiguously ethnic, "obviously augmented"[14] appearance, stemming from American celebrity and entertainment culture. With her tanned appearance, full lips, sharp cheekbones, and prominent posterior, Kim Kardashian was an often-cited example of this ideal (figure 6). These kinds of racially adjacent but not racially explicit labels derived reflected glamour from popular culture, emphasizing customization in terms that were more alluring than the dry, limited labels of medical journal articles.

The Miami and L.A. looks drew on different cultural associations. The Miami look derived meaning from Miami's role as a central cultural and aesthetic hub for Latinos/Latinas in the U.S. and in the Caribbean and South America. According to Dr. June (Black, U.S.), Miami had a kind of "international," "Latin" cachet which patients from all over wanted to emulate. Similarly, Dr. Castañeda (Latino, Miami) identified the Miami look as a brand that drew international patients: "What we are trying to accomplish is the aesthetic of Miami, so patients understand that and that's what they want. If they live in England or Germany [and come here], they want to look like a Miami aesthetic." Dr. Castañeda identified "a very Hispanic influence, sensibility" as suffusing the city's distinctive aesthetic look and style, making explicit the racial undertone. Cosmetic surgeons signaled the Miami brand by emphasizing looks featuring curvy figures, big breasts, and big butts. Similarly, some cosmetic surgeons considered the attention-grabbing, obviously overdone appearance to be the quintessential L.A. look. According to Dr. Solomon, the mantra for the L.A. look was "whatever you can do to get attention where you normally wouldn't, that's the norm. Because [L.A.] is a city where people come to find themselves and get attention." Much like the Miami look, the L.A.-branded look was associated with bigger breasts, plump, tight, wrinkle-free faces, and a skinny figure. In

Figure 6. Kim Kardashian, 2010 Heart Truths Red Dress Collection. *Source:* Tim Lundin for the U.S. Department of Health and Human Services, Wikimedia Commons.

practice, this translated to many of the same physical features as the Miami look—but the urban culture in which each look was enmeshed helped differentiate a surgeon's brand, particularly for medical travelers.

The L.A. and Miami looks were discursive constructions linked to the racialized, gendered, and classed connotations of each city. The Miami look represented a Latina-inspired beauty ideal that was "racially flexible"; it could connote Blackness, whiteness, or brownness depending on other contextual factors and intersections with markers of class and sexuality.[15] Conveniently racially ambiguous, the L.A. look resonated with patients worldwide, made familiar by American popular culture and reality television celebrity. Surgeons touted the L.A. brand as an artificial look that was neither quite Black nor white but constituted a potential model for Black and white women. Kim Kardashian epitomized this racial ambiguity, as someone who was not Black but capable of signifying an "exotic" racial other nonetheless.[16] In resorting to city-named brands, surgeons could selectively call upon collectively shared U.S. racial meanings. Regional connotations were fuzzier, more subjective, and perhaps even more evocative than racial labels, adding another layer of meaning to looks.

Invoking cities and regions also allowed surgeons to hint at more specific constructions of whiteness as part of their brands. That is, instead of calling upon whiteness as a generic referent, surgeons leaned on the gendered, classed, and racialized connotations of places like New York City and the U.S. South to construct different iterations of white femininity. The most noticeable of these was a look corresponding to highly stylized, sexualized white femininity of the Southern belle, epitomized in the extreme by the figure of Dolly Parton.[17] Dr. June (Black) commented that "Texas has historically always liked really large breasts. Bigger and better in Texas. Big boobs, blonde hair, big hair and skinny waist." This look represented a hypersexualized, exaggerated performance of femininity and whiteness that was associated with the American South and West.

Though typically not racially marked by surgeons, it was a brand that represented the American heartland.[18] Other surgeons emphasized their own city brands by contrasting them with the aesthetic norms and classed and gendered reputations of other American places. For example, Dr. Novak (white, NYC) compared "the New York business nose" to a California look: "It's nice and elegant and chic but not overly done. Doesn't look like it's operated on. I think in California some people, they wear their cosmetic surgery on their sleeve like, 'Look at me, I got this done!' It's a little more petite, a little more defined, a little bit smaller nose. It's just a little more feminine [in California] than we do here. I think this is West Coast, East Coast." Dr. Novak defined the New York nose as subtle and androgynous, characterizing it entirely in relation to his image of an overdone, feminine California aesthetic. In turn, L.A. surgeons complained that facelifts, Botox, and fillers in New York were overdone, blaming a subculture of upper-class (and Upper East Side) women. Dr. Carras (white, L.A.) called the average woman's face on Fifth Avenue "too tight, too pulled," adding, "You're not one of the girls unless you look like that, so it's a rite of passage." Like L.A., New York was especially famous as a site of artificial or "fake" cosmetic surgery looks—for white women. Using regional identities to stand in for specific versions of white femininity, surgeons emphasized their different aesthetic senses—and advertised that they had the technical chops and expertise to enact these looks.[19]

In addition to having gendered and raced connotations, surgeons' brands were also inflected by assumptions about socioeconomic status. Cosmetic surgeons distinguished between women professionals and socialites, members of the entertainment industry and suburban moms. For instance, Dr. Mannheim contrasted his "academically affiliated" practice, located in a "more expensive zip code," with a "strip mall breast augmentation, double D's, $29.99 special kind of place." Dr. Mannheim's exaggerated comparison here linked large breasts (an obvious, hypersexualized look) with patients of lower-class status by gesturing to "strip malls" and implausibly cheap prices.

By contrast, he described his practice as comprised of a "more afflu-ent educated clientele," located downtown in a "more expensive zip code." Surgeons had a myriad of strategies for how to characterize looks and brands without explicitly using racial labels. They also con-structed looks and built brands that could be narrated in gendered and classed terms rather than race. When responding to market demand, surgeons could be inventive and expansive in envisioning a niche. However, I do not suggest that surgeons were always fully con-scious of every single racial, gender, and class connotation a brand might have. Rather, surgeons used regional and place names precisely because of the broad penumbra of their cultural meanings.

In asserting and shaping brand identities, U.S. cosmetic surgeons relied on purposefully stylized generalizations. Their descriptions of Miami, New York, or other looks should not be seen as faithful repre-sentations of what people did or should look like. Rather, they indexed popularly accessible racial imaginaries in broad strokes. Using American popular culture depictions of iconic cities and global enter-tainment hubs, U.S. cosmetic surgeons developed brands by stand-ardizing looks to fit a popular discourse rather than rigidly adhering to biomedical discourse. In pursuit of making money, cosmetic sur-geons, like advertising executives, "project the most attractive and appealing versions of race, those that let them play up favorable cul-tural and linguistic attributes compatible with brand identities, but downplay those that would threaten the status quo."[20] Furthermore, by claiming a brand affinity with specific regional aesthetics, surgeons could make a bid for patients to travel to obtain their preferred aes-thetic, potentially even across international borders.

In the U.S., white patients remained the most numerous, acces-sible, and lucrative population in cosmetic surgery, and white patients were the economic foundation of most practices. Ethnic marketing thus remained a niche strategy that some surgeons adopted to stand apart in a competitive market. The primary way that U.S. surgeons incorporated racial categories into their brands was through the form of implicitly racialized looks. In fact, cosmetic surgeons' fear of becoming pigeonholed was the main brake on the production of ever-more racialized looks. If a surgeon's brand was associated too closely with a racialized look, they feared putting off other patients seeking a different appearance. This concern suggested that surgeons were embroidering around the edges of the tapestry of kinds of people rather than weaving a new racially diverse motif.

MALAYSIA

Comparing Malaysia to the U.S. reveals other ways of conceptualizing and capitalizing on racial difference. Malaysian cosmetic surgeons also envisioned a market for cosmetic surgery in terms of racial demographics. Aiming at medical tourists as well as domestic patients, Malaysian surgeons exercised aesthetic and clinical judgment in selectively granting looks from among the many beauty ideals requested by patients. However, rather than constructing different looks to appeal to different racial segments of the population, Malaysian cosmetic surgeons built brands based on cultural sensitivity in the care they provided. This allowed surgeons to maintain a consistent brand that signaled their own cultural dispositions and racial sensitivity.

The current multiracial composition of Malaysia is the legacy of British colonial policy, which assisted—and in some cases, forced—migration of people from what is now China and India to take up specific occupational posts. Today, Malaysia recognizes four racial groups in its constitution: Chinese, Malay, Indian, and Other. After gaining its independence, as Meghann Ormond observes, Malaysia "has begun to revalue and identify national diversity as central to Malaysian identity," with multiracial difference helping plug the country "into lucrative transnational flows and networks."[21] Chinese, Indian, and Malay citizens of Malaysia continue to occupy different economic, social, and occupational positions.[22] In cosmetic surgery, this legacy meant that roughly half of surgeons were Malaysian Indian or Malaysian Chinese, outpacing their representation in the broader population.

Because of Malaysia's distinct colonial trajectory, the way that Malaysian surgeons conceptualized and operationalized racial categories differed from the U.S. For one thing, race as popularly used in Malaysia included traits like language and religion, often associated with ethnicity. Raymond Lee has argued that "in the Malaysian context, 'race' is an inclusive term that covers both physical and cultural characteristics."[23] For instance, the Malaysian Constitution defined the Malay race as a people who practice Islam (the state religion), speak the Malay language, and follow Malay custom. To be Malay was, by statute, to be Muslim—though it is important to note that not all Muslims in the country were Malay.[24] The Malaysian Constitution does not offer definitions for any other racial groups, and the racial boundary between Malay and non-Malay citizens remains politically and socially salient. In applying the term "race" here myself, I am not simply reproducing surgeons' terminology. Instead, I am pointing to the existence of a hierarchy among Malaysian racial categories. Differential access to political power, economic resources, and cultural capital between racial groups influenced the Malaysian cosmetic surgery market and profession.

Malaysia differed in another key respect from the U.S. In contrast to the norm of colorblindness in the U.S., Malaysian cosmetic surgeons were much more comfortable explicitly discussing race. They sought to economically capitalize on racial difference and multiculturalism. Accordingly, surgeons used their familiarity with the languages and cultures of Malaysia's diasporic Indian and Chinese communities to appeal beyond the country's borders to medical tourists. To a greater extent than my U.S. respondents, Malaysian surgeons deployed their own racial heritage to build brand identities highlighting their racial sensitivity. Furthermore, Malaysian cosmetic surgeons considered white patients, who came to their practices as expatriates or medical tourists, as one among the many racial demographics they treated. Malaysian surgeons parlayed their fluent command of the English language, another legacy of British colonial rule, to create a hospitable environment for expatriates and medical tourists from Australia and New Zealand, including white patients. But unlike most U.S. surgeons, Malaysian surgeons handled white patients as a group with specific cultural preferences rather than as a default referent.

Thus, to distinguish themselves in a racial market for cosmetic surgery, Malaysian cosmetic surgeons crafted brand identities based on the provision of racially and culturally sensitive care to patients. Malaysian cosmetic surgeons differed from their U.S. counterparts in eschewing the creation of distinct racial looks for patients, instead implementing cosmopolitan beauty ideals primarily developed elsewhere. To this end, they tested new techniques and materials to remove potential obstacles to cosmetic surgery for Malaysian patients of multiple races and for medical tourists.

The Brand of Cultural Sensitivity

Rather than constructing multiple aesthetics in line with the dominant racial categories in the country, Malaysian cosmetic surgeons promised to translate requests for several beauty ideals, including "Caucasian," "Korean," "Indian," and "Asian" looks, onto the bodies of patients. Drawing on the country's multicultural reputation, Malaysian surgeons built brands based on customizing experiences, tailoring ideals for patients of different backgrounds. To achieve this aim, Malaysian surgeons, like their American counterparts, analyzed the market for their services in terms of racial demographics. In a typical instance, Dr. Bala (Malaysian Indian) explained, "The type of clientele will be much more toward the Malay patients in KL. There's a little bit of variation, regional variations, cultural variations, racial variations depending on the patients." Surgeons like Dr. Bala heralded the growing interest in cosmetic surgery of a younger generation of Malays, who comprised the single largest racial demographic in the country. Though surgeons projected market growth and expansion opportunities among Malays, most of my respondents identified Malaysian Chinese patients as making up the majority of their patients.

To address these "variations," Malaysian cosmetic surgeons claimed cultural sensitivity in meeting religious needs, especially for Malay patients. Regardless of their own religious upbringing, Malaysian surgeons were well versed in anticipating the concerns of Malay patients. For instance, Dr. Bala, who was not Muslim, explained to me: "Islam does not encourage any insertion of foreign material into their body. . . . Because some places, there is a fatwa, that means an edict saying that OK, cannot do that. That precludes any kind of cosmetic, breast implants, forget it, they don't like, they don't do it." Laying out the different conditions and tolerances for Malay patients, he suggested alternatives, such as breast lift procedures, for what they might do to remedy issues like sagging breasts. Religion need not be an obstacle to a patient undergoing surgery if the surgeon could accommodate religious concerns. This was an important considera-tion because fatwas, or religious orders, issued by Malaysian imams based on their interpretation of Islamic teachings, could ban or restrict cosmetic surgical procedures. In 2006, for example, the National Fatwa Council of Malaysia issued a nonbinding advisory against the use of botulinum toxin such as Botox by Muslims.[25] Malaysian surgeons like Dr. Bala encouraged Malay patients to ask imams for guidance before seeking cosmetic surgery.

Anticipating the objection raised by some imams, Malaysian sur-geons ensured that materials used in cosmetic surgery were halal. Referring to compliance with Islamic law and ethics (shariah), the term halal has been applied to anything from food to financial products. Cosmetic surgeons operationalized halal as avoiding any product—implant, filler, injectable—that had ingredients derived from pigs. To Malaysians, this was a familiar stricture; Dr. Bala com-mented, matter-of-factly, "Of course you can't use porcine products for Muslim patients." In practice, this required Malaysian cosmetic

surgeons to pay attention to the ingredients and production processes of implants, fillers, and injectables. Seeing religion as a cultural
factor to accommodate, Malaysian surgeons like Dr. Bala prepared
to treat Malay patients by anticipating religious objections and making slight modifications to their practice.

Going beyond mere avoidance of "porcine content" in aesthetic
materials, one Malaysian aesthetic physician saw this as a business
opportunity. Dr. Christine (Malaysian Indian) was developing a line
of halal skin care products and fillers. Calling herself a "pioneer,"
Dr. Christine was seeking recognition for her products from the
Islamic Development Department of Malaysia, also known as
JAKIM, which conducted halal certification for products and services. Dr. Christine reflected, "It's a very up and coming country,
Malaysia, so everybody is very forward thinking, but there are religious laws as well that we need to abide by. . . . We try to get certification for halal or JAKIM at least. Those kinds of things make it
across-the-board safe for anybody to do. Also for Indian patients,
Chinese. We try not to put in animal products." Halal certification
reassured Muslim patients, but also, she suggested, made products
safer and more appealing to everyone. Thus, while halal aesthetic
products most directly targeted Muslim patients (in Malaysia and
beyond), Dr. Christine believed that the JAKIM certification also
made products more appealing to strict Hindu and Buddhist vegetar-
ians or others with religious restrictions. She developed materials and
techniques that could achieve Asian, Western, or Korean ideals for
the growing numbers of diverse Malaysian patients, from Muslim
Malays to Malaysian Chinese and Indian patients.

Though Dr. Christine was the only Malaysian respondent to float
the idea of a halal line of products, her example highlighted the productive potential of translation work and cultural sensitivity for
establishing a brand. With state support, Malaysia has become a
leader in the production and certification of halal products for cosmetic and personal care,[26] benefiting from a broader global trend
toward halalization.[27] Development of such products, as well as

"modest fashion,"[28] bolstered the Malaysian government's attempts to build an international reputation and encourage medical tourism, particularly from Indonesia and the Middle East. Rather than presuming that all Muslims shared essential traits, they identified specific religious practices that they could accommodate with their racial and cultural sensitivity. This was not such an outlandish thought, given the transnational success of analogous services, like traditional Chinese medicine. However, Malaysian surgeons' efforts were ultimately rooted in and limited by their own heritage and experiences. While they could promise familiarity with Islamic practice, there remained wide cultural gaps between Muslims from Malaysia versus Muslims from other countries in language, dress, and diet—just as with other medical traveler groups, as I explore in more detail later in this chapter. Making the leap from racial sensitivity, honed in a specific national context, to claiming cultural sensitivity and expertise in a global market was easier said than done.

But say it Malaysian cosmetic surgeons did, as did Malaysian bloggers alongside them. On fashion and beauty–centered Instagram, YouTube, and blog accounts, Malaysian social media influencers reviewed beauty practices, including cosmetic surgery, halal cosmetics, and modest fashion for an audience comprised of a larger Muslim world and diasporic Chinese and Indian audiences.[29] And Malaysian surgeons did report gaining travelers from abroad based on this outreach. Malaysian cosmetic surgeons, like other Malaysian entrepreneurs, hoped to parlay their brand of racial sensitivity into success in a global market.

Embodying the Brand

There was some irony in the fact that Malaysian cosmetic surgeons were offering prospective patients racial sensitivity rooted in their experience navigating a multicultural milieu. Malaysian multiculturalism is emblazoned in tourism campaigns and proudly proclaimed on the global stage as part of the national myth of the country, analogous in status to the idea of the U.S. as a melting pot of different immigrant cultures. Yet tension between Malaysian racial groups was also a frequent subject of newspaper articles, social media, and clinic break room conversations.[30] The ability to claim familiarity with patients of Indian and Chinese heritage as well as those professing the Muslim faith furnished Malaysian cosmetic surgeons with a distinct market niche for cosmetic surgery tourism.

Recall that plastic surgeons in Malaysia were generalists. They were also more likely than U.S. surgeons to be members of racial minorities, hailing from Chinese and Indian heritage. This was the result of the British colonial administration's recruitment of physicians from these groups. In the five decades since gaining independence, the Malaysian government has implemented formal affirmative action programs to increase the number of Malay physicians. These policies can be credited with bringing the proportion of Malay physicians up to the proportion of Malays in the general population.[31] However, plastic surgeons were more likely to be Malaysian Chinese (40%, relative to 23% of the population) or Malaysian Indian (14%, relative to 7% of the population) than Malay (46%, relative to 69% of the population). The current racial mix of the profession, compared with the more rapidly changing racial demographics of Malaysian society, provided added incentive for Malaysian Indian and Chinese surgeons to showcase their racial and cultural sensitivity to meet the needs of any Malaysian patient.

Compared with U.S. surgeons, Malaysian cosmetic surgeons were more comfortable foregrounding aspects of their own racial identities as part of their brands. To make connections and establish rapport with patients from across Asia, Malaysian surgeons emphasized their ethnic heritage, language skills, and cultural values. Most of the formal and technical discussions about cosmetic surgery procedures occurred in English. However, in consultations with patients in the clinic, I found that Malaysian surgeons would slip into Bahasa Melayu with Malay patients or Cantonese or Mandarin with Malaysian Chinese patients. This kind of code-switching put patients visibly at ease in the clinic. Surgeons who were unable to code-switch felt comparatively disadvantaged. For instance, Dr. Rajan, who was Malaysian Indian, characterized Malaysian Chinese surgeons as better situated to serve Malaysian Chinese patients: "He has a base, the Chinese doctor, because he knows the language." Surgeons believed that sharing a language brought people together, and they benefited from a presumption that shared language suggested other similarities in values, beliefs, or upbringing.

In a cultural context in which racial identities and backgrounds were often inferred from surnames, the racial identity of Malaysian surgeons could be a salient brand identity that appealed more strongly to some patients and helped establish their cultural sensitivity. Dr. Hsu (Malaysian Chinese) observed, "Sometimes the patient wants to see a particular racial doctor because they feel that it's easier to communicate and there is better understanding from the cultural point of view." Linking race to culture, Dr. Hsu identified the surgeon's racial identity as a component of their brand whether they liked it or not. She clarified, "For the doctor, I know it doesn't matter. But I know some patients would rather have [a doctor of the same race]." Dr. Hsu's reasoning was typical: sharing the race of the surgeon could facilitate communication and comfort for some patients. Again, the value of occupying racial niches in the market was most clear in the breach. Malaysian Indian and Chinese surgeons believed that Malay patients preferred surgeons of the same race. Dr. Fang (Malaysian Chinese) remarked, "I think because of the religious thing, Malays would rather go through a Malay surgeon." Some cosmetic surgeons believed that their personal identity characteristics, including race and religion, helped establish familiarity.

This kind of racial legibility and the overall experience it was thought to connote was important enough that some Malaysian surgeons hired staff with different racial identities and language skills to extend their reach. A multiracial staff complemented the surgeon's own outreach. Dr. Rajan (Malaysian Indian) hired two Malaysian Chinese "assistants," both women, who he thought were well "worth the money that I pay them." In addition to supplementing his language skills, he also found them to be more accessible to his patients, most of whom he described as "middle-class, upper-middle-class Chinese" women. He reckoned that his staff's investment in building relationships paid off, calculating that one assistant had "converted one case into three times or four" as patients returned for additional procedures. Similarly, Dr. Hsu (Malaysian Chinese) underscored the importance and potential of a multiracial team. Describing her operating room, in which one doctor was a member of one race and the nurses of two others, Dr. Hsu commented, "It is important for a team to be as multiethnic as possible so when they look after a patient who is multiethnic, different individuals with different backgrounds can contribute what they think. Maybe I don't know something about a cultural thing, and they can tell me. . . . But [race] shouldn't affect how you manage a patient, there's certain things that you do wrong because you don't understand the patient's culture. But I think we learn as we go along." This robust endorsement of multiethnicism was consistent with the ethos of Malaysian multiculturalism. Here Dr. Hsu argued that a racially diverse team could pool their distinct cultural knowledge to overcome difficulties communicating with patients of different races. Like other Malaysian surgeons, Dr. Hsu emphasized that a medical team reflecting Malaysia's multiracial society enabled them to anticipate, mitigate, and accommodate cultural difference more easily. In Malaysia, surgeons asserted expertise in different Asian cultures as part of their brands. Unlike their U.S. counterparts, Malaysian cosmetic surgeons were more comfortable and forward in marketing their own racial identities in the service of building a brand.

Racializing Cultural Sensitivity

Malaysian cosmetic surgeons promised patients a multicultural-sensitive form of care.[32] In addition to boasting facilities that met or exceeded Western standards, Malaysian cosmetic surgeons welcomed medical travelers with exemplary hospitality. Malaysian cosmetic surgeons promised a smooth surgical experience to patients traveling from abroad rooted in specific aspects of Malaysian culture—like English fluency among educated Malaysians of a certain generation and facility in several other languages. Facilities also advertised their provision of halal food in hospital recovery rooms and access to prayer rooms.[33] Consistent with Ara Wilson's findings in Thailand, medical tourism in Malaysia "leverage[ed] the 'local'— instrumentalized versions of culture, inexpensive material and immaterial labor, contingent expert knowledges . . . to produce the universal elements, the gleaming biotech, five-star lobbies, and accreditation by global/Western standards."[34] That is, Malaysian surgeons could imagine and prepare to cater to patients' every need by dint of both their multicultural expertise and their country's structural position as a site of cheaper labor.

Patients took note. After consulting with surgeons in the U.S., Thailand, and Malaysia, a white American patient, Mindy, who underwent breast augmentation and liposuction procedures in Malaysia, sang her surgeon's praises. Mindy began, "I liked him right away," continuing, "I felt like his communication skills were good, and I was in good hands. Especially having surgery outside the country, I wanted to make sure that their communication skills, that we were on the same level." The fact that her surgeon was fluent in English inspired confidence that he understood what she wanted. Describing the staff as "top of the line," she listed a series of detailed examples of care, from ensuring she was warm enough, helping her get dressed, and even blow-drying her hair after she showered over the course of a four-day hospital stay. Summing up, Mindy enthused, "They took amazing care of me. . . . Now what doctor in the U.S. does that?" Though she had prepared for cultural friction, this medical traveler's care team made her feel pampered, wowing her with five-star service. The hospitality and care in Malaysia exceeded her expectations, providing good value for the money.

In other cases, unfamiliarity between cultures and/or ethnic mismatches could lead to misunderstanding, friction, and bad experiences. Malaysian surgeons reported some difficulties interacting with medical travelers from Australia and New Zealand, who were often of lower socioeconomic status than the average Malaysian cosmetic surgery patient. Dr. Fang (Malaysian Chinese) contrasted these medical tourists, who "can more or less just afford your fees," with Malaysian patients, who "are wealthy, super-rich to the middle class." Purchasing power differences between Malaysia and Australia/New Zealand meant these medical travelers were still "top monetary high value cases," as Dr. Fang put it, in Malaysian practices. Their preference for more expensive surgical procedures like facelifts and tummy tucks, and for undergoing multiple procedures, made them important sources of revenue for surgeons. Cultural differences compounded the differences in socioeconomic status. Dr. Rajan (Malaysian Indian) found white Australian patients to be difficult and demanding, grumbling, "When they go back to Australia and they start calling you, it can be a nightmare. I can't see them. And I don't do Skype consultations because Skype consultations take maybe half an hour and they don't pay you anything." He perceived medical travelers as entitled and insufficiently deferential to his authority. In the context of patients who were scraping together fees, it was possible to also discern anxiety and uncertainty over the expenditure of scarce funds. Like Dr. Rajan, some Malaysian cosmetic surgeons reported breakdowns in relationships with medical travelers, especially those from Australia and New Zealand. Intermediary organizations like medical travel agencies helped bridge the cultural, socioeconomic, and geographic gaps.[35] Cosmetic surgery tourism could require additional translation work and time for surgeons and for patients.

Of course, the emergence of this kind of friction was not exclusive to Malaysia. Misunderstandings transpired between white, lower-middle-class patients from Australia and their Malaysian Indian and Chinese doctors but also between Chinese medical tourists and their South Korean providers, as well as between types of patients, including Indonesian versus Middle Eastern patients.[36] In the context of international travel, as Heng Leng Chee and Andrea Whittaker have called attention to, "suspicions of unacceptable practices also take on racialized narratives."[37] While Malaysian surgeons' capacity to accommodate difference was often celebrated, they could also be stymied and frustrated by the effort.

Medical tourism in Southeast Asia takes place amidst a longer history of colonial and interracial tensions. Shared economic and political arrangements promoted flows across the region, but had not necessarily eroded geopolitical frictions.[38] In fact, doubling down on the assertion and maintenance of racial differences incentivized the entrenchment of cultural difference.[39] Emphasizing "strategic essentialism" to attract medical tourists risked amplifying "certain stereotypes of exoticness."[40] This could reassert and reinforce racial differences along the old colonialist tracks which had given rise to this kind of pluralism in the first place. In touting multicultural expertise and racially sensitive surgical care as central elements of their brand, they sometimes essentialized and racialized culture. To deliver customized experiences, cosmetic surgeons sometimes engaged with cultural difference in shallow, stereotyped ways, perpetuating the notion of cultural difference as racial difference in their appeals to patients.

CONCLUSION

Alongside clinical judgment, mastery of the craft of cosmetic surgery required surgeons to command a place within the market. In both the U.S. and Malaysia, some cosmetic surgeons constructed their brands to pursue racial or "ethnic" niches within the market for cosmetic surgery. In the racial project of cosmetic surgery, racial categories helped make the particular become general and vice versa, transformations that extended surgeons' reach without unduly boxing them in. This is, more generally, how multicultural advertising works. As Arlene Davila has shown, "Individuals are turned into consumers and populations into markets." The ambiguity of racial meanings takes on an added versatility in the medical marketplace. In scaling up, assertions of "supposed intrinsic differences of particular populations"[41] could be baked in.

This took different forms across the U.S. and Malaysia. In the U.S., cosmetic surgeons constructed brands around different kinds of racialized looks, marketing "ethnic" aesthetics. By contrast, in Malaysia, surgeons constructed brands based on the delivery of racially and culturally sensitive care, marketing kinds of experiences. A broader social norm of colorblindness in the U.S. made it a more uncertain prospect for surgeons to center race as part of their brand—whether explicitly, through claims to being an "ethnic specialist," or by emphasizing their own racial background. Thus, some U.S. surgeons relied on regional signifiers and icons with implicit racial meaning instead. In Malaysia, a country where people were far more willing to discuss race and where colorblindness was not a norm, surgeons took for granted that their own racial background could be a potential foundation for a brand. Moreover, Malaysian surgeons drew on the country's multicultural ethos to signal their cultural sensitivity, differentiate themselves from competitors within Asia, and appeal to medical tourists. Comparing cosmetic surgeons in the two countries illustrates the proliferating possibilities of race to signal customization in a global marketplace.

The specific histories and racial structures of each country shaped how surgeons could mobilize racial categories. In the U.S., cosmetic surgeons presumed a tradeoff between appealing to white patients, who comprised the bulk of the current patient population, and patients of other races, whom they treated as a niche with future market potential. In Malaysia, cosmetic surgeons sought to expand from their success with Malaysian Chinese and Malaysian Indian patients into appealing to more (Muslim) Malay patients. They further hoped to translate their familiarity with the customs and needs of Malaysian racial groups into appeals to medical tourists, especially Muslims from other countries—though it was not clear that racial identities could be so easily transported. Across the two countries, there were different costs and benefits for surgeons using racial categories to establish brands and market niches. In the U.S., many surgeons concluded that the costs of marketing of racial looks outweighed the benefits, and cosmetic surgeons instead turned to more implicit racial images and associations in marketing their services. In Malaysia, where multiculturalism served as a springboard to participating in regional and even global markets, cosmetic surgeons were far more forward in declaring the utility and relevance of their own racial identities as part of the package that distinguished their practices. Emphasizing their own racial sensitivity, rather than advertising specific looks, also ensured that Malaysian cosmetic surgeons did not run afoul of legal prohibitions against the marketing of medical services.

While much of this chapter focuses on the differences between the U.S. and Malaysia, the similarities between the countries are also instructive. In both cases, cosmetic surgeons were inventive. In the U.S., this was evident in the kinds of racialized looks on offer, from a Miami silhouette to a Kim Kardashian transformation. In Malaysia, surgeons were similarly inventive in the experiences they promised patients, from halal cosmetics to five-star hospitality. Though the looks and experiences that U.S. and Malaysian cosmetic surgeons discussed were rooted in their respective contexts, the strategies behind them are more broadly relevant—especially for surgeons aiming to convince prospective patients to travel for care. In using racial categories to establish their brands, cosmetic surgeons elaborated and riffed on racial difference, setting themselves apart from competitors by emphasizing what Joan Fujimura and Ramya Rajagopalan have called "different differences."[42]

Cosmetic surgeons adapted racial categories in use in very different social worlds—from government discourse to popular culture to biomedicine to tourism—and rendered them into physical, embodied form on patients. They essentialized physical and cultural differences, shoring up and embellishing the idea of racial difference. This expanded and broadened aesthetic standards, while also creating more boundaries to police. In building a brand for the cosmetic surgery markets, surgeons used racial categories to calibrate the balance between customization and standardization. Already, in the marketplace, racial categories became fuzzier and sometimes implicit, as with the racially ambiguous L.A. or Miami looks. Because the value of some looks was both derived from and potentially comprised by their proximity to race, a degree of implicit racial connotation could help resolve the contradiction. That way, race could be invoked when it added value, as it suited the needs and desires of surgeons and patients. And race could be elided or denied when it did not. In the next and last chapter, I examine how this was accomplished within the walls of the cosmetic surgery clinic, zooming in to the micro level.

5 Customizing Bodies

SEEING RACE ON THE BODY

Cynthia, a young woman of Chinese descent, gently eased into a chair in front of Dr. Huang's desk for an initial consultation. A television anchor, Cynthia requested that Dr. Huang modify her eyelids to create a clearer eyelid fold. As she looked at herself in a mirror, Cynthia emphasized that she wanted to maintain a natural look. To illustrate, she showed Dr. Huang an image on her phone of a woman with a small but visible eyelid fold. Dr. Huang nodded, gestured for Cynthia to move closer, and handed her a mirror. While Cynthia looked at herself in the mirror, Dr. Huang used a small metal tool to simulate different eyelid heights, directing Cynthia to indicate when she liked what she saw. After a few movements, Cynthia signaled Dr. Huang to stop. Dr. Huang made a note, took a photograph, and the two began to discuss the logistics of a surgical procedure. Thus concluded a typical initial consultation, one of several I witnessed in Dr. Huang's neat, clinically white office in Kuala Lumpur.

Most of this book has focused on how cosmetic surgeons engage in a racial project by generalizing about racial categories—in medical journal articles, at conferences, in conversations and in marketing. This chapter traces the racial project one step further to the micro level, where surgeons and patients enacted race on bodies. In the clinic, surgeons had to translate from abstract generalities to the specifics of a prospective patient's body. There, features like eyes, which cosmetic surgeons described as "ethnically sensitive" in journal articles, were often not discussed in racialized terms. Even the Asian double eyelid surgery, which was the procedure that Cynthia sought above, did not necessarily have that moniker attached. That is, surgeons selectively rendered racial categories visual and material on the bodies of prospective patients or in photographs. Instead of focusing on racial standards, or on adjudicating the symbolic meanings of racial categories, surgeons used racial categories to signify how they would customize looks for patients. Sometimes, racial categories fell out of the picture entirely, as cosmetic surgeons turned to images to implicitly discuss the racialized associations with different looks. In consultations with patients, surgeons exercised their clinical and aesthetic judgment in discerning and enacting race on the body.

In one-on-one sessions, cosmetic surgeons sometimes used overtly racial terminology in narrating what they saw on patients' bodies. But more often, they described noses of various lengths, widths, heights, projection angles, and hues. They considered skin of different degrees of thickness and elasticity. They were trained to deconstruct the patient's physical features and consider how the parts contributed to the whole. With a patient in front of them, surgeons deconstructed visual and physical appearance into more specific variables.

SEEING THE PATIENT
The Professional Vision of Cosmetic Surgeons

Anthropology and sociology have discussed professional vision as a regime of attention. Charles Goodwin defines it as "socially organized ways of seeing and understanding events that are answerable to the distinctive interests of a particular social group."[1] In cosmetic surgery, professional vision was the product of mastery and manipulation of instrumentation as well as the development of an approach to conceptualizing patient anatomy and possible surgical solutions. In clinical encounters, cosmetic surgeons visualized patients with their eyes, digital cameras, and software tools that "morphed," or modified, photographs of patients' bodies. Their gaze was trained by techniques taught in medical school but also by conventions of popular culture. Investigating the racial implications of cosmetic surgeons' professional vision, I show how cosmetic surgeons saw (and did not see) race on bodies using specific technologies of visualization and representation. Whether or not race was openly discussed in the clinic, surgeons' aesthetic judgment and the technologies they used shaped how patient race could appear in the clinical encounter.

My point here is renewed emphasis on the "social practices that produce our very ability to see race."[2] Cosmetic surgeons adopted a standard approach to visualizing patients' bodies:[3] they eyeballed patients, took photographs of them, and simulated surgical outcomes with computer software. In both the U.S. and Malaysia, surgeons often incorporated technologies, mundane and sophisticated, into their professional vision, including mirrors, cameras, and simulation software. Techniques for honing professional vision were codified in textbooks and passed on in residency and fellowship training programs. They were further perfected after repeated use in years of practice, shaped by the kinds of patients that surgeons saw and by their engagement with sources of aesthetic inspiration like popular culture.

Examinations in the Clinical Encounter

Almost every cosmetic surgeon used images to communicate with patients. Images constituted a lingua franca between surgeons and patients, eliminating slang or highly technical language and enabling them to negotiate the problem and solution. Clinical consultations were suffused with images, as my observations of Dr. Huang's clinic illustrated. One afternoon, Patricia, a white, middle-aged woman from New Zealand came in for an initial consultation with Dr. Huang, a Malaysian Chinese surgeon, about rejuvenating her eyes. In the corner of the clinic, Dr. Huang had set up a small photo studio with a three-legged stool and neutral background. After a few minutes of casual conversation with the patient about her desired outcome, Dr. Huang asked her to sit on the stool. Frowning as she adjusted the camera and using a bright flash for illumination, she snapped photographs of the patient with a tripod-mounted digital SLR camera.

Once finished, Dr. Huang transferred the images to a computer monitor on her desk. Wincing as her face filled the large screen, Patricia whispered, "Oh God, I look awful." On the screen, Dr. Huang directed the cursor to parts of the face where the light from the flash bounced off. She then pointed to a darker area under the eyes, highlighting the loss of volume in the face. Quickly toggling back and forth between photographs taken with and without flash to illustrate her analysis of the deficiencies of the face, Dr. Huang tailored her recommendations for how to enhance her under-eye region. Patricia asked a few questions and then stood up, saying she would think about it and get back in touch.

This encounter was typical. In the initial consultation, cosmetic surgeons almost always begin by asking a patient what bothers them or what they are looking for. And patients told them. In interviews, patients reported asking surgeons to look "healthier," "natural," "balanced," or "more symmetrical." Peter, a white rhinoplasty patient in the U.S., instructed his surgeon, "Fix it, it's crooked, and I want it to look nice. . . . I want it a little bit smaller here." Patients gestured to specific points on their bodies to illustrate what they thought was wrong. Many provided aspirational "wish pics," or images of people with a desirable physical feature or overall appearance that illustrated the ideal, to flesh out their desires further and explain to sur-

Figure 7. A cosmetic surgeon's office. Photo credit: Alka Menon.

geons their desired aesthetic. Wish pics were photographs of influencers, models, and celebrities that patients sourced from social media sites like Instagram as well as magazines and catalogues.[4]

Initial consultations generally took place inside surgeons' offices within the clinic. Figure 7 depicts a common view from the patient's seat: scattered forms, textbooks and journals, albums illustrating different looks, and lots of mirrors. In the consultation, cosmetic surgeons listened to patients' requests and examined the patient. In front of a mirror, cosmetic surgeons pinched, poked, and pored over patients' bodies, using their professional vision to evaluate whether to operate. They took photographs of their patients, which then served as a launching pad for discussion. As the patient watched, the surgeon modified their photographs with image-editing software (like Adobe Photoshop) to simulate the changes the surgeon suggested. After back-and-forth discussion, if the surgeon and patient came to an agreement, the surgeon invited the patient to schedule a procedure or an additional appointment.[5] And after the patient healed from surgery, surgeons took photographs to document their transformation.

For Patricia, like many patients, photographs suggested deficiencies that were not necessarily obvious to the naked eye. And like many surgeons, Dr. Huang used the camera flash as a diagnostic tool, literally shedding light on previously invisible faults on the patient. And just as happened here, patients often had strong negative reactions, bordering on revulsion, when presented with their own images. Several cosmetic surgeons found the act of showing a patient a photograph of themselves to be "very instructive and very traumatic," in the particularly apt phrasing of Dr. Horn. He wryly concluded, "People don't usually like to look at themselves." This was not merely an observation but a strategy. Dr. Donati, a white surgeon practicing in L.A., made this explicit: "It is very important to try and objectify the face for the patient." He continued, "In a mirror you're actually looking at a mirror image. And by looking at photographs, you're looking at your real image, which read our way is different, which helps you to objectify your own face. You have to snap out of what you normally see and see something else and then see it in a clinical way. And then have somebody clinically point out objectively, the features of your nose and what's going on." Dr. Donati guided the patient to disregard what they saw in the mirror as biased because it was not how they appeared to others. Retraining the patient eye from the familiar self-image in the mirror to a different vantage point, the surgeon directed the patient to the photographs as more "objective" and a better reflection of how others saw the person. The mediation of a camera helped patients distance themselves and take on a clinical gaze, allowing them to temporarily adopt a surgeon's perspective and professional vision.

To help guide the patient to see things their way, cosmetic surgeons often narrated what they saw in photographs back to their patients. Dr. Huang explained,

I told [Patricia], "When I took this picture, your entire face looks pretty flat. I want to create a multidimensional, a little bit of volume." I explained to her, and she couldn't really see the difference. But I said, "Look, when I took this, both pictures were taken with flash. In this picture, everything was flat. Not a single thing captured the flash because everything was flat. So all the flash hit the face and got bounced back. But if you see in this picture, you can see this point here actually captured the flash." After I explained it, then she understood, because she couldn't really see the difference.

Images were not self-evident. Rather, cosmetic surgeons deployed the photographs they took to make arguments for a particular diagnosis or intervention. Patients could and did push back with their own images, requests, and questions. However, they relied on surgeons' patience in being able to negotiate in real time. Just as scientists carefully selected which images to publish to advance a particular argument, images used as before-and-after photographs by surgeons were also presented "to make particular points and to illustrate the argument" or vision of the surgeon, having a "rhetorical" object.[6]

MAKING RACE PHYSICAL AND MATERIAL IN THE CLINIC

It is important to emphasize that racial categories were submerged rather than entirely absent from the clinical encounter. Surgeons could decide whether and how to excavate racial associations. An extended visit to Dr. Silber's rhinoplasty clinic helped make this apparent to me. One wall of his office was comprised entirely of mirrors. A large Mac monitor was perched on his desk, facing away from him and toward the patient's seat, where I was sitting. I asked Dr. Silber (white, L.A.) about a phrase I had encountered on online discussion boards about cosmetic surgery: what did it mean for patients to "to keep the ethnic character" of their noses? In response, Dr. Silber scoffed, "Bullshit. . . . What they're saying, to translate, is, 'I don't want a nose that looks like Michael Jackson.' Not even Michael Jackson—let's say Michael Jackson before his last couple of rhinoplasties." Turning to his computer, he added, "Where what they don't want is this look." He rapidly flipped through a series of before-and-after photographs of revision rhinoplasty procedures, primarily in Black patients.[7] As he pointed to different parts of the nose with his cursor, he remarked, "I made that bigger, I made that smaller, I made this stick out more but not up more and then took that part off and then grafted that on the other side to get to that. . . . That's what they mean when they say 'I don't want to change it too much.' What they're saying is, 'I don't want *that.*'" I do not expect this running verbal commentary to get the reader far, but I include it as an example of how race *could* be materialized and translated in the clinical encounter. Eschewing racial terminology, Dr. Silber translated the patient's body into corporeal and visual elements. Indeed, without the photographs, the words themselves convey fairly little.

Within the clinic, when surgeons were interacting one on one with a patient, racial categories could be too broad to characterize an actual patient's body or adequately elaborate their requests. Walking me through the motions of an initial consultation, Dr. Silber presented a show-and-tell of several photographs of past operations. Pointing to one spot on a digital image, he identified "a pancake of tissue that [he] peeled from under the skin and off of the cartilage." He explained, "That's the difference between a Caucasian nose and a non-Caucasian nose; that [pancake] would be more like a piece of paper in thickness" rather than "a flapjack." Dr. Silber made racial difference palpable on this patient by highlighting the amount and placement of tissue on the nose. This exercise in diagnosing and explaining specific physical features, however, also called into question the very existence of a standard Black or white nose. While scrolling through additional photographs, Dr. Silber reflected, "It depends how much Caucasian you have in that ethnic rhinoplasty. I've seen Black noses that are as Caucasian as any Caucasian." Dr. Silber here acknowledged that patients' racial self-identification and their physical features did not always align, to his mind. Though he had just generalized that "non-Caucasian" noses had more fatty tissue than "Caucasian" noses, that made little difference to a patient presenting with the opposite pattern. Actual patients' bodies departed from standard textbook depictions, especially in the extent to which they conformed to racial expectations.[8] For surgeons like Dr. Silber, deciding whether and how to perform a rhinoplasty procedure on a Black patient, the amount of fatty tissue present was as salient as their racial self-identification. When a body itself was present, racial categories were no longer useful as proxies for physical features. The imperfections and limitations of racial categories as a proxy for physical difference became clear in the context of the clinical encounter. Surgeons could choose when and how to make race explicit in part because racial categories were too general to be useful in the clinic.

NEGOTIATING OUTCOMES IN CONSULTATIONS WITH PATIENTS

Patients usually had the first word in the initial consultation. But surgeons had several tools and strategies at their disposal in responding to patient requests. First, they could criticize or disqualify patient wish pics as ideals, narrating what they saw and why it was a good model or not for the specific patient. Second, they took their own photographs of patients and, in their words, "educated" or coached patients to view themselves as a surgeon might. In addition to taking digital photographs, some surgeons employed more sophisticated 3D imaging and technology, which defamiliarized patient bodies.

Third, surgeons presented patients with their own set of aspirational images, namely before-and-after photographs documenting procedures that surgeons had themselves performed in the past. In what follows, I show evidence of how cosmetic surgeons used each of these strategies to retrain and focus the gaze of patients on what surgeons believed to be feasible, desirable, and possible outcomes.

Pushing Back on Wish Pics

Wish pics helped make patient requests for surgery more concrete. Cosmetic surgeons often used images as a starting point to delve into the specifics of patients' requests, zooming in on past generic racial categories. Dr. Keller (white, Chicago) told patients, "I can't make you look like that picture, but at least I'll know what you're talking about when you say, 'I want a smaller nose.' Or 'I want my nose shorter'—what does that mean? Does that mean shorter in a vertical direction? Or shorter in terms of how far it projects from your face? If she shows me a picture of a nose that she thinks is good . . . it's a point where the discussion can start." Dr. Keller here identified the various ambiguities inherent in verbal communication about physical appearance. Without a referent, it was unclear what terms like "shorter" signified. Describing a patient-selected photograph as a starting point for discussions with patients, Dr. Keller described photographs as grounding the conversation with a patient in a concrete image. In narrating what they saw in wish pic photographs to patients, cosmetic surgeons bolstered their diagnosis by pointing to traits in the wish pic that the patient could discern themselves. In initial consultation with prospective patients, cosmetic surgeons toggled from general, population-based thinking to the individual level. For example, in characterizing ideal looks in general terms, Dr. Rajavi (Persian, U.S.) told me that "a huge big Bill Cosby nose" could not be transformed into a "petite Charlize Theron nose." Foregoing the generalization that a certain stereotypically Black nose could not be transformed into a small, feminine, white nose, Dr. Rajavi took the wish pic of Charlize Theron and said to the patient, in effect, "This nose shape will not work on *your* body." Surgeons could use wish pics to push back on patient requests that they perceived as transgressions of racial boundaries and to reinforce their own aesthetic and physician authority.

Moreover, surgeons decided which wish pics were viable models and in which ways. Dr. Bala (Malaysian Indian) perhaps put it best in calling himself a "guru of the face." As "gurus" or experts of the face, cosmetic surgeons could always lay claim to their professional vision. Some directed patients to vetted websites like implantinfo.com to look for appropriate models. Others guided patients to bring in photographs of family members, setting bounds on who was an appropriate model for a prospective patient.

Cosmetic surgeons chose whether to bring out race when evaluating wish pics for realism and aesthetic value. Surgeons could suggest the infeasibility of a given ideal by systematically differentiating their patients' physical characteristics from those of their photographed models. Dr. Keller used wish pics as an entry point to discuss "surgical limitations to producing that look," pointing out what he thought "would look good on her, and the things on that picture that I can't achieve surgically, because they may have too thick a skin or some other reason, or their age or various things." While surgeons often spelled out thick skin, age, and "various things" as being related to race when asked to generalize (as in chapter 3), they avoided making these racially explicit claims in initial consultations. In the clinic, they just needed to show patients how their bodies differed from their wish pic models to suggest the impossibility of achieving an ideal.

Using Cameras and Photographs to Align the Gaze of Surgeon and Patient

Visualization technologies were used to train patients to adopt the professional vision of the surgeon. Unlike other kinds of visualization technologies in medicine, like MRI machines or CAT scans, digital cameras and software programs like Adobe Photoshop were familiar, even mundane technologies in an era of ubiquitous smartphones and the selfie. This was part of their appeal: surgeons used familiar technologies of visualization to make patients' bodies unfamiliar to them, enjoining patients to see themselves as others did. In consultations, interviews, and journal articles, cosmetic surgeons hailed the diagnostic power of the camera and photograph. In the preface to their textbook on photography for facial plastic surgery, Drs. Tardy and Brown declared, "It is constantly a source of amazement that defects, asymmetries, and irregularities, undetected or overlooked during even the most careful physical examination, are exposed blatantly when the patient is viewed through the camera lens."[9]

In the clinic, surgeons trained patients how to look at their own bodies with the aid of visualization technologies.[10] Dr. Castañeda (Latino, Miami) ticked off a list of questions to address with patients using the visual aid of photos and tester breast implants: "Looking at pictures, what look are you looking for? What projection, what profile? Do you want a more natural shape? Do you want a more fake shape?" Aesthetic ideals like "natural" and "fake" were specified visually through photos. These photos linked specific images to words that had both clinical and lay meanings.

Cosmetic surgeons also used software to "morph" patients' photographs in order to simulate surgical outcomes, visually defining and testing racial boundaries. By manipulating images in software programs, cosmetic surgeons could pin down abstract ideals while still allowing for nuance and ambiguity. These manipulations also afforded surgeons a way to more gracefully reject patients' requests. For example, Dr. Ghorbani (Persian, U.S.) waved his hand when asked about patient requests for maintaining the "ethnic character" of the nose, saying, "That's such a vague statement." He continued, "You tease out exactly what they want, and that's where the morphing comes in to show them what to do.'" Morphing of images allowed for more subtlety and specificity in communicating about possible surgical looks with respect to race. Surgeons used visual simulations of surgical outcomes to show rather than tell patients how unattractive an outcome might appear. Dr. Berman (white, L.A.) described how this unfolded with a patient: "They'll say, 'I want it smaller.' Then we show them how it looks smaller, and I don't think it looks good. It becomes, looks unnatural, I would never seek to do that and they think that's OK. . . . That's at least a yellow light, and maybe a red light, not to do it." Surgeons hoped that patients would choose to abandon a request on their own when shown an exaggerated representation of a small nose, past the point of what the surgeon found to be aesthetically pleasing. Surgeons assessed reactions to simulated outcomes to determine whether or not the patient had "realistic expectations" and were a good fit for their practice and brand. Exchanges between surgeon and patients over imaging was a test run for whether and how a patient would respond to surgical intervention. If it did not go well, the discrepancy was a red flag for a doctor, indicating a divergent aesthetic sense or a difficult-to-satisfy customer.

Diagnostic photographs and morphed images illustrated racial boundaries in the limits and materiality of the patient's own body—without using racial language. For all patients, the decision to operate depended on what surgeons believed to be safe and feasible, as well as aesthetically pleasing. The anatomy of individual patients posed material constraints on safe surgical intervention. Dr. White (white, Houston), a rhinoplasty specialist, began, "Take the nose. . . . [With] different people's skin, different structure, you're going to be able to do different things. There are some things you can't do. I've had someone with very thick skin and I'm just not going to be able to get it really small. . . . And that's not going to look good anyway. There's some people that want it really, really skinny. You have to say, 'You don't want to do that. This is what's going to look natural and that's as far as I'll go.'" Discussing skin thickness, which was associated with racial difference by U.S. and Malaysian surgeons, Dr. White positioned herself as the custodian and guardian of the patient's bodily integrity, rather than as an arbiter of racial boundary policing. She expressed a technical inability ("I'm just not going to be able to get it really small") and aesthetic evaluation ("not going to look good") in the same breath. The features of patients' bodies—especially those recognized as racially implicated, like skin color and thickness, or eye or nose shape—were presented as material constraints that could lead to disfiguration if not accounted for. Ultimately, cosmetic surgeons marshaled evidence in images to "educate" patients, helping patients see bodies the way they did.

Though patients were very familiar with the idea of photographing themselves, camera systems could also be reconfigured as a tool for surgeons to assert their medical authority. Working at an academic medical center, Dr. Murta (white, Chicago) proclaimed, "We take our own photos in a dual-strobe professional photo setup with a fixed lens and a fixed focal length. It's super. We are [University] Medical Center. We don't fool around." Using impressive-sounding, high-tech descriptions of visual simulation technologies, Dr. Murta highlighted his command of the latest tools of the trade, distinguishing himself from less scientifically minded or able competitors. However, in a tacit acknowledgment of the authoritative feel of such technologies, surgeons employing 3D imaging technologies were more cautious about the claims they made about simulated images. They required patients to sign a waiver indicating that the simulated image implied no guarantee. Accordingly, cosmetic surgeons could enroll the camera as an ally, conscripting it into their arsenal of biomedical tools.[11]

In the 1990s, feminist scholars warned against the new prospect of simulating surgical outcomes with images in cosmetic surgery. Anne Balsamo cautioned, "The digital transformation of one's own face produces a magical liquid simulation that is difficult to reject."[12] As her work chronicled, images in cosmetic surgery had resilience and staying power. But cosmetic surgeons could also turn that "magical liquid simulation" to the opposite effect, to seek to dissuade patients, eliciting disgust instead of hope. In fact, images in cosmetic surgery required interpretation—by surgeons and patients. Cosmetic surgeons could decide whether to screen ostensibly racially neutral requests—"shorter," "more refined," "smaller"—for their racialized implications. Incremental modifications to racialized features that resulted in a white(r) appearance could perhaps pass muster absent an associated narrative of racial boundary crossing and transformation. Relying on their clinical and aesthetic judgment, cosmetic surgeons each sought to identify their own line as to where racialized requests became Trojan horses for wholesale racial transformation. When communicating with pictures, patients and cosmetic surgeons could choose whether, when, and how to see race, and whether to read between the lines to assess the racialized implications of apparently neutral requests.

Representing Race in Before-and-After Photographs

Cosmetic surgeons displayed their own before-and-after photographs to train the gaze of patients as to what was desirable and possible for them to accomplish. In addition to aiding diagnosis, before-and-after photographs taken in standardized poses became part of a patient's record. With patients' permission, they were shared with prospective patients as models of what surgery could achieve. Before-and-after photographs fixed bodies in time and space. During interviews, surgeons shared before-and-after photographs with me, pulling out albums, mobile phones, iPads, or monitors to illustrate their points. These carefully curated collections revealed the extent to which cosmetic surgeons operated on patients of color or wanted to advertise that fact. While flipping through an iPad containing before-and-after photographs that he presented to prospective patients during the initial consultation, Dr. Stone (white, L.A.) noted, "Just today I was looking on my little iPad that I show people and I realized I don't have a Black face on there. And this [patient] is a Black woman, I want to show some pictures. I guess we have a pretty, I wouldn't say homogeneous, a lot of Latinos [but] they're mostly white out here—the ones that come to me." Many surgeons had few if any before-and-after photos featuring Black patients. Before-and-after photographs were an opportunity for surgeons to curate their aesthetic sense and brand. Surgeons only highlighted their best work, that which they wanted to be known for. Many performed relatively few operations on Black patients or did not want to represent their practice with images of Black patients. Surgeons' handpicked before-and-after photographs thus offered clues for patients into surgeons' expertise and experience operating on people of different races. The inclusion of racially marked patients (Black, Latina, or Asian) in before-and-after photograph collections reflected surgeons' attention to and familiarity with communities of color.

Before-and-after photographs documented the results of procedures that a surgeon had personally conducted, giving patients a sense of the surgeon's own aesthetic sense. Cosmetic surgeons accorded before-and-after photographs privileged status among different images as the most representative of a surgeon's brand and ability. Dr. Forrat (white, Chicago) told patients, "Look at my real pictures. If you like what you see there, then let's talk." Surgeons portrayed before-and-after photographs as "bare facts," enabling patients to perceive change "with their own eyes," just as scientists once presented X-rays.[13] Such photographs were thought to be so enticing as to violate rules against the advertisement of medical services in Malaysia, where surgeons could only show them within the context of an initial consultation.[14]

Though cosmetic surgeons claimed that before-and-after photographs were the best indicators of what was possible through surgical intervention, they were also mediated and sometimes manipulated. Differences between the "before" and "after" photos often had more to do with the staging of the photograph than with surgical intervention. For instance, patients in the "after" condition were sometimes subject to different lighting conditions and heavier makeup. The backdrop behind patients in the photos changed color, affecting the outline and silhouette. Cosmetic surgeons had less control over the "after" photograph, taken as a courtesy to them months after a surgical procedure. But some placed more importance on consistency (or standards for clinical photography) than others.[15] Even before-and-after photographs could be gamed to mislead patients and make a surgeon, outcome, or procedure look better. Cosmetic surgeons across the board admitted that they only showed prospective patients their best outcomes. They were obligated to discuss possible complications with prospective patients, and they did—verbally. Few showed their patients photographs of them for fear of scaring off squeamish patients. Recognizing the visceral potential of images to disgust as well as entice, cosmetic surgeons worried that images of complications would communicate perhaps too honestly about the risks of an invasive elective procedure for beautification.[16]

Racial Assumptions within Visualization Technologies

Surgeons' reliance on cameras made them subject to the limitations built into the machines. Existing scholarship in science and technology studies has made it clear that cameras and digital photography do not represent an unmediated reality. Rather, they contain assumptions about the relevant characteristics of the object under depiction. That is, the way that surgeons used technologies such as cameras, and features and settings within cameras, filtered how the body could be represented. Lorna Roth has shown how photography, both analogue and digital, has failed to represent darker-skinned and Black photographic subjects with the same richness and specificity as lighter-skinned or white photographic subjects. Bias in skin tone is built in to "the actual apparatuses of visual reproduction," as with cards used to coordinate color in Kodak film.[17] Historically, the cards featured white models to guide and calibrate color balance in film development. The advent of digital photography did not eliminate these issues. Scholars of race and technology like Ruha Benjamin note that color-correcting software still does not always recognize or account for the full range of human skin tones today.[18] Algorithms can fail to parse Black or darker-skinned faces and accordingly misapply or fail to generate flashes. Digital cameras circumscribe how bodies can appear, systematically erring in the direction of assuming what Simone Browne has called a "prototypical whiteness."[19] The affordances of visualization technologies set the terms for how bodies can be comprehended. This is true even as purveyors of digital imaging technologies privilege tools like cameras or biometric fingerprint readers as representational tools that reveal some inner essence or truth.

Surgeons' reliance on cameras meant that these biases likely entered the cosmetic surgery clinic, even as it is difficult to surface them by drawing on surgeons' accounts alone. The material and virtual affordances of computer software in digital cameras could lead to the misrepresentation of patients of color. The images generated of people of color by digital cameras could be "off" and constrained in ways that could misdirect the attention of surgeons and patients and lead to greater alienation for patients of color—especially Black patients. In recognition, some surgeons discussed the need to adjust for the shortcomings of the camera, along with strategies to better capture a full range of patients. For instance, cosmetic surgeons writing in the journal *Plastic and Reconstructive Surgery* warned their colleagues that they faced issues with "digital color management, color accuracy, and color reproducibility," which they recognized as "challenging to even the most seasoned professionals."[20] To compensate, they suggested adjustments via image-editing programs such as Adobe PhotoShop. More recent updates in digital imaging technologies, along with greater awareness of lighting effects, also improved surgeons' ability to capture darker skin tones. The point is not that digital cameras were irredeemably biased. Rather, digital photography, like other visualization technologies, filtered bodies in ways that could systematically constrain the visual representation of race. Cameras and digital imaging processing invisibly calibrated surgeons' and patients' ability to perceive race in the clinical encounter.

SETTING EXPECTATIONS: SURGEONS' ENGAGEMENT WITH POPULAR CULTURE AND MEDIA

Cosmetic surgeons are producers and consumers of images in the clinic. However, it is important to recognize that the beautiful bodies and images that they construct and produce circulate well beyond the clinic walls into popular culture and the media. At the intersection of the worlds of medicine, beauty, and entertainment, cosmetic surgery profits from a "symbiosis between scientific and popular imaging technologies," with medicine also adopting "the representational conventions of popular entertainment."[21] Cosmetic surgeons produced and disseminated images in several popular venues. In the U.S., some surgeons had appeared on cosmetic surgery reality television programs; others were featured on morning news segments. In Malaysia and the U.S., surgeons were active on social media sites like Instagram or Snapchat, displaying photographs consistent with their brand and creating filters. With patient consent, a few even live-streamed surgical operations.[22] Cosmetic surgeons were wise to the traffic between popular culture and medicine, and they participated in an economy of visual beauty. All of the clinics I visited in both Malaysia and the U.S. displayed images of beauty in some form, from high-end fashion magazines resting on tables in waiting rooms to discreet, leather-bound albums of before-and-after surgery photographs of past patients. In some clinics, a television displayed videos of past procedures. All of these images of beauty, and the beauty ideals they represented, were embedded in a racial structure that set expectations about what kinds of appearances were valued.[23]

Cosmetic surgeons were also consumers of images from popular culture. In particular, they used celebrity examples to index specific looks or features. Given the continuing stigma associated with cosmetic surgery, celebrities provided a convenient shorthand for surgeons. Widely believed to have undergone surgery, though most denied it, celebrities were prominent examples of what was possible. U.S. surgeons gestured primarily to white celebrities such as Mickey

Rourke, Jane Fonda, Renée Zellweger, and Burt Reynolds. By comparison, they only mentioned a handful of celebrities of color, including Beyoncé, a Black musical artist, Jennifer Lopez, a Latina actress and singer, and Kim Kardashian, a celebrity and reality television star. Michael Jackson was repeatedly indexed as a worst-case scenario in cosmetic surgery. As other examples of looks to avoid, cosmetic surgeons offered the names of older white women like Joan Rivers and Carol Burnett.

Malaysian surgeons invoked a deeper bench of celebrity examples from all over the world. In addition to Malaysian celebrities (like famous chefs or DJs), Malaysian surgeons also cited Bollywood actresses, K-pop icons, and American entertainers. They were prepared to evaluate wish pics from around the world with an eye toward their local Asian patients. Dr. Huang (Malaysian Chinese) told me, "If patients come in having a Justin Bieber picture or Angelina Jolie picture, I'd be like, 'Look, hang on, just wait a second.'" She laughed, then continued, "I usually do a lot of counseling for them. In the process of doing that, I would be able to pick up if there is body dysmorphic syndrome or if there are any other social issues to be dealt with. Because eventually, if they have underlying other social issues that they are facing, they will not be happy with whatever results you give them." The wrong celebrity model could signal issues in the patient, including immaturity or fixation. Senior surgeons who were Malaysian Chinese or Malaysian Indian men seemed surprised by the turn in popularity to Korean stars, and were less familiar with their names. Cosmetic surgeons were wary of becoming known for an aesthetic that they did not recognize or understand. If wish pics depicted a body that was outside of mainstream beauty or a cosmetic surgeon's aesthetic, he or she might refuse to operate.

The value and viability of wish pics and celebrity looks depended on their legibility to cosmetic surgeons. As discussed in chapters 3 and 4, cosmetic surgeons' aesthetic sense and judgment was shaped by local mores and familiarity with different segments of popular culture. In the U.S., white surgeons did not always share a pop cultural space with patients of color. Celebrity references were culturally specific and could quickly become outdated, especially for the continuing stream of young patients. A few cosmetic surgeons described systematic efforts to keep up with beauty trends. Dr. Weisman (white, NYC) counted "a lot of popular culture magazines" alongside the academic journals that she regularly perused to stay au courant. Reading these magazines was both "relevant to what I do," according to Dr. Weisman, and something she enjoyed. She explained, "You gotta know when someone comes in referring to something." Similarly, Dr. Rodriguez (Latino, Miami) turned to Instagram to stay abreast of a broader range of looks. After daily check-ins, he called himself "sensitized" to "pictures of Instagram models with fake butts," noting that "every girl comes in and says, 'This is what I want to look like.'" For Dr. Rodriguez, beauty trends on social media helped him understand which "fake" or obviously surgical looks were in vogue.

However, Drs. Rodriguez and Weisman were unusual in taking such steps to train their own gaze this way. Even as cosmetic surgeons credited popular culture with generating beauty ideals, most surgeons did not discuss how they kept up with popular culture or acknowledge how it might shape their aesthetic sense. Indeed, many U.S. cosmetic surgeons expressed some bewilderment with changing trends in communities of color. As Dr. Kozlowski (white, Chicago) put it, "If you would've asked me ten years ago about fat transfer to the butt—I would have been like, 'Yeah, someone's going to pay for that?!'" Curvier figures and bigger butts, in particular, had been ideals for Black beauty for even longer than the period he outlined. In the absence of close connections to communities of color, white U.S. surgeons seemed surprised by the requests arising from them.

Media supplied surgeons and patients with both models and moral and aesthetic valuation of racialized looks. Editorial magazines, from Black lifestyle magazines like *Ebony* or *Essence*, portraying curvier figures as a quintessential form of Black beauty, to *Vogue* and *Vanity Fair*, showcased multipage spreads of beautiful actresses. Tabloid magazines and reality television shows offered wide-ranging coverage speculating about which celebrities had undergone which procedures, and what had gone wrong. For example, Joan Rivers and Donda West, the mother of rapper and producer Kanye West, garnered extensive coverage after they died following cosmetic surgery procedures.[24] Such stories emphasized errors and disasters, including the complications resulting from procedures performed outside of clinics. Whether or not surgeons were altogether conscious of it, input from popular culture also informed their professional vision and clinical judgment—all the more so for racialized procedures like buttocks augmentation.

Reshaping Racial Imaginaries: The Feedback Loop of Social Media

Less than 10% of my respondents directly contributed to traditional media by appearing on television or in glossy magazine spreads. But by the time I conducted interviews in 2014–2016, almost every cosmetic surgeon had a direct presence on social media sites like Instagram or Snapchat.[25] On social media, cosmetic surgeons acted as producers, gatekeepers, and consumers of beauty ideals. As media ecosystems fractured and diversified, social media sites were important sources of beauty ideals. With a lower bar to entry than traditional media and different gatekeepers, more alternative standards of racial or "ethnic" beauty circulated on social media. Social media helped accelerate a feedback loop between cosmetic surgery, beauty ideals, and race; patients and surgeons did not just take inspiration from social media, but actively contributed content to it. Both surgeons and patients shared images of surgically modified bodies, sometimes acknowledging that work had been done, and sometimes not. By sharing surgically inspired looks, they helped up the ante and created new models and pressures for beauty.

Most used social media sites like Instagram not only as a source of beauty ideals, but also as a platform to develop and signal their brand and aesthetic sense. Limited by professional norms and ethics that generally prevented surgeons from breaking patient confidentiality, surgeons did not post their own before-and-after photographs. Rather, they shared images of their clinic, or of celebrities, or of their friends to convey their brand and aesthetic. In addition to searching for new inspiration for surgical looks on Instagram, Dr. Rodriguez (Latino, Miami) sought opportunities to meet influencers and expand and build his social network, which he documented online to further express his aesthetic and brand identity. On Instagram, Dr. Huang posted photos of herself and of the occasional patient with their permission. By advertising particular looks online and successfully recruiting more patients, these cosmetic surgeons increased the salience of those looks and drove up demand for them. Surgeons with active social media presences could post or encourage content that trained patients' vision and heightened expectations of cosmetic surgery.

Patients sometimes shared photographs of themselves after surgical modification—and sometimes made a career or brand out of sharing their cosmetic surgery experiences online. As one example, Malaysian celebrity entrepreneur and DJ Leng Yein posted on Facebook, Instagram, and blogs promoting products that aligned with her lifestyle. Starting out as a celebrity entrepreneur and DJ, she achieved greater fame by publicizing her multiple cosmetic surgery procedures on Facebook and Instagram. She posted photographs of her "fake" look, featuring big breasts, double eyelids, and a v-shaped face.[26] In some cases, cosmetic surgeons provided influencers like Leng Yein with free or discounted aesthetic procedures in return for coverage of their experience to their social media followers. Discussing a colleague's experience with the practice, Dr. Huang (Malaysian Chinese) explained: "They actually pay beauty bloggers, or they have them come in and give them a free treatment and blog about it and really boast about the treatment services and all that. Because of a lot of women, youngsters nowadays love to go to look at the blogs. They trust bloggers more than anything else." Cosmetic surgeons enlisted the cultural authority and embodied experience of the most active social media users to familiarize and advertise their services. Influencers were incentivized to disseminate surgically altered images of beauty as widely as possible to prospective patients, and could become the basis for patient wish pics. In the U.S. and Malaysia, cosmetic surgeons recognized and capitalized on the growing power and importance of social media in circulating surgical looks.

At the time of my research, none of my respondents reported cultivating a relationship with influencers, despite the visibility of this economy. Many were ambivalent about how to navigate social media. Some worried that it promoted unrealistic expectations about how patients saw themselves and what could be done to the body. They argued that the ascendance of social media and the internet had changed both how people wanted to look and how they justified their requests in a way that was ultimately "good for business, bad for society," as Dr. Rajavi (Persian, U.S.) remarked.[27] They believed that social media had retrained how patients saw themselves and how they compared themselves to others.[28] Dr. Rajavi explained, "With Instagram, social media, and the increased selfies and all this stuff, I think people are more critical and I think it's actually gonna increase the demand for what I do, for better or worse." Dr. Rajavi thought that increased social media usage and the ways of viewing the body that it facilitated—the angle of the lens in selfies, filters that widened and brightened eyes—would not only increase demand for cosmetic surgery procedures but also raise expectations for them. The very existence of a platform involving visual check-ins and a wide audience created a pressure, he believed, for "reassurances from self and others on how good you look. Maybe that's increasing the demand or just also proportionately decreasing satisfaction rates from cosmetic surgery." The concern was that such constant attention and distributed evaluation of appearance might make patients dissatisfied even after surgical alteration of their bodies. Confronted with more critical, image-savvy social media users, surgeons worried that the associated uptick in business would result in more patients who were impossible to satisfy.

Surgeons were not altogether comfortable with this state of affairs. In an echo of the critique surgeons leveled at "surgery junkies," people who returned repeatedly for procedures seeking ever greater perfection,[29] Dr. Solomon (Persian, U.S.) lamented: "Social media capitalism is driving what women want, what they should get, and it's become a commodity." Though physicians, in his story, "are trying to keep up with it," Dr. Solomon noted, "We can't because there's a limit to biology and physiology." Linking cosmetic surgery and capitalism, Dr. Solomon characterized desires as stretching the limits of patients' bodies and cosmetic surgeons' own abilities. While Dr. Solomon was unique among my respondents in naming capitalism as the relentless driver behind changing media and beauty trends, the idea of insatiable, media-driven demand resonated with surgeons in the U.S. and Malaysia. Through their engagements with social media, from following aesthetic trends to posting beautiful images, cosmetic surgeons shaped and perpetuated racialized beauty ideals.

The broader range of looks circulating on social media represented a pluralization of aesthetics, rather than a wholesale democratization of beauty ideals. As sociologist Forrest Stuart has pointed out, "Although the means of cultural production are now more open than ever, some people are better equipped to exploit them than others."[30] Groups that had less access to traditional forms of media, including young women and young Black men, could generate content and obtain recognition online, but faced significant headwinds in gaining attention.[31] Social media afforded new opportunities for people to, as bell hooks put it, "eat the other."[32] Communication scholar Wesley Stevens argues that "because the platform privileges visual content, Instagram is a space in which racial identity's aesthetic performativity is especially evident," making it a key site for negotiating racial meaning.[33] In addition to promoting the consumption of Black aesthetics, social media also provided more avenues for people to capitalize on Black aesthetics, including those who did not identify as Black. Cosmetic surgeons steered clear of discussions about cultural appropriation of Black or other racialized looks by people of other racial backgrounds. But their active social media presence and engagement with sites like Instagram made them part of a larger economy that traded on the cultural and economic value of racialized bodies.

Cosmetic surgeons balanced between capitalizing on the growing awareness of their services engendered by social media and raising expectations of what it was possible to look like. Surgeons maintained that they could not guarantee that patients would appear just like the images that inspired their dissatisfaction with their bodies. Dr. Milstein (white, L.A.) noted, "When you give those two visuals, that's their expectation. And unfortunately the computer isn't doing the cutting and the computer isn't doing the healing." Noting that images were easier to manipulate than bodies, cosmetic surgeons regarded images from social media with some wariness.

CONCLUSION

At the micro level, within the clinic, racial standards were too general to be useful, and racial categories took on different forms from their exposition in journal articles or in surgeons' discussions. When a patient was physically present before surgeons, the abstraction of race did not adequately capture the particularities of the body. Accordingly, in interpersonal interactions with patients, surgeons chose when and how to make race visible and material in their discussions of patients' features. Race flickered in and out of view, as Amade M'charek writes, "oscillating between a presence and absence between relevance and irrelevance, or between it being above the surface and beneath it."[34]

In the initial encounter and afterward, images, including photographs, wish pics, and computer simulations of possible outcomes, facilitated surgeon-patient communication. Generating, interpreting, modifying, and disseminating images was central to the craft of cosmetic surgery, alongside well-honed aesthetic judgment and an understanding of the fundamentals of human anatomy. Using images, surgeons made arguments for patients' faults and possible solutions, selectively invoking race. Patients also illustrated their requests with images, including wish pics and celebrity references. They negotiated with surgeons by suggesting tweaks to simulated images. In an era in which every patient carried a camera in their pocket and many crafted carefully curated representations of themselves online, the visual tools of cosmetic surgery could seem comprehensible and even familiar to patients. Far from being magical, visualization tools enabled patients to communicate in visual terms, even as they also filtered information and structured the boundaries of racial representation.

Though cosmetic surgeons heralded the potential of images to improve communication with patients, some claimed an ambivalent relationship with the popular culture and social media that disseminated them. On the one hand, social media publicized a continuous stream of beauty ideals and induced patients to reexamine their bodies in a different light. Social media reinforced the idea of race as a visual phenomenon and offered surgeons more opportunities to develop niches along racial lines. On the other hand, surgeons were concerned that social media elevated patient expectations of surgical transformation to unrealistic heights. To manage expectations, surgeons used their own professional vision and judgment to push back on patients' wish pics. They limited which pictures they deemed acceptable and desirable as wish pics, "educated" patients to perceive their bodies differently, and countered patients' requests with their own before-and-after photographs. Cosmetic surgeons shored up their authority by invoking technological aids like 3D imaging, to which patients lacked access.

Cosmetic surgeons were not simply at the mercy of entertainment culture and social media, however. Despite their stated misgivings, they also directly contributed their own images of beauty in their online posts. Like patients, surgeons actively circulated images of beauty, weighing in and asserting in visual terms what was aesthetic and what was not. Cosmetic surgeons were part of a feedback loop consuming and producing racially legible looks. Surgeons were thus joint authors of the visual world they had come to inhabit. And with years of formal training and technical skill, they were better positioned than patients to navigate this image economy; surgeons could usually recognize whether celebrity models for wish pics had themselves undergone surgery. As gatekeepers and experts, surgeons could ensure that they maintained the upper hand in clinical encounters.

Surgeons' aesthetic judgments were pronouncements but also enactments—on the bodies of patients and in visual representations. Scholars have described the "technological gaze" in cosmetic surgery as gendered and paternalistic.[35] I find it is also embedded with assumptions about race: trained primarily on white patients, visualization tools could sometimes fail to properly represent patients of color, especially Black patients. Utilizing visual technologies, cosmetic surgeons remade and produced differences even as they purported to catalogue them.

Conclusion **The Art and Science of Racial Difference in Global Cosmetic Surgery**

In revisiting my initial preconceptions at the end of my fieldwork, I realized I had come to agree with Dr. Alizadeh's remarks to the *New York Times*: in some key respects, cosmetic surgeons *are* like amateur sociologists. Like sociologists, cosmetic surgeons claim expertise about social identities like race and gender and use these categories to generalize about groups of people. Cosmetic surgeons are attentive to social boundaries, including those between racial groups, between femininity and masculinity, socioeconomic statuses, and nationalities. Surgeons' analysis of cultural worlds arguably makes them like sociologists.

However, cosmetic surgeons have their own professional and economic motivations for producing knowledge using social identity categories. To navigate a transnational discipline spanning biomedicine and popular culture, cosmetic surgeons wear many hats. As surgeons noted, they are also scientists who generate standards using racial categories. They are clinicians who decide how to apply standards to patients in practice and adopt professional vision in visualizing patient complaints and solutions. They are artists who exercise aesthetic and moral judgment in deeming "ethnically congruent" looks to be natural and racial boundary-crossing looks to be artificial. And they are businesspeople searching for a niche (like offering specific kinds of racialized looks or cultural sensitivity in care) to establish themselves in the global market for cosmetic surgery.

To this list of roles that cosmetic surgeons themselves claim, I add another. Cosmetic surgeons are professionals who act as a kind of racial broker, linking macro racial structures to meso-level racial meanings and micro, interpersonal racial interactions. In each of the above roles, they draw upon and construct racial meanings, contributing to racial projects that stabilize racial hierarchies. This is not to say that they are racist or that they are racial ideologues. I argue that cosmetic surgeons reshape race—literally, on patients' bodies, but also at the level of broader culture. This book traces the role of medical professionals in maintaining and incrementally changing the broader racial structure of societies.

Past research emphasizes how cosmetic surgery standardizes norms of appearance to a white, feminine ideal; my findings complicate this narrative. When I compared expert discourse and practice in cosmetic surgery, and discourse about cosmetic surgery in the U.S. and Malaysia, I found multiple "standard" looks by race. In fact, the *use* of racial categories across the transnational field of medicine is increasingly standard, but not the *content* of the categories. Cosmetic surgeons not only measure and report racial difference in their efforts to be scientific but also preserve and elaborate upon racial difference as a form of art. Cosmetic surgeons have developed procedures for a "macho" nose (one with a bump) for Latino male patients and an hourglass, curvy figure for Black women, among others. Cosmetic surgeons engage in niche standardization to promise customization to an increasing array of consumers.

With this expansion of ideals, cosmetic surgery may seem to offer patients the prospect of liberatory self-authorship, consistent with Donna Haraway's exposition of the "cyborg." Theoretically, plastic surgery could be "a means toward individual authenticity and self-actualization," as anthropologist Eric Plemons writes. The growing number of race-specific looks, alongside other uses of plastic surgery, as with gender confirmation procedures, highlights this expressive potential.[1] The story I tell of race-specific standards of beauty emphasizes the role of medical professionals in changing cultural meanings of race. However, imagination and potential must contend with the gatekeeping of cosmetic surgeons in actual practice. Surgeons' willingness and ability to act is shaped by standards, their clinical judgment, their place within a medical market, and legal and cultural structures. Cosmetic surgeons assessed patient requests for surgery for their conformity to racial, gender, and class boundaries. Cosmetic surgery thus provides a good case for examining the production and maintenance of these boundaries, even as it reveals them to be specious.

COSMETIC SURGERY AS A TRANSNATIONAL RACIAL PROJECT

Racial projects are well documented in social science and humanities scholarship, but largely within the context of one society.[2] Comparing the use of racial categories in cosmetic surgery across the macro (global), meso (national), and micro (interpersonal) scales, this book demonstrates how racial projects are formed by the interplay between transnational clinical and economic exchanges and local practice. Conceptualizing racial projects as scalar yields a richer understanding of how globalization and globalized industries support racial power structures. This is theoretically useful for characterizing phenomena from social movements to cultural products (like television or film) to biomedical or scientific projects (like national genome sequencing efforts). This book portrays how a kind of medical professional, the cosmetic surgeon, engages in a transnational racial project.

Through my exposition of cosmetic surgery, I present an analytic and methodological framework for conducting global and transnational research on biomedicine, science, technology, and popular culture. When conducting research about a global phenomenon, where should one focus? Anthropologists and sociologists have often situated themselves in particular local places, generalizing up to global processes. In my research, I spent shorter periods of time in multiple different places in order to make several comparisons. To trace the journey from journal science to popular knowledge, I compared transnational, expert discourse about race with local clinical practice in two multiracial societies, the U.S and Malaysia.[3] I also compared clinical practice in the U.S. to practice in Malaysia. This asymmetrical juxtaposition illustrates how race and multiculturalism manifested under different historical trajectories and economic structures. Finally, I compared cosmetic surgeons' generalizations about patients and race in the U.S. and Malaysia with a more focused analysis of how they discussed the faults of and fixes for specific patients. As a result, I am able to show how ideas about race circulate transnationally from the U.S. to Asia and back again.

This book presents a snapshot in time of how cosmetic surgeons incorporated racial meanings into their scientific knowledge production and clinical practice. I expect those racial meanings to change, if they have not already. Rather than presenting a definitive portrait of beauty, I show how cosmetic surgeons anticipate, shape, and respond to changing racial meanings. Comparing how cosmetic surgeons discuss their practices in the U.S. and Malaysia affords a vantage point into the intersections of race with gender, nationality, and socioeconomic status in a particular historical moment. Building on work that considers racial projects as developing over time, I offer a method for analyzing racial projects across space.

The racial project of cosmetic surgery also supports conformist iterations of gender and other social identity categories, like age and/ or socioeconomic status. In cosmetic surgery, racial categories and gender are closely entangled: efforts to create racial standards also specify ideal configurations of femininity and masculinity. Ultimately the transnational racial project is also a gendering one. While my aim is to identify mechanisms sustaining and shaping racial categorization in biomedicine, this scalar and site-specific method is also potentially applicable to other social categories, especially gender. The evidence presented here suggests that gender could also serve as a standard coordinating action across the micro, meso, and macro levels. Future research might foreground whether and how efforts to standardize sex and gender in other biomedical disciplines exhibit a similar trajectory.

Expert Discourse and Clinical Practice

In my research, I found a clear contrast between how racial categories were used in expert discourse compared to clinical practice. In expert discourse like medical journal articles and conference presentations, racial categories facilitated standardization. They made it easier for surgeons to exchange information transnationally and helped surgeons build scientific and technical reputations. In medical journal articles, written by surgeons for other practitioners, surgeon-authors developed multiple, race-specific standards for the appearance of noses. Attempts to communicate transnationally prompted some surgeons to revert to outdated, biologized typologies of racial difference that enshrined the idea that noses exist in racial types. Other surgeons grafted new social and cultural racial meanings onto descriptions of physical difference. They offered explanations and origin stories for racial categories. And they explicitly defined a growing number of racial categories, including kinds of whiteness.

Furthermore, in expert discourse, surgeons used racial categories to characterize standard sets of techniques, like "Asian cosmetic surgery." Asian cosmetic surgery delineated a particular style or craft that incorporated a consideration of how institutional as well as cultural differences could impact practice. Describing a set of techniques as "Asian cosmetic surgery" helped surgeons package together a preference for specific kinds of implants, surgical procedures, and even beauty ideals under a legible rubric. Racial labels stood in for cultural differences, which were reconceived as opportunities for arbitrage across borders. Such labels also organized and promoted travel between countries for surgery. In expert discourse, racial categories helped coordinate surgeons' communication and allowed surgeons to situate their expertise within a larger, competitive field.

In clinical practice, cosmetic surgeons also standardized looks by racial category. But in practice, surgeons embraced the opportunities racial categories afforded for customizing looks. Considering the intersection of racial categories with gender, nationality, and socioeconomic status, surgeons exercised clinical and aesthetic judgment in deciding which standards of appearance to apply when. Though they upheld a "natural," racially legible look as the preferred outcome of surgery, they also showcased their artistry by presenting patients with a host of options. However, surgeons did not stray far from a set of conventional ideals for fear of alienating their existing customer base. In clinical practice, racial categories were expedient because they struck a balance between standardization and customization. Racial categories were amorphous and subjective enough to leave ample room for discretion and clinical judgment. This was especially clear in surgeon-patient consultations, where niche standardization and niche marketing largely gave way to a close focus on customizing bodies. In consultations, patients and surgeons used images to coordinate communication and action. Though racial terminology was mostly absent in the clinical encounter, images often had racial connotations and meanings from popular culture—which could selectively be excavated and scrutinized. And after surgery, the patient themselves, or their "after" photographs, became a model for future racial, gender, and other ideals.

Comparing the U.S. and Malaysia

It may be easy to see how Malaysian cosmetic surgery is imbricated in transnational exchange, especially given its aspirations to attract cosmetic surgery tourists from around the world. But the U.S. is equally enmeshed. Many of the surgical implants that U.S. cosmetic surgeons rely on are manufactured outside the country.[4] Despite having a large domestic market, the U.S. is also subject to global trends and exchanges. U.S. patients cite some of the same beauty icons as inspirations and foils, including Korean pop stars, Bollywood actresses, Latin American models, and American entertainers. By comparing the U.S. and Malaysia, I situate cosmetic surgery as a transnational enterprise, underpinned by state regulations, investments in medical tourism, and global cultural flows.

The differences between the U.S. and Malaysia are instructive for understanding how racial structures shaped the conditions of possibility for racial meaning in cosmetic surgery. In the U.S. and Malaysia, orientations to multiculturalism, and positions within the global market for cosmetic surgery, helped explain how and why cosmetic surgery looks ultimately differed in each country. In the U.S., cosmetic surgeons upheld and policed racial boundaries between U.S. groups (like white, Latino, Asian, and Black Americans) in determining ideal, racially legible appearances. In the process, they developed some looks that differed from a white standard—a departure from the past default of assimilation. A subset of U.S. surgeons, including the increasing number of surgeons who identify as people of color, built an aesthetic sense and brand around highlighting and reclaiming physical markers associated with race. In clinical practice, U.S. surgeons used racial categories that had broad resonance in popular culture and American society. However, adhering to a norm of colorblindness, some surgeons were reluctant to use racial labels to advertise their practices for fear that any explicit discussion of race could be taken as racist.

Racial norms governed acceptable narratives of change in cosmetic surgery. In the U.S., most surgeons refused to operate on patients of color who asked to look white. But surgeons did not necessarily object to making patients of color appear whiter than the average member of their racial group, should a patient request this in a colorblind way. The construction of distinct, race-specific looks in the U.S. reflected a desire for racial authenticity for some and an approximation of a whiter appearance for others. Most surgeons sidestepped debates occurring within different racial communities about attractiveness, colorism and whitening.[5] In contrast to a single universal beauty ideal, the development of multiple race-specific standards of appearance led to the possibility of indefinitely proliferating, competing standards. I follow Maxine Craig's call to think "about competing beauty standards and their uses by men and women in particular social locations."[6] The stories that surgeons and patients told about beauty standards and race reflected the different (and variable) cultural meanings of race and indexed rapidly changing politics.

By contrast, Malaysian cosmetic surgeons maintained and policed a racial boundary between Asian and white looks. To a greater extent than their U.S. colleagues, Malaysian cosmetic surgeons recognized beauty ideals as relational in a global context. They identified purportedly neutral norms of cosmetic surgery as in fact white, Western, or U.S. specific. Moreover, a preference for "Asian" looks situated Malaysian surgeons as part of the biopolitical project of a rising Asia. With an eye to serving medical tourists as well as their fellow Malaysians of all races, surgeons promised cultural and racial sensitivity when translating beauty ideals onto the bodies of patients. To this end, they anticipated religious, cultural, linguistic, and economic barriers to cosmetic surgery and sought to circumvent them.

Similarities between cosmetic surgery in the U.S. and Malaysia illuminated how racial categories at the national level functioned in relation to the global level of expert discourse in a transnational medical consumer market. Surgeons evaluated patients' requests for what they wanted to change about themselves and why alongside concerns about feasibility and safety. In both countries, racial categories in cosmetic surgery were often central to narratives about bodily change. Ultimately, cosmetic surgeons in both places prized requests for "natural" looks that amounted to incremental changes "preserving" a patient's racial legibility. To reach different market segments, surgeons created brands differentiated along the lines of race and its intersections with identities of gender, class, and nationality. Using racial categories to promise customization, surgeons in the U.S. and Malaysia distinguished themselves as artists celebrating and emphasizing difference.

MAKING RACE MATERIAL AND VISIBLE IN THE CLINIC

Just as it can be difficult to "see" the global, it can sometimes be difficult to "see" race. Drawing from existing sociological conceptions, I envision race and racism to be hierarchical structures that may be present even when absent from explicit discourse. In cosmetic surgery, race may be implied, or salient to some parties but not others, making it tricky to tease out. I elucidate processes of racialization in biomedicine, showing how clinical technologies and practices can racialize physical features and/or patients. To be clear, surgeons' negotiations with patients were not always or only about race; to some extent, cosmetic surgeons chose whether and how to incorporate race into the discussion.

At the micro scale, racial categories were enacted in the clinical encounter. Using their trained professional vision, aided by cameras and mirrors, surgeons diagnosed faults in patients' physical features and proposed surgical solutions. In the process, surgeons chose whether and how to make racial categories explicit, subject to the material affordances of patients' bodies and their visualization tools. Negotiating race as a visual and aesthetic phenomenon, surgeons and patients communicated through images, which had racial meaning and legibility supplied by popular culture. In the clinic, patients used images and narratives of transformation to negotiate with cosmetic surgeons to get closer to their desired appearance. Patients' requests for looks sometimes challenged or expanded surgeons' awareness of racialized aesthetics.

Cosmetic surgeons elaborated upon racial difference not always or simply as a science, but also as an art. In both professional discourse and the clinic, cosmetic surgeons effected categorical alignment between physical features and cultural schemas—but often using different discursive maneuvers because of the distinct social and political histories of each racial group. These competing definitions and configurations of racial categories in cosmetic surgery coexisted rather than displaced one another.

THE CONSEQUENCES OF USING RACIAL CATEGORIES TO STANDARDIZE AND CUSTOMIZE BODIES

Cosmetic surgery is a craft that spans a biomedical science of the body and the art of its manipulation. I revive the concept of "craft" to refocus scholarly attention on clinical judgment and practice in addition to biomedical knowledge production and standardization. I find that in clinical practice, surgeons do not use racial categories to reduce the variation in the world or to objectify patients. Instead, racial categories function as a shorthand for injecting subjectivity and variation into beauty standards. Racial categories gesture broadly to human differences, and necessarily build in a role for aesthetic and clinical judgment. Cosmetic surgeons maintain practice variation to reflect the racial differences they see in social life in the hope of maximizing market niches. Thus, for cosmetic surgeons, using racial categories can be a process of subjectification and cultural meaning making that preserves complexity.

The use of racial categories in cosmetic surgery has material consequences. Standards in cosmetic surgery refashion racial meaning both materially and culturally. Through cosmetic surgery, bodies can literally become what the standard is defined to be—subject to material constraints and the resistance of patient features, a potentially recalcitrant source of "surgical anxiety" for both the patient and the surgeon.[7] Individual patients navigate this uncertainty by seeking a relationship with other patients, carefully crafting pitches and shopping multiple surgeons in pursuit of a good experience. Fleshing out racial boundaries in cosmetic surgery standards, literally and figuratively, lends more substance to those boundaries, particularly when backed by the imprimatur of biomedicine. The existence of race-specific standards and their realization on the bodies of patients leads to a transformation of physical appearance and of racial meaning.

What is concerning about cosmetic surgery is that the racially inflected stereotypes of cosmetic surgeons can be physically engraved onto the bodies of patients of all genders. In cosmetic surgery, bodies are racialized in two senses: first, in the assumption that the bodies of members of different racial groups can be distinguished in key respects with reference to skin, bone and cartilage structures, and fat layers; and second, in the way that cultural notions of what is beautiful for a given racial group are brought to bear in reshaping the body toward new racialized ideals. Attempts to reach out to racial groups to ensure representation in cosmetic surgery have the paradoxical consequence of reinforcing their otherness and reinvigorating racial stereotypes. Rather than constituting a new, fully inclusive reenvisioning of bodies, surgeons' racial sensitivity is a means of articulating the social and physical boundaries of surgical procedures to patients. Though outreach to patients of color has transformative potential, seeing color and taking it explicitly into account does not necessarily translate into a "culturally competent" intervention.[8] The embrace of a multicultural logic in cosmetic surgery allows cultural stereotypes to become tools for interaction across lines of presumed racial difference.

Cosmetic surgeons acknowledge and capitalize upon the fact that what is considered an ideal physical appearance varies, to some extent, according to cultural norms and trends. The craft of cosmetic surgery reinscribes intersecting social categories of race, nationality, class, and gender on the physical body, in line with the prevailing social mores of the moment. Building on sociological studies on how racial categorization schemes have shifted,[9] this book draws attention to the role of professionals in mediating this process. This is important in biomedicine, in which physicians might discipline bodies to fit into racial categories and conform to physical standards. That cosmetic surgery has become an outlet for racial expression demonstrates society's faith in the power and authority accorded to medicine; cosmetic surgery is also an investment in the physical body as the bedrock of identity.

Race and the physical body have been connected in ways ranging from the eugenic to the empowering. Sociologists have uncovered these linkages in studies of hairstyle, clothing, fashion, egg and sperm donation, and pharmaceutical drug development.[10] Genetic explanations of human similarity and difference have, if anything, further re-animated the popular association between race and the physical body.[11] The idea that race is encoded in our DNA has been extensively explored in studies of genetics, genomics, and biotechnology research.[12] However, the practice of cosmetic surgery challenges genomic understandings of race, returning our attention to phenotype, or physical traits presumed to be associated with race. By investigating a case in which race is made to appear on the surface, this book contributes to a larger body of research examining how people interpret and make distinctions based on physical appearance.[13]

In response to consumerist trends,[14] medicine is conscripted into the building and realization of modern identities—like race—on the body.[15] This is the case even despite a norm of colorblindness. Counter to that norm, cosmetic surgeons did claim to "see" race, as with their discussions of niche marketing by racial category. And some cosmetic surgeons argued that they treated people differently as a result, with the aim of ensuring better quality care. But they did not always discuss race explicitly, choosing to invoke it selectively. In contrast to narratives of scientific progress that hail the imminent irrelevance of race, I expect race to remain salient in medicine as a category that easily circulates between science, art, and consumer markets.

DIRECTIONS FOR FUTURE RESEARCH

Scholarship on cosmetic surgery has often focused on normative questions about beauty. This book uses the case of cosmetic surgery to explore the generation of clinical and cultural knowledge about race at the nexus of medicine and the market. In departing from a normative frame, this book opens up several directions for future research in medical sociology, science and technology studies, the sociology of race, and the sociology of the body. I outline three potential directions here.

First, by analyzing cosmetic surgery as a medical specialty, this work raises questions about expertise in transnational medical fields. How clinical knowledge about race is generated in other medical disciplines, and the relationship between knowledge about race and clinical practice, is worth examining, especially in disciplines with similarly transnational footprints. Existing scholarship on the relationship between medicine, technology, and race, in particular, is largely based on cases and examples from the U.S. and Europe—places where biomedicine is imagined to be at its pinnacle.[16] However, biomedicine has a global footprint. Aided by international collaborations and transnational exchange in journals, American-style reporting of differences by race in research has traveled beyond U.S. borders.[17] What are the implications and consequences of transnational circulation of these categories, and how is clinical knowledge conditioned by engagements outside the West? Future studies might compare how clinicians contend with clinical knowledge produced in societies with different racial formations that must be made relevant in their clinical practice.

Future research might also explore the ramifications of this way of thinking about racial projects and racial formation. In Omi and Winant's exposition, racial projects and formations are distinct to societies, informed by historical and political trajectories. Cosmetic surgery is a good case to empirically examine what happens when racial formations from multiple countries come into contact. In my research, I found that specific racial categories, like the category "Asian," help temporarily align racial formations across countries, and even contribute to transnational or regional racial formations. This process can be explored in other contexts or knowledge systems. Furthermore, this book conceptualizes racial projects as capable of spanning multiple scales, from the micro (how surgeons read and write racial categories onto the bodies of patients), to the meso (how surgeons generalize about race in the context of specific societies), to the macro (how surgeons standardize about racial categories in the pages of journals). Systematically tracing race throughout a biomedical discipline like cosmetic surgery illustrates how ideas (like expertise and aesthetics) come together with things or objects (like bodies and technologies) to stabilize cultural meaning.

Finally, by examining a biomedical discipline embedded firmly within consumer markets and popular culture, this research raises broader questions about the intersection of expertise, professionalism, consumer markets, and race. On the one hand, as surgeons who have taken the Hippocratic oath, most cosmetic surgeons take their professional obligations to patients seriously, weighing patient requests against the risk of bodily harm rather than against considerations for future business. On the other hand, cosmetic surgery realizes the dream of healthcare driven by patient choice, given the field's greater insulation from insurance restrictions and associated price controls. I find that cosmetic surgeons adopt the strategies and market differentiation mentality of advertising agencies,[18] grouping patients together based on presumed cultural traits that can be as essentializing as explanations of biological difference. Generating expertise about race and selling racial imaginaries can garner some surgeons, and perhaps other professionals, a measure of fame and fortune. It remains to be explored whether patients in fact share these imaginaries. My findings suggest that consumerism might reinvigorate the use of racial categories in biomedicine. To what extent does this happen in other medical specialties, and under what conditions? This book provides a framework for investigating these questions.

FROM RACIAL DIFFERENCE TO RACIAL JUSTICE IN BIOMEDICINE

When I began this research in 2012, it was sometimes difficult to have frank conversations about race in the U.S., in notable contrast to Malaysia. I found this to be true even of cosmetic surgeons who prided themselves on being blunt. At the time, U.S. cosmetic surgeons engaged with racial difference but operated within a broader norm of colorblindness. Since then, U.S. biomedical institutions have begun to move beyond mere description of racial difference and racial inequity to engage more seriously with its role in sustaining racial inequalities—particularly amidst the racial reckoning prompted by George Floyd's murder in 2020. For instance, in summer 2021, the editor-in-chief of *JAMA*, a world-renowned medical journal, resigned after content disseminated by *JAMA* denied the existence of structural racism or racist physicians in healthcare.[19] After several years of advocacy by medical trainees for increasing the racial diversity of the physician workforce, the profession of plastic surgery is now organizing efforts to achieve this. In fall 2020, a global open access publication associated with the flagship journal *Plastic and Reconstructive Surgery* included an article titled "How to Embrace Antiracism as a US Plastic Surgeon." The essay opened by defining race "as a social construct used to refer to a group of people who share physical traits and ancestry," and racism as "the practice of subordinating other races believed to be inferior." The authors called on the profession to diversify its ranks and to take "an active role to examine power imbalances and promote change of a system for equity."[20]

What implications do these shifts have for the future of racialized aesthetics, biomedical expertise, and clinical practice? Undoubtedly, discussing race and acknowledging hierarchies is an important step. However, the example of Malaysian cosmetic surgery, where such critiques were raised even at the time of research, suggests that talking about race is not itself a panacea to remedy racial inequalities. My research suggests that outdated racial typologies have staying power. It remains to be seen what biomedicine maintains from the logic of racial difference as it pivots to address changing expectations.

By providing an in-depth empirical account of how cosmetic surgeons discuss and enact race, I draw attention to processes by which cultural meaning is fashioned and refashioned within biomedicine and popular culture. Analyzing cosmetic surgery as a scalar racial project, this book highlights the mechanisms that link structural racism and culturally shared meanings of race and gender to interpersonal interactions and to the body itself. Forces at the micro, meso, and macro levels together support racial categorization in cosmetic surgery, and the hierarchies that go along with it. At the same time, trends within each sphere (and across them) provide leverage with which to question and challenge those hierarchies.

Methodological Appendix

I began this project by examining how cosmetic surgeons generated expertise about race, focusing on expert discourse in medical journal articles and international conferences. It became clear from these findings that there was not one white universal standard of beauty, as previous sociological research suggested, but multiple. I became interested in how surgeons applied these multiple standards and their race-specific expertise to patients in practice. So I conducted interviews with cosmetic surgeons, asking questions about how they navigated between different race-specific beauty ideals, patient requests, and learned to address them in practice. Finally, I spent time observing consultations between cosmetic surgeons and patients in the clinic, including during surgical procedures, to see for myself how surgeons and patients came to decide on specific looks. Combined, these methods yielded a snapshot of how surgeons used racial categories across the macro, meso, and micro levels. This perspective was given cross-sectional depth by the comparison of the U.S. with Malaysia. This appendix provides more details about my research methods and the analysis of the qualitative data used in this book. In what follows, I discuss how my methodology addressed different parts of my sociological puzzle. I conclude with a reflection on conducting transnational research.

EXPERT DISCOURSE

To answer my research questions about how cosmetic surgeons generate and apply clinical knowledge about race, I analyzed the content of medical journal articles about nose jobs and observed the proceedings of four plastic surgery professional society conferences.

Content Analysis of Medical Journal Articles

I collected and analyzed articles about rhinoplasty (nose jobs) in cosmetic surgery journals published between 1993 and 2019. This captured the moment of attention to race in clinical research in the aftermath of a 1993 National Institutes of Health mandate to include women and racial minorities in federally funded clinical research.[1] To identify articles, I searched the PubMed database to select articles that explicitly used racial and/or geographic labels in the title (e.g., the following verbatim terms combined with the phrases rhinoplasty and plastic surgery: race, ethnic, Asian, African American, Hispanic, Korean, etc.). The references in these articles were consulted to identify other relevant articles. From this corpus, I selected articles published in English in peer-reviewed journals, including the flagship journal of ASPS, *Plastic and Reconstructive Surgery*. The resulting 203 articles about rhinoplasty were written by facial plastic surgeons/otolaryngologists (52%) and plastic surgeons (47%) from 27 different countries.[2] While a majority of senior authors were affiliated with academic medical institutions (58%), several reported primary affiliations at large hospitals (16%) and private clinics (25%).[3] Forty-one percent of senior authors reported an institutional affiliation in the U.S.; most other senior authors were based in South Korea (22%), Brazil (4%), Taiwan (4%), China (3%), Colombia (3%), and the UK (3%). Several surgeons wrote multiple racial-specific articles, and several appeared together in special issues of plastic surgery journals.[4]

I uploaded all articles in the corpus to the qualitative coding software Atlas.ti and assembled a codebook inductively based on themes that emerged in the data. These included the racial definitions used by surgeons, invocations of procedures as "masculine" or "feminine," whether surgeons advocated for a single, universal ideal of beauty or whether they advocated for multiple beauty ideals, reference categories they used for race, and challenges or limitations that surgeons associated with racial categories. A team of two student coders aided me in downloading and coding the articles. Quotations presented in the text are chosen for their typicality unless otherwise noted.

Ethnographic Observation of Plastic Surgery Professional Meetings

In addition, between 2014 and 2016, I observed conferences of four plastic surgery professional societies in the U.S. and Asia.[5] These organizations overlapped in membership and affiliated with one another. By observing these meetings, I could see how cosmetic surgeons framed and communicated their expertise to one another and get a sense of the global business side of cosmetic surgery. The conferences I attended varied not just in their sponsoring organization and location, but in their audience, size, and scope.

The two meetings I attended in Asia were primarily attended by surgeons in the region and featured more presentations about patients or procedures labeled "Asian." This included the small International Confederation for Plastic, Reconstructive and Aesthetic Surgery Congress in Singapore in August 2014 (two days) and the larger and longer ISAPS Congress in Kyoto in October 2016 (five days). The Association of Southeast Asian Nations (ASEAN) IPRAS Congress was a regional biannual plastic surgery meeting, with the 2014 iteration cohosted by the Singapore Association of Plastic Surgeons. This conference featured one presentation track for the hundred or so surgeons in attendance. Attendees came from Southeast Asia, Europe, Australia, and South Korea. By contrast, ISAPS organized a large international congress every other year for its membership of 3,200 plastic surgeons from 103 countries, focusing on cosmetic and aesthetic procedures.[6] The 2016 ISAPS Congress that I attended was cohosted by the Japan Society of Aesthetic Plastic Surgery (JSAPS), with a special track on "Asian aesthetic surgery." At both conferences, almost every session was in English, though a few sessions in Kyoto co-occurred in Japanese.

The large annual plastic surgery conferences of the U.S. professional societies were better attended by U.S. surgeons and catered more to U.S. audiences, though international surgeons were also present. I observed the 2015 ASPS meeting in Boston (five days) and the 2016 ASAPS meeting in Las Vegas. Both of these meetings drew thousands of cosmetic surgeons from around the world as presenters and attendees. An organization representing the big tent of plastic surgery, ASPS is one of the largest professional societies in the field. It had over 8,000 plastic surgeon members, most of whom were board-certified plastic surgeons in the U.S.[7] ASAPS, by contrast, was devoted to aesthetic procedures. Founded in 1967, ASAPS had approximately 2,500 members in the U.S. and Canada in 2016.[8]

At all of the conferences, I gained permission to attend from the organizers and identified myself as a researcher in small groups, one-on-ones, and in the exhibit hall. I observed several kinds of interactions at the conferences, including networking opportunities for surgeons and medical device and service vendors, ongoing clinical education, scientific sessions, and business sessions that gave marketing advice. At the larger meetings where several sessions occurred simultaneously, I attended scientific sessions and business sessions, focusing on events with racial and/or geographic labels in the title. Taking notes on my laptop and smartphone during sessions, I captured quotes verbatim. I also spent time in the exhibit hall, examining products, listening to sales pitches, collecting advertisements and informational brochures aimed at both cosmetic surgeons and patients, and informally interviewing fourteen vendors. After each day of observation, I wrote up additional fieldnotes.

CLINICAL PRACTICE

To answer my research questions about what looks cosmetic surgeons found appropriate and desirable, I conducted interviews with cosmetic surgeons.[9] I triangulated the narratives told by surgeons by conducting a limited number of interviews with patients, analyzing the content of online reviews authored by patients, and by observing surgeons interact with patients in the clinic.

Interviews with Cosmetic Surgeons

I conducted in-depth, semi-structured interviews with 60 cosmetic surgeons in the U.S. (46) and Malaysia (14) between 2014 and 2016. Surgeons hailed from sites within each country in order to sample for regional diversity and account for the distribution of racial minorities across each country. All sites were social and economic centers that hosted concentrations of cosmetic surgeons and educational institutions that trained surgeons. In the U.S., surgeons hailed from five metro areas: Chicago (the location of 16 interviews), New York (11), L.A. (12), Miami (4), and Houston (3). In Malaysia, most surgeons were based in Kuala Lumpur (8), with five from other cities around the country.

My resulting sample of interview respondents was more racially diverse and had more women than the demographics of the larger profession of plastic surgery (table 3). In the U.S., most respondents were white (72%), though over 28% self-identified as a member of another racial group, including Hispanic and/or Latino (7%), Black (4%), Persian (9%), and

Asian (9%).[10] This breakdown was roughly reflective of the demographics of U.S. plastic surgery residents, who more closely resembled the racial demographics of the U.S. population than did the rest of the field: 67% identified as white; 22% as Asian American, 8% as Latino/Hispanic American, 3.5% as African American, and less than 1% identified as Native American/Native Hawaiian/Native Alaskan.[11] Approximately 16% of ASPS members were women in 2016.[12] Most of my respondents were men in both the U.S. (37 compared with 9 women) and in Malaysia (9 men, 5 women). In Malaysia, demographic statistics about plastic surgeons are not officially reported. Using the membership of Malaysian plastic surgery professional societies as a rough proxy for the demographics of the field, about 46% of Malaysian plastic surgeons were Malay, 40% were Chinese, and 14% were Indian. Approximately 25% of Malaysian plastic surgery specialists were women.[13]

On average, respondents had been in practice for about twenty years. Respondents were trained as board-certified plastic or facial plastic surgeons. Having undergone medical residency in their respective surgical specialties followed by a fellowship in many cases, these physicians had undergone the most rigorous and lengthy training available to practice cosmetic surgery. To recruit participants, I mailed and emailed letters to members of national and regional plastic surgery and facial plastic surgery professional societies based on public rosters of their membership. The study was advertised as an interview-based project on social identities, cosmetic surgery, and expertise. Interviews lasted between thirty minutes and one hour on average and were recorded and transcribed verbatim. I conducted them face to face in cosmetic surgeons' clinics and offices, allowing me a glimpse of the facilities as well as promotional materials, office forms, and before-and-after photographs. Surgeons did not receive compensation for their participation.

In interviews, I first asked surgeons about how they became interested in becoming cosmetic surgeons. I then asked surgeons to articulate the goals of cosmetic surgery and what they thought was beautiful. Further questions investigated what surgeons found to be a "good" or "successful" surgery, and asked surgeons to characterize the demographics of their patients and describe their efforts to attract patients. I asked surgeons to describe initial consultations and presented them with hypothetical patient requests, particularly around race and ethnicity. My last set of questions asked surgeons to reflect on their position within the medical profession and in the market, inquiring about their perceptions of medical

Table 3   Demographics of Interview Respondents (Cosmetic Surgeons)

	U.S.	*Malaysia*
Average age	54	52
% female	20	36
% racial minority	28	86
Average years in practice	21	19
Total respondents (*n*)	46	14

tourism, business, and their competition. At the end of each interview, I opened up the floor for surgeons to ask me questions or elaborate on any issue that had come up.

Interviews with Patients and Content Analysis of Online Reviews

To gain a perspective on patients' motivations for undergoing surgery, I conducted a limited number of interviews with cosmetic surgery patients (8 from Malaysia, 6 from the U.S.). Patients ranged in age from 19 to 41. All but two respondents were women. To recruit patients, I distributed flyers in cosmetic surgery clinics and contacted patients who had written online reviews directly through review platforms. Interviews with patients allowed me to assess the extent to which patients shared surgeons' goals and view of the relationship between social identities such as race, nationality, gender, and the body. Interviews averaged forty minutes and were audio-recorded and transcribed verbatim. Respondents received $15 gift cards for their participation. To reflect my goals of understanding how cosmetic surgeons shaped racial meaning, I asked patients several questions about their surgeons: how they found a surgeon, how the consultation worked, what surgical procedures they wanted (particularly as it related to their race and gender), and what they thought of their surgeon.

I supplemented patient interviews with online reviews of cosmetic surgery procedures from the medical aesthetics platform RealSelf. RealSelf, modeled after the travel review platform TripAdvisor, is the largest review platform for cosmetic procedures in the U.S. Surgeons often mentioned it in interviews. Collectively, my 46 U.S. respondents received 1,004 star rankings on RealSelf on or before April 1, 2016. In addition to star rankings, some posters provided reviews and photographs, narrating their experiences from finding a surgeon through to postsurgical recovery. I analyzed the qualitative content of reviews from a randomly selected subset of ten of my U.S. respondents. This yielded 130 reviews across respondents. I consulted online reviews about procedures, like the "Brazilian butt lift," on RealSelf to obtain additional insight into patients' desired looks. Based on previous research, I recognize that the people posting on an online review platform likely differ from cosmetic surgery patients as a whole. Previous research suggests that reviewers might be expected to be younger, more technologically savvy, and more likely to have strong positive or negative experiences than the average patient.[14]

Ethnographic Observation in Clinics

For more insight into how surgeons navigated from patient requests to a racialized look, I observed clinical consultations between surgeons and patients in two Malaysian clinics. I shadowed one female cosmetic surgeon and one male cosmetic surgeon during their daily activities and in all consultations for which patients first consented to my presence. Over the course of two weeks in each clinic, I observed several initial consultations, some surgical procedures (including for blepharoplasty), and follow-up appointments for postsurgical care and assessment. The observations allowed me to compare what surgeons and patients reported in interviews with what they did in the clinic. Particularly since illustrations, pictures, and computer imaging technologies were critical to the cosmetic surgery encounter, observing initial patient-doctor interaction gave me a better sense of how patients and doctors arrived at a desired look, with what goals or intentions, capturing how social identities could be implicated visually even when not explicitly discussed. In the clinic, I jotted notes on my smartphone, and at the end of each day of observation, I wrote detailed fieldnotes.

I had planned to also shadow U.S. surgeons, but found them considerably more reluctant to grant access to clinical encounters. A few agreed and subsequently changed their minds. In one case where I gained access, no patient consented to my presence in the consultation room on the first day, leading the surgeon to decide against inviting me back. This is perhaps not surprising. Most of my respondents held initial consultations and follow-up appointments in private, exclusive clinics rather than bustling hospitals. In the absence of doctors-in-training and the many support staff typical of a teaching hospital setting, my presence stood out. Even aspiring cosmetic surgeons could have difficulty obtaining opportunities to engage in the

kind of apprentice-like observations and bedside training in aesthetic procedures that characterized the rest of their plastic surgery training. For
instance, Dr. Donati, of Los Angeles, told me in an interview, "In residency,
hopefully the attending is letting you do at least some of the cosmetic surgery. In reconstructive surgery, it's the other way around. You're doing most
of it and then the attending is watching and helping you. He's your assistant. When it's a private cosmetic patient, it's a little different. You get little
bits and pieces of a surgery." Surgeons were wary of making cosmetic
patients feel uncomfortable. They did not want to jeopardize relationships
with patients by taking a chance incorporating surgeons-in-training—or
ethnographic observers, even those affiliated with the local medical school.

    To compensate, I spent time observing U.S. professional socialization
efforts in cosmetic surgery, from medical school classes to special events
for residents and cosmetic surgeons at professional conferences. This gave
me a sense of how U.S. cosmetic surgeons discussed clinical encounters
and prepared the next generation to specialize in aesthetics.

DATA ANALYSIS

Interview transcripts, fieldnotes from my clinic observations, and online
reviews written by patients were compiled in Atlas.ti, a qualitative data
analysis software. I began by coding surgeon interview transcripts. Following Kathy Charmaz's application of constructionist grounded theory,[15] my
coding process underwent multiple iterations. I first performed a descriptive layer of coding, focusing on, for instance, which beauty ideals cosmetic
surgeons invoked, their characterizations of patients, and their descriptions of their own training, practice, and brand amidst the larger field. I
added items to the codebook as I analyzed more transcripts, incorporating
new insights as they arose. In a second round of coding, completed after I
finished conducting interviews and had reengaged with sociological litera-
tures, I added more analytic codes that allowed me to leverage layers of
comparison, including between U.S. and Malaysian surgeons and between
what surgeons said they did (clinical practice) versus what they were taught
in training, journals, and conferences (expert discourse). I incorporated
concepts like judgment, standards, and customization and natural versus
artificial looks, and justifications for why surgeons chose to operate or not.
I used an abbreviated version of the codebook and the same strategy to
subsequently code patient interview transcripts, clinic fieldnotes, and fieldnotes from conferences. Using the inductive descriptive to analytic strategy

outlined above, I developed another codebook to analyze online reviews by patients. The codes for this analysis focused on patient satisfaction and discussions of aesthetic and economic value, in addition to the themes listed above. In writing up my findings, I presented illustrative quotations that were typical exemplars of the themes being discussed, unless otherwise noted. Interview excerpts have been edited for brevity and clarity.[16] All interview respondents were identified by pseudonyms as per my agreement with the university Institutional Review Board.

THE NUTS AND BOLTS OF TRANSNATIONAL RESEARCH

This project necessitated extensive travel, time, and funding. I began data collection in 2012 and completed my last trip to the field in early 2020, as the COVID-19 pandemic prompted countries to close borders. Between 2014 and 2016, I spent six months in Southeast Asia. Interspersed in between visits to Malaysia, I conducted interviews with cosmetic surgeons and patients in Chicago, where I lived. In 2015 and 2016, I also spent several weeks at a stretch in Miami, L.A., New York City, and Houston to conduct in-person interviews with surgeons. In the same period, I traveled to Boston, Las Vegas, and Kyoto, Japan, to attend plastic surgery conferences. Pursuing this kind of travel-intensive research led me to spend months living out of a suitcase. But based on my experiences, there is a case to be made for in-person interviews in the clinic. I took notes while waiting in cosmetic surgeons' clinics and wrote fieldnotes after every interview about the surroundings and staff. These aggregate observations of cosmetic surgery clinics and their waiting rooms enriched the study. Many Malaysian surgeons, in particular, were impressed by the fact that I had traveled so far to see them and were generous with their time.

Recruitment was a lengthy and continuous process. At any given research location, in addition to conducting interviews and attending conference sessions, I was also reaching out to potential respondents for my next trip. For this study about experts, some aspects of my strategy and my academic background facilitated my access. Cosmetic surgeons in the U.S. and Malaysia cited my affiliation with Northwestern University's Feinberg School of Medicine as driving their interest in participating in the study. My knowledge of basic anatomy and biology, a function of my bachelor's degree in the biological sciences, also helped me build rapport with respondents. I kept in touch with key informants, sending them scientific articles upon their request and comparing notes on changing trends and new developments in the field.

All of the surgeons in my fieldwork spoke English, the lingua franca of global cosmetic surgery. And in Malaysia and Singapore, fluency in English was one of the advantages surgeons promised to patients. The language of instruction in training programs was also English. Accordingly, I conducted all interviews myself in English. Though most surgeons in Malaysia reported speaking only English with their patients, I discovered otherwise when shadowing them in the clinic. One surgeon did speak only English with patients; the other chatted in Mandarin and code-switched some Malay phrases when building rapport with patients. Surgeons also code-switched with staff members. While I am confident in the transnationally oriented story I tell about Malaysia, my limited facility to speak Malay or Mandarin likely limited my access to some spaces and encounters. I am sure that another researcher, with different identities and skills, would uncover additional insights about race, gender, and cosmetic surgery.

Notes

INTRODUCTION. FROM STANDARDIZATION TO
CUSTOMIZATION

1. Dolnick (2011, A17).

2. I use the term "cosmetic surgery" to highlight procedures that are primarily aesthetic in nature. Surgeons have come to refer to these procedures as "aesthetic surgery." The line between the reconstructive and aesthetic or cosmetic side of plastic surgery can be blurry. See Gilman (2000); Haiken (1997).

3. Kwan and Graves (2020, 14).

4. For scholarship that analyzes the implications of cosmetic surgery with respect to patients, especially in gendered terms, see Kwan and Graves (2020); Morgan (1991); Pitts-Taylor (2007); Blum (2005).

5. Sullivan (2001).

6. In my analysis, I conceptualize expertise using Gil Eyal's (2013, 875–76) framework: "as a network that produces, reproduces, and disseminates expert statements or performances." This definition encompasses those who claim or have knowledge and skills, the tools they rely on, and "the mechanisms that secure the cooperation of the clients, as well as the other parties involved." In Eyal's model, following Foucault (1980), power comes

from the extension, rather than the restriction, of expertise beyond the jurisdiction of a credentialed few.

7. I adopt Mears's (2011, 6) definition of a "look" as a "unique appearance and personality that appeals to a particular client at a particular time," a function of personal taste and evaluations of the physical body.

8. See Morning (2011, 17–19) for a discussion of social constructivist versus essentialist positions on racial categories. My use of "race" as a category of analysis is consistent with the constructivist tenet that "racial classification is at its root an instrument of power, meant to establish social hierarchy" (19). In line with previous research, I expected to find that cosmetic surgeons would primarily adopt an essentialist perspective on race. However, my findings show that they mixed essentialist and constructivist conceptualizations.

9. Omi and Winant (2014, 13).

10. While sociologists define race and ethnicity this way, cosmetic surgeons use these terms, too, with different definitions. I discuss this at greater length in chapter 1. In this book, I typically use the terms "race" and "racialized" to emphasize my analytical perspective. Surgeons often used more specific racial labels, including "Caucasian," "Asian," "African American," "Hispanic," and so on. I adopt their usage when discussing quotes or examples from interviews, observations, and journal articles, usually with quotation marks. But on occasion, I use some of the same racial labels, especially "Asian" and "white," to make my own points. Sociology and cosmetic surgery are part of the same racial structures.

11. Omi and Winant (1994, 55–56) refer to racial structures as racial formations.

12. M'charek (2013); Pollock (2012).

13. Roth (2016, 1313) offers a typology of six dimensions of race, from subjective self-identification to ascribed characteristics based on appearance and/or ancestry.

14. Nelson (2008, 776) further identifies site, scale, and subjectification as factors to investigate to understand the relationship between race and technology.

15. Korver-Glenn (2021, 12) defines race brokers as "gatekeeping individuals in any social sphere who are more influential than most other people in shaping what race means and whether and how ideas about race are connected to resources." In addition to expressing and acting on opinions about race, they occupy professional positions of authority that enable them to be particularly influential in maintaining or enacting racial hierarchies.

16. Cohen, Wilk, and Stoeltje (1996, 5).

17. Peiss (1998, 95).

18. Edmonds (2010); Balogun (2020). Though racial and beauty hierarchies are often parallel, I do not think that beauty hierarchies are ultimately reducible to racial hierarchies. As Alvaro Jarrín (2017, 18) argues, beauty can be understood as a form of symbolic capital that depends on "the transference of the meanings attributed to one set of relationships (race, class, and gender hierarchies) to a second set of relationships (beauty and ugliness)" by means of what he calls "the transitive properties of affect."

19. Hoang (2014); Holliday and Elfving-Hwang (2012, 58).

20. International Society of Aesthetic Plastic Surgery (2019, 1115).

21. American Society of Plastic Surgeons (2019, 3). Estimate for 2019 includes both surgical procedures and minimally invasive procedures.

22. Berry (2008); Pearl (2017); Talley (2014); Schweik (2010).

23. MacGregor (1967); Haiken (1997); Gilman (2000).

24. Blum (2005); Pearl (2017).

25. Misra and Walters (2022).

26. Bourdieu (1984) addresses cultivation of the body to build capital in *Distinction*. Sociologists of the body have further spelled this out. See Hoang's (2015) *Dealing in Desire* and Loic Wacquant's (2006) *Body and Soul* for different treatments. As this book focuses on the role of cosmetic surgeons and their gatekeeping efforts, body capital and the motivations of patients are less central to my analysis.

27. Gimlin (2002).

28. See Kuipers (2015) for an analysis of status as it relates to physical appearance. See Wacquant (2006) for more on body work. The requirement of body work and investment in body capital by employers for employees has been analyzed as "aesthetic labor" (Misra and Walters 2022, 13).

29. Strings (2019, 147).

30. Berkowitz (2017); Brooks (2017).

31. ASPS (2010, 1).

32. Heyes (2009, 191).

33. Delinsky (2005); Swami and Tovee (2005).

34. Tait (2007).

35. Blum (2005); Sullivan (2001); Pitts-Taylor (2007); Jones (2008).

36. Timmermans and Epstein (2010, 71).

37. Freidson (1970, 343).

38. See Carmel (2013, 734) for a discussion of the craft of medicine.

39. Epstein (2007, 138).

40. Timmermans and Berg (2003).

41. Timmermans and Angell (2001).

42. Armstrong (2002).

43. Geltzer (2009). Cosmetic surgery is perceived by other physicians and some members of the public as on the margins of ethical medical practice. See Sullivan (2001) and Kwan and Graves (2020) for discussions of the reputational stigma faced by cosmetic surgeons.

44. Essén and Sauder (2017, 514).

45. Bowker and Star (1999).

46. Pearl (2010).

47. See Gould (1996); Fabian (2010). For anthropology's role, see Stocking (1990). Cosmetic surgeons draw on anthropometry to describe types of bodies.

48. Edmonds (2010, 27).

49. Henderson (2014); Gilman (2000).

50. Because U.S. laws once mandated that anyone with "one drop" of Black blood was to be categorized as Black under slavery and afterward, Blackness was and remains a broad category that presented in many different ways. See Hunter (2005) and Hobbs (2014).

51. Craig (2002); Banet-Weiser (1999).

52. Bonilla-Silva (2010, 2).

53. Shankar (2020, 115).

54. Haraway (1990, 104). Haraway further argues for the collapse of boundaries between human and animal, human and machine, and physical and nonphysical things.

55. Davila (2001, 110–11).

56. Mears (2010); Kuipers, Chow, and van der Laan (2014).

57. Epstein (2007, 135).

58. Epstein (2007).

59. Epstein (2007, 91).

60. Timmermans and Berg (1997).

61. Armstrong (2002).

62. Shuster (2016, 322).

63. Timmermans and Angell (2001).

64. Timmermans and Berg (2003, 19).

65. Sullivan (2001); Haiken (1997).

66. Panofsky and Bliss (2017) write about the productive nature of ambiguity in scientific discourse; Epstein (2022) explores this further in his genealogy of "sexual health."

67. In my fieldwork, I found that plastic surgeons considered all of these social identities to be potentially malleable on the body. However, while I trace efforts to standardize looks by race, I did not find analogous efforts to standardize looks by gender and socioeconomic status. It is possible such schemes may emerge for procedures that aid patients in transitioning from one gender to another, like facial feminization surgery. See Plemons (2017), Aizura (2018), and Shuster (2021) for detailed discussions of gender confirmation procedures, which are performed by a distinct set of reconstructive plastic surgeons (rather than cosmetic surgeons).

68. Morning (2011); Loveman and Muniz (2007); M'charek (2013).

69. Duster (2015); Roberts (2011).

70. Menon (2017b).

71. Holliday et al. (2017).

72. Jarrín (2017); Edmonds (2010).

73. Pitts-Taylor (2007); Berkowitz (2017); Leem (2016a); Wen (2013); Miller (2006).

74. Braun (2014); Sun (2016); Ong and Chen (2013).

75. Epstein and Timmermans (2021, 250).

76. Clarke et al. (2003, 182).

77. Sullivan (2001).

78. Holliday, Jones, and Bell (2019); Ackerman (2010).

79. Edmonds (2010); Davis (1995); Haiken (1997).

80. Kane (2019).

81. Malaysia and the U.S. are both multiracial states; they also have both been described as multicultural. However, the U.S. is more consistent with what Bloemraad, Korteweg, and Yurdakul (2008) have identified as "passive multiculturalism," whereas Malaysia's multiculturalism is borne out of British colonial rule and a legacy of pluralism, the uneasy coexistence of racial groups (who were seen as having essentially different cultures). In Malaysia, multiculturalism is ultimately linked to the achievement of modernity and postcolonial status, whereas for the U.S., multiculturalism is often opposed to the pole of assimilation. See Goh (2008).

82. ISAPS (2018).

83. Holliday et al. (2015).

84. Malaysian racial groups are also associated with particular religions: Typically, most *bumiputera* are Muslim, Indians are Hindu, Muslim, or Christian, and Malaysian Chinese are often Buddhist or Christian. Chapter 3 discusses religion and cosmetic surgery in more depth.

85. Chin (2013); Khoo (2014). Countries of origin for noncitizens include the U.S., Europe, Indonesia, Bangladesh, and the Philippines.

86. Sun (2016, 81).

87. Hoffstaedter (2011). Sun (2016) argues that while British colonial policy played a role in migration and racial differentiation, the colonization of Malaya also helped fix racial identities in place during World War II.

88. Chee (2008).

89. Bonilla-Silva (1997); Lee and Bean (2010).

90. Hispanic/Latino is technically an ethnic category as defined by the U.S. Census. However, census statistics increasingly adjust to include it alongside the racial categories.

91. Omi and Winant (1994) cite several specific pivotal events, including the dispossession and genocide of Native Americans by European settlers, chattel slavery from Africa and the subsequent abridgement of the rights of African Americans, and the exclusion of Asian and other immigrants from the continental U.S.

92. Immerwahr (2019).

93. Butler, Britt, and Longaker (2009); Silvestre, Serletti, and Chang (2016).

94. Demographic statistics about plastic surgeons have not been officially collected by the government or by professional bodies. I analyzed the membership of two relevant professional societies, the Malaysian Society of Plastic and Reconstructive Surgery (MSPRS) and the Malaysian Association of Plastic, Aesthetic and Craniomaxillofacial Surgeons (MAPACS) as a proxy for the demographics of the field.

95. Bucknor et al. (2018); Brotherton and Etzel (2015, 2016). Approximately 16% of American Society of Plastic Surgeons members were women in 2016. Though women comprised over half of all medical students in both the U.S. and Malaysia, they were underrepresented in surgical specialties, particularly in the U.S. See Boulis and Jacobs (2008, 67) (data from AMA Physician Masterfile); see also Cassell (1997).

96. These figures should be taken with a grain of salt. They are commissioned by professional societies primarily as a marketing tool, and cosmetic surgeons told me they were sometimes reluctant to share data from their practices. In the case of the ISAPS statistics, data from some countries is simply missing altogether: for instance, South Korea, which has one of the highest per capita rates of cosmetic surgery in the world, was not included in the 2017 ISAPS Global Statistics report. Over the years, meth-

odology changed and some reports were edited after publication. In the absence of centralized data collected by governments, however, these sources provide some of the best estimates available.

97. IMCAS (2014).

98. These numbers are skewed by what is counted as cosmetic surgery. For instance, sources vary on whether they include hair implantation procedures, which would increase the proportion of men represented. See Holliday and Elfving-Hwang (2012).

99. ASPS (2018, 6); ASAPS (2017, 21); ASPS (2013).

100. Though FDA scrutiny or lack thereof has become a subject of political debate in the U.S., some U.S. cosmetic surgeons described FDA guidelines as too stringent for medical devices. They noted, correctly, that at the time only four companies were cleared to sell breast implants in the U.S., though many more companies offered products worldwide.

101. World Tourism Organization (WTO) and European Travel Commission (ETC) (2018, 68).

102. WTO and ETC (2018).

103. The 5% estimate averages the median percentage of medical travelers reported by U.S. surgeons in ISAPS reports for the years 2016, 2017, and 2018.

104. ASPS (2019).

105. Board-certified specialists reported that prices for cosmetic surgery also vary regionally within the U.S., but systematic figures were not publicly available.

106. Though these figures are not representative of all U.S. or all Malaysian cosmetic surgeons, they are largely consistent with ASPS and ASAPS estimates. The GDP per capita figures are constant 2010 US dollars as reported by the World Bank (Malaysia, $12,487; U.S., $55,753). See https://data.worldbank.org/indicator/NY.GDP.PCAP.KD.

107. Papanicolas, Woskie, and Jha (2018).

108. Lunt et al. (2011, 12).

109. Bookman and Bookman (2007); Wilson (2011).

110. According to the policy at the time of research, visitors from 163 jurisdictions could enter visa free for periods from 14 to 90 days; 43 other jurisdictions, mostly in Africa and South Asia plus China, required visas to enter (http://www.imi.gov.my/index.php/en/main-services/visa/visa-requirement-by-country).

111. Lunt et al. (2011).

112. Lamont and Swidler (2014, 157).

113. Hunter (2005); Morgan (1991); Bordo (2000); Kaw (1993); Dull and West (1991).

114. Kaw (1993); Rondilla and Spickard (2007); Davis (2003).

115. Menon (2019).

116. My respondents were fairly conservative in their practice. Only two surgeon respondents in the U.S. and Malaysia reported conducting gender confirmation or facial feminization procedures (out of 60 respondents). This may reflect the fact that gender confirmation procedures are emerging as a distinct specialty within the larger umbrella field of reconstructive plastic surgery. Many plastic surgeons who conducted gender confirmation procedures did not see themselves as "cosmetic surgeons," which was the phrase I used in my recruitment materials.

117. Dull and West (1991).

CHAPTER 1. STANDARDIZING NOSES IN GLOBAL COSMETIC SURGERY

1. This chapter developed out of an earlier article, Alka Menon, "Reconstructing Race in American Cosmetic Surgery," *Ethnic and Racial Studies* 40 (2017):597–616.

2. Haiken (1997); Gilman (2000).

3. MacGregor (1967).

4. Kaw (1993); Hunter (2005).

5. Rondilla and Spickard (2007).

6. Gulbas (2012); Hoang (2014); Lenehan (2011).

7. About 75% of rhinoplasty patients are women. But the gender gap for rhinoplasty is less pronounced than for other cosmetic surgery procedures.

8. Kridel and Rowe-Jones (2010, 62).

9. Only a small subset of cosmetic surgeons wrote medical journal articles; many authors were affiliated with academic medical centers.

10. Fausto-Sterling (2008); Stocking (1990); Strings (2019). Especially for racial and ethnic minorities, efforts to write race on the body often also made assumptions about ideal presentations of sex and gender.

11. Tapper (1999).

12. Almeling (2011); Thompson (2006).

13. Duster (2015).

14. Lee (2009).

15. Ong (2016); Coopmans and Hua (2018).

16. Sunder Rajan (2006); Waldby and Mitchell (2006).

17. Epstein (2007).

18. Epstein (2007, 91).

19. Bliss (2012); Epstein (2007).

20. The U.S. (41%,), South Korea (22%), and Brazil (4%) were the most common locations.

21. See Porter and Olson (2001) for an example of population averages for African American women; see Porter and Lee (2002, 343) for a discussion of ideal facial proportions in historical perspective and across racial groups.

22. Carvalho et al. (2012, 445).

23. Barkan (1993).

24. Fullwiley (2008); Lee (2009); Montoya (2011).

25. Yellin (1997, 236); Cobo (2011, 467–68).

26. Strings (2019).

27. Barkan (1993).

28. Patel and Kridel (2010a, 131).

29. The idea of pure racial types is a logic that genetics and genomics has also drawn upon and perpetuated. See Fujimura and Rajagopalan (2011).

30. Cobo (2003, 257).

31. The language of "correcting" racial features is not confined to the U.S. context. Jarrín(2017) and Edmonds (2010) discuss examples of similar constructions among Brazilian plastic surgeons.

32. Gruber, Kuang, and Kahn (2004, 424).

33. Eight percent of the articles presented whitening as an acceptable goal for cosmetic surgery, and the remaining 31% of the articles offered both goals as options.

34. Cobo (2010, 188).

35. Rohrich and Ghavami (2009, 1343).

36. Mears (2010); Kuipers, Chow, and van der Laan (2014).

37. Wimalawansa, McKnight, and Bullocks (2009, 160).

38. ASPS (2013).

39. ASAPS (2016, 23); according to the report, Hispanic patients received 9.7% of total procedures, African Americans comprised 7.3%, Asians comprised 5.5%, and other groups constituted 2.1%.

40. Chee, Whittaker, and Yeoh (2017).

41. See Rodríguez-Muñiz (2021) for a robust engagement with the politics of demographic projection in an electoral context. Entities releasing

the statistics and projections were typically industry boosters like professional organizations who also had an interest in making cosmetic surgery seem more common (Ormond, Mun, and Khoon 2014, 2).

42. Zelken et al. (2016, 287).

43. Cobo (2011, 467).

44. Epstein (2007).

45. Porter and Olson (2003, 620).

46. Zelken et al. (2017, 136).

47. Timmermans and Epstein (2010).

48. Lipsitz (2006).

49. Sexton (2008).

50. Edmonds (2010).

51. Lohuis and Datema (2015); Boccieri (2010).

52. Niechajev (2016).

53. Rowe-Jones and van Wyk (2010, 83).

54. Lee and Song (2015, 262).

55. Rohrich and Muzaffar (2003, 1322).

56. Patel and Kridel (2010b, 143–44).

57. Jang and Kim (2018); Aung, Foo, and Lee (2000).

58. Patel and Daniel (2012, 526e).

59. Gruber, Kuang, and Kahn (2004, 423).

60. Bergeron and Chen (2009).

61. Mehta and Srivastava (2017); Nagarkar, Pezeshk, and Rohrich (2016).

62. Ofodile, Bokhari, and Ellis (1993).

63. Lam (2009, 216).

64. Lam (2009, 215–16).

65. Ishii (2014, 2).

66. Li et al. (2014, 24e).

67. Some articles, published without racialized labels, also catalogued differences between male and female bodies in facial operations, e.g., Barone et al. (2019).

68. This is a conservative estimate. This reflects roughly the proportion of men versus women undergoing rhinoplasty internationally according to ISAPS statistics. See also Hamilton and Hobgood (2005). Cosmetic surgeons did not identify any patients as nonbinary or trans in the articles in my corpus.

69. Holliday and Elfving-Hwang (2012) urge scholars to pay more attention to men seeking cosmetic surgery.

70. Rohrich and Ghavami (2009, 1343).

71. These gender conformity efforts were for cis patients. Facial feminization surgery (FFS) is a reconstructive set of procedures to help those born male transition to becoming women. Plemons (2017) discusses this, touching on race.

72. Lam (2005, 319).

73. Chen (1999).

74. Gruber, Kuang, and Kahn (2004); Patel and Daniel (2012).

75. Patel and Kridel (2010b, 144).

76. Patel and Kridel (2010b, 143–44).

77. Rowe-Jones and van Wyk (2010).

78. Dull and West (1991); Davis (2003).

79. Patel and Daniel (2012, 526e).

80. Pitts-Taylor (2007).

81. Bordo (2000).

82. Wang (2003, 249); see also Daniel (2010).

83. Dworkin and Wachs (2009).

84. Niechajev and Haraldsson (1997, 140).

85. Darrach et al. (2019).

86. Leong and Eccles (2010, 65).

87. Epstein (2007).

88. Bowker and Star (1999).

89. Timmermans and Epstein (2010, 83).

90. Braun (2014).

91. Reardon (2004); Jordan-Young (2010); Richardson (2013).

92. Scott (1986); Fausto-Sterling (2000, 2008).

93. Barkan (1993).

94. Bliss (2012).

95. For more on the emergence of facial feminization surgery, which may involve rhinoplasties, see Plemons (2017).

96. Tate (2007).

97. Bliss (2012).

98. Cottom (2019).

CHAPTER 2. STANDARDIZING TECHNIQUES

1. It should be noted that this event took place a few years before the 2019 debut of *Leaving Neverland*, the documentary that led to a wider

reevaluation of Michael Jackson's legacy. Kobayashi, like the other names of surgeon-presenters in this chapter, is a pseudonym.

2. Davis (2003).

3. For this insight, I am indebted to Parthasarathy's (2007) idea that national toolkits shape technologies and their regulation.

4. Craft is an analytic category rather than a term used by my respondents. For a more in-depth theorization about craft as related to medicine, see Carmel (2013); Pope (2002).

5. Smart et al. (2008). Smart et al. apply Star and Griesemer's (1989) metaphor of boundary object to racial classification systems used in genetics.

6. Ong (2016).

7. Liu (2010, 255).

8. Fullwiley (2008); Bliss (2012).

9. See Ong (2016) for a discussion of how cosmopolitan science is playing out in Asia, especially Singapore.

10. Scientists have also struggled with how to ethically represent the genetics of Indigenous peoples, using labels such as "Human Genome Diversity Project" and "Native American DNA." See Wade et al. (2014); TallBear (2013); Ong (2016).

11. Gilman (2000).

12. Millard (1955, 322).

13. See Gilman (2000). Some of the earliest accounts of Asian cosmetic surgery by U.S. surgeons were written by Hawaii-based surgeons, including Dr. John McCurdy. Hawaiian surgeons emphasized their experience with Asian patients, since the state was majority Asian/mixed race. Early on, they argued that patients were seeking enhancement but not necessarily Westernization with their requests for eyelid surgeries.

14. In the 1950s, U.S. media featured the story of a young group of Japanese women who traveled to the U.S. for reparative surgeries following injuries sustained as a result of the bombing of Hiroshima. The "Hiroshima Maidens" were an early example of international medical travel for plastic surgery (Serlin 2004, 17).

15. Miller (2006); Chen (2016).

16. Dr. Khoo's training in Japan was somewhat unusual for the immediate post–World War II years. For this longer Asian historical trajectory of cosmetic surgery, see Heyes (2009); Zane (1998).

17. Some notable highlights: Khoo (1963, 1964, 1966, 1969).

18. Though many foreign doctors (including from Japan, Vietnam) observed his practice, Dr. Khoo mentored only cosmetic surgeons from

other countries. He did not teach locally in Singapore because he worried about competition. He commented that if "you have a colleague, he will go and open a clinic next to you and charge half the price." It is perhaps a testament to his singular influence that neither Singapore nor Malaysia became cosmetic surgery powerhouses.

19. Khoo (1963).

20. DiMoia (2013); Leem (2016a).

21. Holliday et al. (2017).

22. In the years prior, ISAPS congresses were held in Miami and Sao Paulo; neither had ethnoracial or geographical themes.

23. Sun (2016); Ong (2016).

24. Aizura (2009); Miller (2006); Holliday et al. (2017).

25. On Botox, see Berkowitz (2017).

26. Khoo (1963); Chen (2016). Cosmetic surgeons sometimes disagree about what techniques can be subsumed under this name.

27. Millard (1955, 335). Dr. Millard was not concerned with maintaining a natural appearance in patients; it was acceptable to him if it looked like patients had been operated upon.

28. It may also encompass alarplasty, which reshapes the nostrils, or interventions that modify the tip of the nose.

29. Bergeron and Chen (2009, 16).

30. Another choice, which did not vary so systematically along Asian/non-Asian lines, was whether to conduct the surgery using a closed approach, which was slightly less invasive and did not require an incision across the columella, or an open approach, which made the interior of the nose visible to the surgeon.

31. At the ISAPS meeting, cosmetic surgeons from China also discussed the potential use of "xeno" implants derived from animal tissue (often rabbits or goats). But this was a fleeting mention, and not referenced in most articles, textbooks, and conference presentations. Allogenic implants, derived from human cadavers after processing, were more commonly discussed as "natural" alternatives to autogenous materials, particularly by U.S. and European cosmetic surgeons. Most often, the comparison was between autogenous cartilage and synthetic implants.

32. Davis (1998).

33. Lee, Unger, and Rohrich (2011, 545e).

34. I use "women" deliberately here; worldwide, breast augmentation was mostly performed by male cosmetic surgeons on women patients.

35. Leem (2016a).

36. U.S. Food and Drug Administration (2011). Regulatory changes included a minimum age for receiving breast implants (age 18 for saline implants, which had less serious potential consequences in case of rupture, and age 21 for silicone implants) and an estimated lifespan for the medical devices (about 10 years).

37. De Boer et al. (2018).

38. U.S. Food and Drug Administration (2019).

39. Rather than seeing breast reduction as reconstructive surgery, cosmetic surgeons in countries from Brazil to Malaysia considered it to be a cosmetic procedure. Breast reduction procedures were sometimes covered by insurance, including in the U.S., as a treatment for back pain resulting from large, heavy breasts. Breast reduction referred to people born female asking for breast tissue removal (but still identifying as women). Removal of excess breast tissue in men was a distinct procedure called gynecomastia. The removal of breast tissue for patients as part of gender confirmation surgery was generally performed by different kinds of plastic surgeons in the U.S.

40. Cosmetic surgeons reported that rhinoplasty procedures were occasionally covered by U.S. insurance plans if a breathing obstruction could be demonstrated or if an accident had taken place. A "deviated septum" diagnosis is one way some Americans have gained access to insurance reimbursement for rhinoplasty.

41. Bookman and Bookman (2007, 95).

42. World Tourism Organization and European Travel Commission (2018, 109).

43. Ormond (2013); Chee (2008).

44. Bookman and Bookman (2007); Wilson (2011). Promotion of international travel can also hamper healthcare affordability and limit access in developing countries by contributing to an internal brain drain from the public healthcare sector to the private sector and the creation of a dual-track or two-tiered medical system.

45. Bookman and Bookman (2007).

46. Holliday et al. (2017, 190).

47. Ong and Chen (2013); Leem (2016b); Edmonds (2010).

48. Jarrín (2017); Aizura (2009).

49. DiMoia (2013, 8).

50. Balogun and Hoang (2018, 954).

51. This had overtones of the display of and voyeurism around Sarah Baartman (Henderson 2014).

52. Okamoto and Mora (2014); Mora (2014).

53. Alvaro Jarrín (2019, 146–49) writes at length about the discourse of "corrections" of the "negroid nose" conducted by surgeons in Brazil. While this language appeared in medical journal articles, it was largely absent from the conference stage.

54. Timmermans and Almeling (2009).

55. For more discussion about how the ambiguity of racial classification schemes can be productive, see Panofsky and Bliss (2017).

CHAPTER 3. "LOOKING RIGHT"

1. Portions of this chapter and the next appeared in a different form as Alka Menon, "Cultural Gatekeeping in Cosmetic Surgery: Transnational Beauty Ideals in Multicultural Malaysia," *Poetics* 75 (2019): 1–11.

2. In part 2, I provide surgeons' racial self-identification and city of practice alongside quotations, except in cases where it would potentially compromise confidentiality. I exclude city for respondents in favor of including information about racial identification, which means Malaysian respondents are identified only by race.

3. Haiken (1997).

4. These considerations were often linked to evolutionary biology (see Etcoff 2000). Even here, however, cosmetic surgeons recognized the cultural contingency and historical evolution of these terms (see chapter 1).

5. Bosk (2003 [1979], 45).

6. Haiken (1997).

7. Gilman (2000).

8. Bonilla-Silva (2010).

9. Jena et al. (2011). Cosmetic surgery represented the lion's share of lawsuits in plastic surgery, though few surgeons ultimately faced court sanctions. The threat of a malpractice lawsuit and court judgment influenced how surgeons approached cases. See Sarmiento et al. (2020).

10. Dull and West (1991).

11. Here I combine Mary Waters's (1990) notion of ethnic options, which refers to the choice some white Americans have made about how to identify ethnically, with Kathy Peiss's (1998) insight about how white women have used makeup to selectively put on or take off racial markers.

12. The celebration of an imagined future mixed-race melting pot is well encapsulated in a 1993 special issue of *Time* magazine. The cover features a

composite image of a woman generated by a computer from "a mix of several races." The caption proclaims, "The New Face of America: How Immigrants Are Shaping the World's First Multicultural Society" (Gaines 1993). The historical merits of this argument can be debated, but the same visual logic of mixed-race beauty and inevitability periodically appears in magazines. More recently, for its 125th anniversary issue in 2013, *National Geographic* assembled photographs of multiracial Americans and printed them under the banner "What Average Americans Might Look Like in 2050" (Norris 2013).

13. Writing about Brazil, Jarrín (2017) discusses how cosmetic surgeons have framed some procedures as a solution to miscegenation gone astray.

14. For more on cultural intermediaries, see Kuipers (2011); Bourdieu (1984).

15. Zane (1998, 162).

16. Aizura (2009); Miller (2006); Holliday et al. (2017).

17. Ong (1999, 59).

18. Jha (2016).

19. Gimlin (2013).

20. Miller (2006, 76); see Cottom (2021) for a more in-depth discussion of Dolly Parton's look.

21. Hoang (2014); Gimlin (2013).

22. Clarke and Griffin (2007); Gilman (2000).

23. The anatomic shape was less round, and surgeons argued it more closely resembled the "natural" breast. This shape was also popular in Europe.

24. Medical device vendors confirmed the U.S. average implant size in informal conversations at conferences. A Chicago-based cosmetic surgeon told me that he was taught "that any woman who wants an implant smaller than 250 cc doesn't know what she really wants; that's a waste of everybody's time and she's never going to be happy."

25. Gimlin (2013).

26. Hoang (2014); Holliday et al. (2017).

27. Glenn (2008); Kaw (1993); Rondilla and Spickard (2007).

28. Leem (2016b).

29. Lee (2016).

30. Foucault (1980, 135–59) described biopolitics as a concern that states have in governing the health of their populations as part of the administrative project.

31. Here I am extending Darling-Wolf's (2015, 12) insight about the role of gender constructions in beauty ideals in Japan to a consideration of the intersections of race and gender afforded by the Malaysian case.

CHAPTER 4. RACE AND CUSTOMIZATION IN
THE MARKET FOR COSMETIC SURGERY

1. Kahn (2013, 17); Sun (2016); see also TallBear (2013); Montoya (2011).
2. The same language appears in the code of ethics for both societies.
3. Malaysian guidelines carve out an exemption for educational content, but explicitly prohibit advertisements featuring photographs of patients.
4. For more on colorblindness, see Bonilla-Silva (2010).
5. The American Society for Aesthetic Plastic Surgery (2017) reported that American surgeons performed 333,392 breast augmentation procedures, 140,834 tummy tuck procedures, and 38,659 rhinoplasty procedures, compared with 23,115 buttocks augmentation procedures (including implants and fat transfer).
6. Pitts-Taylor (2007, 4) also observed the "plastic" look in her work. See also Gimlin (2013) for a discussion of the "obviously augmented" breast.
7. A 2018 report by authored by a plastic surgery task force about Brazilian butt lifts warned, "The death rate of approximately 1/3000 is the highest for any aesthetic procedure," citing three deaths in one state in 2017 alone. See Inter-Society Gluteal Fat Grafting Task Force (2018).
8. For a tabloid example, see Shea (2019).
9. The mistaken belief that Black women have larger buttocks dates back to at least Sarah Baartman, a Black woman who was displayed throughout Europe as the exotic, sexualized, and racialized "Hottentot Venus." See Henderson (2014) and also hooks (2015).
10. Just as I was conducting interviews with U.S. surgeons in June 2015, Rachel Dolezal attracted significant media attention and public outrage for passing as Black despite having white heritage. Though Dolezal did not claim to undergo cosmetic surgery procedures to appear Black, she did apply tanning lotions and style her hair in accordance with Black fashion trends. Though this was ubiquitous in the news, no cosmetic surgeon respondent listed her as an example in our interviews, or raised any other example of cultural appropriation, let alone used the term. For a sociological analysis of the ramifications of the Dolezal affair for gender and race, see Brubaker (2016).
11. Bonilla-Silva (2010).
12. hooks (2015).
13. Wealthy elites from around the world traveled to the U.S. for treatment; my respondents from L.A. and Miami boasted up to 50% or more

foreign patients visiting from abroad, whereas respondents in Houston, Chicago, and New York reported that foreign patients constituted under 10% of their practice. Eighty-three percent of U.S. respondents reported having some patients who flew in to their cities from other parts of the U.S. for treatment.

14. Gimlin (2013).

15. See Molina-Guzman (2010, 58) for a discussion of the Latina beauty ideal using the case of Jennifer Lopez for a more in-depth discussion of how race and ethnicity can function as a symbol in the media.

16. Hobson (2005:97) as quoted in Appleford (2016). For a more detailed discussion of Kim Kardashian, see also Tate (2015).

17. For an excellent discussion of the role of Dolly Parton in American beauty culture, see Tressie McMillan Cottom's (2021) essay "The Dolly Moment."

18. Cottom (2021).

19. This was reminiscent of the claims made by cosmetic surgeons about Asian cosmetic surgery at international plastic surgery conferences discussed in chapter 2. Different looks or aesthetics required different techniques, and paved the way for technical specialization.

20. Shankar (2015, 41).

21. Ormond (2013, 13).

22. Race in Malaysia is a fascinating and complicated matter, and I am offering a condensed history and snapshot of its sociopolitical trajectory here. As a juridical category in Malaysia, race was inherited at birth from the father, regardless of the race of the mother. And in addition to Malay, Chinese, Indian, and Other, the Malaysian government also recognized (and some argue, created) a larger ethnic category, *bumiputera*, to establish a larger political majority after gaining independence (Milner 2008; Hirschman 1986). *Bumiputera*, which include Malays, receive special privileges written into the Malaysian Constitution to redress their treatment under British colonialism (Hoffstaedter 2011; Shamsul 2001). Lee (2004, 127) argues, "Being Malay means not only being a legitimate heir of political power once held by the British, but also being an exclusive claimant of privileges not explicitly available to the Chinese and Indians."

23. Lee (2004, 120).

24. Some Malaysian Indians professed the faith of Islam as well. It should be noted that though identity as a Muslim has been racialized in different times and places (see Rana 2011), in Malaysia, the Islamic faith itself was not racialized; rather, it was a racial identifier for the racial cat-

egory Malay. While Malays were Muslim by statute and custom, the constitution did not specify religions for other races. Generally, Malaysian Chinese were Buddhist or Christian, and Malaysian Indians were Hindu, Muslim, or Christian; each of these religions was less salient as a racial identifier than was Islam for Malays.

25. This attracted global press at the time, appearing in the *New York Times*, among other publications. The then-head of the National Fatwa Council, Professor Datuk Shukor Husin, cited the use of a pig-derived substances in the manufacture of Botox and the prevalence of fake products that could harm users as reasons for the decision. The council consulted reports and fatwas issued in other Muslim countries in making its decision. Fatwas—opinions based in religious law—can vary by scholar and organization within the same sect. See Aglionby (2006).

26. Fischer (2016).

27. Calder (2020).

28. These were clothing lines featuring garments that covered much of the body and are now offered at mass market retailers (see Lewis 2013).

29. See chapter 5 for a more extended discussion of influencers.

30. This is a staple of pluralist societies. But the gap between image and practice characterizes many multicultural contexts; for instance, the multiracial harmony that the U.S. projects to the world is different from the concerns and conversations about race that take place in newspapers and bars.

31. Chee (1982); Ormond (2013).

32. Aizura (2009) outlines a hospitality strategy emphasizing service and Oriental attention to care and comfort in the case of international medical travel for gender confirmation procedures in Thailand. Malaysian cosmetic surgeons did not play up "Orientalized" care or hospitality to quite the same degree.

33. Chee (2008).

34. Wilson (2010, 136).

35. Holliday, Jones, and Bell (2019).

36. Holliday, Jones, and Bell (2019); Chee and Whittaker (2020).

37. Chee and Whittaker (2020, 14).

38. Holliday, Jones, and Bell (2019, 151).

39. Goh (2008).

40. Buzinde and Yarnal (2012, 786).

41. Davila (2001, 7).

42. Fujimura and Rajagopalan (2011).

CHAPTER 5. CUSTOMIZING BODIES

1. Goodwin (1994, 606).

2. Osagie (2014, 2–3).

3. "Visualization" is a two-fold process inherent in the professional vision of cosmetic surgeons. I use Michael Lynch and Steve Woolgar's (2014, vii) definition of visualization as "connot[ing] practices of making visible—fashioning and exhibiting witnessable and accountable material and virtual displays." As discussed by science and technology studies scholars, visualization refers to both the mechanical means of representation and the interpretation of a phenomenon en route to explaining it. It is often used to describe the process by which phenomena are rescaled for presentation—think photographs of distant stars or microscopic molecules. Here, visualization is occurring at the level of organs and body parts.

4. One American patient brought a Victoria's Secret catalogue to our interview to highlight one of the model's noses as her ideal.

5. The cosmetic surgeon and/or staff also took a medical history of the patient during the consultation.

6. Dumit (2004, 16).

7. Revision rhinoplasty refers to any nose job procedures after the first.

8. The multiplicity of the body, and the enactments that bring different embodiments into being, is similar to the points made by Annemarie Mol (2002) in her book *The Body Multiple*.

9. Tardy and Brown (1992, 1).

10. Anne Balsamo (1996) has written about the clinical, technological gaze as normative and gendering. The very act of photographing patients in the cosmetic surgery clinic set up and reinforced a certain kind of gendered relationship between the masculinized surgeon (viewer) and the feminized patient (object). This remains the default pattern in the clinic. But one change I observed is how some surgeons also encouraged patients to take their own photographs—both in the clinic (of surgeons' photographs, of themselves in different poses or with different markings) and out in the world. Surgeons encouraged patients to adopt a technological gaze, but the ubiquity of digital cameras in smartphones enabled them to be viewers and producers of images as well.

11. I here lean on Latour's (2007) actor network theory, which characterizes scientific actors as "enrolling" objects, or even microbes, in service of explaining the natural world.

12. Balsamo (1992, 225).

13. Golan (1998, 447).

14. Direct-to-consumer advertising of medical devices, services, and pharmaceuticals is illegal in most countries (but not in the U.S.).

15. Journals specify broad standards about photographs included in publications. For instance, *Plastic and Reconstructive Surgery* notes that "before-and-after photographs should be identical in terms of size, position, and lighting." From "Instructions for Authors," *Plastic and Reconstructive Surgery* (http://edmgr.ovid.com/prs/accounts/ifauth.htm, accessed 23 January 2020). In interviews, cosmetic surgeons decried the images used in conference presentations as some of the least rigorous.

16. See Taussig (2012) for a discussion of the grotesque in cosmetic surgery.

17. Roth (2009, 114).

18. Benjamin (2019).

19. Browne (2015, 113).

20. Galdino, DaSilva, and Gunter (2002, 1428).

21. Treichler, Cartwright, and Penley (1998, 3).

22. Jarvis et al. (2016).

23. Cottom (2019).

24. Salas-Rodriguez and Mustafa (2020).

25. U.S. surgeons were slower to make this transition than Malaysian surgeons, and often relied almost entirely on their staff to maintain a social media presence in 2015–2016.

26. Barnes (2018).

27. This is also a phenomenon that has been discussed by cultural commentators. See, for instance, Tolentino (2019). If anything, the movement of life and work online during the initial phase of the COVID-19 pandemic exacerbated this trend, increasing demand for cosmetic surgery procedures (Richtel 2020).

28. This concern was articulated in interviews in 2015–2016 but also in a series of editorials and literature reviews in plastic surgery journals published in 2018 onward and showcased on the American Society of Plastic Surgeons website. See, for instance, Rajanala, Maymone, and Vashi (2018).

29. For more on this phenomenon, see Pitts-Taylor (2007).

30. Stuart (2020, 5). In his book *Ballad of the Bullet,* Stuart writes about Black youth's efforts to gain fame by releasing drill music online and curating social media presences.

31. Duffy (2017).

32. hooks (2015).

33. Stevens (2021, 2). One important form of cultural appropriation is blackfishing, which refers to efforts by non-Black people to take on physical, behavioral, or cultural markers of Blackness online to build brands and a livelihood based on income received for product endorsements. People who practice blackfishing arguably perform a kind of intermediary work, too: they selectively depict what they think of as the most desirable iterations of Blackness in search of profit. For more on blackfishing, see Stevens (2021).

34. M'charek (2013, 436).

35. Balsamo (1996).

CONCLUSION. THE ART AND SCIENCE OF RACIAL DIFFERENCE IN GLOBAL COSMETIC SURGERY

1. Plemons (2017, 152); Plemons also offers a more in-depth discussion of gender and facial feminization procedures.

2. E.g., Omi and Winant (2014); Nelson (2008); Mora (2014); Rodríguez-Muñiz (2021); Shankar (2015).

3. The importance of this path is laid out by Fleck (1981 [1935], 22).

4. The dependence of U.S. cosmetic surgeons on events abroad was thrown into relief in 2015, when Brazilian regulators shut down a factory producing implants for the up-and-coming company Sientra. This was a subject of discussion among vendors at the two U.S. conferences I attended (see also Mittelman 2015).

5. For more on colorism and competing beauty standards, see Hunter (2005); Craig (2006).

6. Craig (2006, 160).

7. Leem (2016a).

8. Shaw and Armin (2011).

9. Loveman and Muniz (2007); Bowker and Star (1999).

10. Craig (2002); Banks (2000); Mears (2011); Kang (2010); Almeling (2011).

11. Fujimura and Rajagopalan (2011); Duster (2015).

12. Liu (2010); Ong (2016); Fullwiley (2008); Fujimura and Rajagopalan (2011); Ong and Chen (2013).

13. See, for instance, Monk (2015).

14. See Tomes (2016) for a historical analysis of patient consumerism in the U.S.

15. Davila (2001); Edmonds (2010); Epstein (2007); Sunder Rajan (2006).

16. Clarke (2010).

17. Bliss (2012); Epstein (2007, 274).

18. For more on the intersection of advertising with medicine and/or race, see Tomes (2016); Shankar (2015); Mora (2014).

19. Mandavilli (2021).

20. Bradford et al. (2020, 2).

METHODOLOGICAL APPENDIX

1. Epstein (2007).

2. The medical specialty could not be ascertained for three authors. Rhinoplasty is a core specialty for facial plastic surgeons (also known as ear, nose, and throat surgeons) as well as general plastic surgeons.

3. Over time, the same author's affiliation might change, so this reflects a snapshot based at the time of article publication. Affiliations could not be discerned for four articles (published in the 1990s), about 2% of the total.

4. At least three journals published multiple special issues on race-specific themes during this period: *Facial Plastic Surgery Clinics in North America* ("Ethnic Variations in Facial Plastic Surgery" [2002], "The Asian Face" [2007], "Considerations in Non-Caucasian Facial Plastic Surgery" [2010], "Multicultural Aesthetics in Facial Plastic Surgery" [2014], and "Ethnic Variations in Facial Plastic Surgery" [2018]); *Seminars in Plastic Surgery* ("Aesthetic Surgery in Asians" [2009], "Cosmetic Asian Rhinoplasty" [2015], "Cosmetic Asian Blepharoplasty and Periorbital Surgery" [2015]); and *Facial Plastic Surgery* ("The Ethnic Nose" [2003], "Ethnicity in Facial Plastic Surgery" [2010], "Facial Plastic Surgery in Latin America" [2013], and "Worldwide Perspectives in Facial Plastic Surgery" [2016]). Only articles with a strong substantive discussion of noses or rhinoplasty were included in the sample, so not every article from the special issues was included in this corpus. Verbatim reprints were deduplicated in the sample.

5. All members were required to obtain medical degrees followed by several years of specialist training, though the precise requirements differed across organizations. Nonmembers could attend also attend conferences with documentation verifying their status as medical professionals, clinic staff, residents, or students.

6. These numbers are from the ISAPS website, accessed 25 February 2018 (https://www.isaps.org/about-isaps/).

7. ASPS counted 94% of all U.S. board-certified plastic surgeons among its ranks. These figures are from the ASPS website, accessed 25 February 2018 (https://www.plasticsurgery.org/about-asps).

8. Sullivan (2001). ASAPS was a breakaway group from the organization that was a precursor to ASPS. It has since rebranded as The Aesthetic Society and expanded its membership criteria.

9. For purposes of this study, "cosmetic surgeons" were board-certified plastic surgeons and facial plastic surgeons (also known as otolaryngologists)—or the equivalent in Malaysia. Respondents had undergone advanced and extensive training in surgery and many had pursued cosmetic fellowships. Though other kinds of physicians also call themselves cosmetic or aesthetic surgeons, and who counts has been a subject of contestation (see Sullivan 2001), operationalizing cosmetic surgeons in this way allows me to make claims about a global field and compare expert discourse and practice in accordance with my research questions.

10. In the U.S. and Malaysia, I asked surgeons to report their racial identification as one of several demographic questions at the end of the interview. I include their own self-identifications, alongside where they practiced, in the text, except in cases where it would make respondents too easily identifiable.

11. Butler, Britt, and Longaker (2009); Silvestre, Serletti, and Chang (2016). Statistics for the racial and gender diversity of U.S. otolaryngology residents closely resemble those for plastic surgery (Schwartz et al. 2013).

12. Women had more representation in the ranks of current U.S. medical residents (33%). See Bucknor et al. (2018).

13. I calculated the Malaysian figure based on 2016 membership in MSPRS and MAPACS.

14. Hargittai and Walejko (2008).

15. Charmaz (2002).

16. I quoted from online reviews in such a way as to make excerpts less immediately searchable while maintaining meaning.

Bibliography

Ackerman, Sara. 2010. "Plastic Paradise: Transforming Bodies and Selves in Costa Rica's Cosmetic Surgery Tourism Industry." *Medical Anthropology* 29 (4):403–23.

Aglionby, John. 2006. "Malaysian Muslims Told not to Use Botox." *Guardian*, 28 July. https://www.theguardian.com/world/2006/jul/28/islam.religion.

Aizura, Aren. 2009. "Where Health and Beauty Meet: Femininity and Racialisation in Thai Cosmetic Surgery Clinics." *Asian Studies Review* 33:303–17.

———. 2018. *Mobile Subjects: Transnational Imaginaries of Gender Reassignment*. Durham, NC: Duke University Press.

Almeling, Rene. 2011. *Sex Cells: The Medical Market for Eggs and Sperm*. Berkeley: University of California Press.

American Community Survey Demographic and Housing Estimates. 2016. ACS 5-Year Estimates Data Profiles (Table DP05). U.S. Census Bureau. https://data.census.gov/cedsci/table?tid=ACSDP5Y2016.DP05. Accessed 14 July 2020.

American Society for Aesthetic Plastic Surgery. 2016. "2016 Cosmetic Surgery National Data Bank Statistics." https://cdn.theaestheticsociety

.org/media/statistics/2015-TheAestheticSocietyStatistics.pdf. Accessed 5 October 2022.

———. 2017. "2017 Cosmetic Surgery National Data Bank Statistics." https://cdn.theaestheticsociety.org/media/statistics/2017-TheAesthetic SocietyStatistics.pdf. Accessed 5 October 2022.

American Society of Plastic Surgeons. 2010. "Report of the 2010 Plastic Surgery Statistics." http://www.plasticsurgery.org/Documents/news -resources/statistics/2010-statisticss/Top-Level/2010-US-cosmetic -reconstructive-plastic-surgery-minimally-invasive-statistics2.pdf. Accessed 5 October 2022.

———. 2013. "Briefing Paper: Plastic Surgery for Ethnic Patients." https:// www.plasticsurgery.org/news/briefing-papers/briefing-paper-plastic-surgery-for-ethnic-patients. Accessed 5 October 2022.

———. 2018. "2018 Plastic Surgery Statistics Report." https://www .plasticsurgery.org/documents/News/Statistics/2018/plastic-surgery -statistics-full-report-2018.pdf. Accessed 5 October 2022.

———. 2019. "2019 National Plastic Surgery Statistics." https://www .plasticsurgery.org/documents/News/Statistics/2019/plastic-surgery -statistics-report-2019.pdf. Accessed 5 October 2022.

Appleford, Katherine. 2016. "'This Big Bum Thing Has Taken over the World': Considering Black Women's Changing Views on Body Image and the Role of Celebrity." *Critical Studies in Fashion and Beauty* 7 (2):193–214. DOI: 10.1386/csfb.7.2.193_1.

Armstrong, David. 2002. "Clinical Autonomy, Individual and Collective: The Problem of Changing Doctors' Behavior." *Social Science and Medicine* 55:1771–77.

Aung, S. C., C. L. Foo, and S. T. Lee. 2000. "Three Dimensional Laser Scan Assessment of the Oriental Nose with a New Classification of Oriental Nasal Types." *British Journal of Plastic Surgery* 53 (2): 109–16. https://doi.org/10.1054/bjps.1999.3229.

Balogun, Oluwakemi. 2020. *Beauty Diplomacy: Embodying an Emerging Nation.* Stanford, CA: Stanford University Press.

Balogun, Oluwakemi M., and Kimberly Hoang. 2018. "Political Economy of Embodiment: Capitalizing on Globally Staged Bodies in Nigerian Beauty Pageants and Vietnamese Sex Work." *Sociological Perspectives* 61 (6):953–72.

Balsamo, Anne. 1992. "On the Cutting Edge: Cosmetic Surgery and the Technological Production of the Gendered Body." *Camera*

Obscura: Feminism, Culture, and Media Studies 10 (1):206–37. DOI: 10.1215/02705346-10-128-206.

———. 1996. *Technologies of the Gendered Body: Reading Cyborg Women.* Durham, NC: Duke University Press.

Banet-Weiser, Sarah. 1999. *The Most Beautiful Girl in the World: Beauty Pageants and National Identity.* Berkeley: University of California Press.

Banks, Ingrid. 2000. *Hair Matters: Beauty, Power, and Black Women's Consciousness.* New York: New York University Press.

Barkan, Elazar. 1993. *The Retreat of Scientific Racism: Changing Concepts of Race in Britain and the United States between the World Wars.* Cambridge: Cambridge University Press.

Barnes, Jordan. 2018. "Who Is Leng Yein, 'Malaysia's Hottest DJ' and Alleged Abuse Victim?" *Malaymail*, 24 March. https://www.malaymail .com/news/malaysia/2018/03/24/who-is-leng-yein-malaysias-hottest-dj- and-alleged-abuse-victim/1606141. Accessed 18 May 2021.

Barone, Mauro, Annalisa Cogliandro, Rosa Salzillo, Emile List, Vincenzo Panasiti, Stefania Tenna, and Paolo Persichetti. 2019. "Definition of 'Gender Angle' in Caucasian Population." *Aesthetic Plastic Surgery* 43 (4):1014–20. DOI: 10.1007/s00266-019-01366-w.

Benjamin, Ruha. 2019. *Race after Technology: Abolitionist Tools for the New Jim Code.* Medford, MA: Polity.

Bergeron, Leonard, and Philip Kuo-Ting Chen. 2009. "Asian Rhinoplasty Techniques." *Seminars in Plastic Surgery* 23:16–21.

Berkowitz, Dana. 2017. *Botox Nation: Changing the Face of America.* New York: New York University Press.

Berry, Bonnie. 2008. *The Power of Looks: Social Stratification of Physical Appearance.* Burlington, VT: Ashgate.

Bliss, Catherine. 2012. *Race Decoded: The Genomic Fight for Social Justice.* Stanford: Stanford University Press.

Bloemraad, Irene, Anna Korteweg, and Gokce Yurdakul. 2008. "Citizenship and Immigration: Multiculturalism, Assimilation, and Challenges to the Nation-State." *Annual Review of Sociology* 34:153–79.

Blum, Virginia. 2005. *Flesh Wounds: The Culture of Cosmetic Surgery.* Berkeley: University of California Press.

Boccieri, Armando. 2010. "The Surgical Approach to the Mediterranean Nose." *Facial Plastic Surgery* 26 (2):119–30. DOI: 10.1055/s-0030-1253498.

Bonilla-Silva, Eduardo. 1997. "Rethinking Racism: Toward a Structural Interpretation." *American Sociological Review* 62:465–80.

———. 2010. *Racism without Racists: Color-Blind Racism and Racial Inequality in Contemporary America*. Lanham, MD: Rowman & Littlefield.

Bookman, Milica Z., and Karla R. Bookman. 2007. *Medical Tourism in Developing Countries*. New York: Palgrave Macmillan.

Bordo, Susan. 2000. *The Male Body: A New Look at Men in Public and in Private*. New York: Farrar, Straus and Giroux.

Bosk, Charles. 2003 [1979]. *Forgive and Remember: Managing Medical Failure*. 2nd ed. Chicago: University of Chicago Press.

Boulis, Ann K., and Jerry A. Jacobs. 2008. *The Changing Face of Medicine: Women Doctors and the Evolution of Health Care in America*. Ithaca, NY: Cornell University Press.

Bourdieu, Pierre. 1984. *Distinction: A Social Critique of the Judgement of Taste*. Cambridge, MA: Harvard University Press.

Bowker, Geoffrey, and Susan Leigh Star. 1999. *Sorting Things Out*. Cambridge, MA: MIT Press.

Bradford, Perry S., Brent R. DeGeorge, Steven H. Williams, and Paris D. Butler. 2020. "How to Embrace Antiracism as a US Plastic Surgeon: Definitions, Principles, and Practice." *Plastic and Reconstructive Surgery Global Open* 8 (9):e3185. DOI: 10.1097/GOX.0000000000003185.

Braun, Lundy. 2014. *Breathing Race into the Machine: The Surprising Career of the Spirometer from Plantation to Genetics*. Minneapolis: University of Minnesota Press.

Brooks, Abigail T. 2017. *The Ways Women Age: Using and Refusing Cosmetic Intervention*. New York: New York University Press.

Brotherton, Sarah E., and Sylvia I. Etzel. 2015. "Graduate Medical Education, 2014–2015." *Journal of the American Medical Association* 314 (22):2436–55.

———. 2016. "Graduate Medical Education, 2015–2016." *Journal of the American Medical Association* 316 (21):2291–2310.

Browne, Simone. 2015. *Dark Matters: On the Surveillance of Blackness*. Durham, NC: Duke University Press.

Brubaker, Rogers. 2016. *Trans: Gender and Race in an Age of Unsettled Identities*. Princeton, NJ: Princeton University Press.

Bucknor, Alexandra, Parisa Kamali, Nicole Phillips, Irene Mathijssen, Hinne Rakhorst, Samuel J. Lin, and Heather Furnas. 2018. "Gender

Inequality for Women in Plastic Surgery: A Systematic Scoping Review." *Plastic and Reconstructive Surgery* 161:1561–78.

Butler, Paris D., L. D. Britt, and Michael T. Longaker. 2009. "Ethnic Diversity Remains Scarce in Academic Plastic and Reconstructive Surgery." *Plastic and Reconstructive Surgery* 123:1618–28.

Buzinde, C. N., and C. Yarnal. 2012. "Therapeutic Landscapes and Post-colonial Theory: A Theoretical Approach to Medical Tourism." *Social Science and Medicine* 74:783–87.

Calder, Ryan. 2020. "Halalization: Religious Product Certification in Secular Markets." *Sociological Theory* 38 (4):334–61.

Carmel, Simon. 2013. "The Craft of Intensive Care Medicine." *Sociology of Health and Illness* 35 (5):731–45.

Carvalho, Bettina, Annelyse Christine Ballin, Renata Vecentin Becker, Cezar Augusto Sarraff Berger, Johann G. G. Melcherts Hurtado, and Marcos Mocellin. 2012. "Rhinoplasty and Facial Asymmetry: Analysis of Subjective and Anthropometric Factors in the Caucasian Nose." *International Archives of Otorhinolaryngology* 16 (4):445. https://doi .org/10.7162/S1809-97772012000400004.

Cassell, Joan. 1997. "Doing Gender, Doing Surgery: Women Surgeons in a Man's Profession." *Human Organization* 56 (1):47–52.

Charmaz, Kathy. 2002. "Qualitative Interviewing and Grounded Theory Analysis." In *The Sage Handbook of Interview Research: The Complexity of the Craft*, edited by Jaber F. Gubrium and James Holstein, 675–94. Thousand Oaks, CA: Sage.

Chee, Heng Leng. 1982. "Health Status and the Development of Health Services in a Colonial STate: The Case of British Malaya." *International Journal of Health Services* 12 (3):397–417.

———. 2008. "Ownership, Control, and Contention: Challenges for the Future of Healthcare in Malaysia." *Social Science and Medicine* 66 (10):2145–56.

Chee, Heng Leng, Andrea Whittaker, and Brenda S. A. Yeoh. 2017. "International Medical Travel and the Politics of Transnational Mobility in Asia." *Asia Pacific Viewpoint* 58 (2):129–35.

Chee, Heng Leng, and Andrea Whittaker. 2020. "Moralities in International Medical Travel: Moral Logics in the Narratives of Indonesian Patients and Locally-Based Facilitators in Malaysia." *Journal of Ethnic and Migration Studies* 40 (20):4264–81.

Chen, Anthony S. 1999. "Lives at the Center of the Periphery, Lives at the Periphery of the Center: Chinese American Masculinities and

Bargaining with Hegemony." *Gender and Society* 13 (5):584–607. DOI:10.1177/089124399013005002.

Chen, William Pai-Dei. 2016. *Asian Blepharoplasty and the Eyelid Crease.* 3rd ed. Edinburgh: Elsevier.

Chin, Christine B. N. 2013. *Cosmopolitan Sex Workers: Women and Migration in a Global City.* Oxford: Oxford University Press.

Clarke, Adele E. 2010. "Thoughts on Biomedicalization in Its Transnational Travels." In *Biomedicalization: Technoscience, Health, and Illness in the U.S.*, edited by Adele E. Clarke, Laura Mamo, Jennifer Ruth Fosket, Jennifer R. Fishman, and Janet K. Shim, 380–406. Durham, NC: Duke University Press.

Clarke, Adele E., Janet K. Shim, Laura Mamo, Jennifer Ruth Fosket, and Jennifer R. Fishman. 2003. "Biomedicalization: Technoscientific Transformations of Health, Illness, and U.S. Biomedicine." *American Sociological Review* 68 (2):161–94.

Clarke, Laura Hurd, and Meredith Griffin. 2007. "The Body Natural and the Body Unnatural: Beauty Work and Aging." *Journal of Aging Studies* 21 (3):187–201.

Cobo, Roxana. 2003. "Mestizo Rhinoplasty." *Facial Plastic Surgery* 19 (3):257–68. https://doi.org/10.1055/s-2003-43161.

———. 2010. "Hispanic/Mestizo Rhinoplasty." *Facial Plastic Surgery Clinics of North America* 18 (1):173–88.

———. 2011. "Ethnic Considerations of the Crooked Nose." *Facial Plastic Surgery* 27 (5):467–82.

Cohen, Colleen Ballerino, Richard Wilk, and Beverly Stoeltje. 1996. "Introduction: Beauty Queens on the Global Stage." In *Beauty Queens on the Global Stage: Gender, Contests, and Power*, edited by Colleen Ballerino Cohen, Richard Wilk, and Beverly Stoeltje, 1–12. New York: Routledge.

Coopmans, Catelijne, and Margaret Tan Ai Hua. 2018. "On 'Asian' Distinctiveness and Race as a Variable: The Case of Ophthalmic Epidemiology in Singapore." *Science, Technology and Society* 23 (2):252–70.

Cottom, Tressie McMillan. 2019. *Thick: And Other Essays.* New York: The New Press.

———. 2021. "The Dolly Moment: Why We Stan a Post-Racism Queen." *Essaying*, 24 February. https://tressie.substack.com/p/the-dolly-moment. Accessed 17 May 2021.

Craig, Maxine. 2002. *Ain't I a Beauty Queen? Black Women, Beauty, and the Politics of Race.* Oxford: Oxford University Press.

———. 2006. "Race, Beauty, and the Tangled Knot of a Guilty Pleasure."
    Feminist Theory 7 (2):159-77. DOI:10.1177/1464700106064414.

Daniel, Rollin. 2010. "Middle Eastern Rhinoplasty: Anatomy, Aesthetics,
    and Surgical Planning." *Facial Plastic Surgery* 26 (2):110-18. DOI:
    10.1055/s-0030–1253503.

Darling-Wolf, Fabienne. 2015. *Imagining the Global: Transnational
    Media and Popular Culture beyond East and West*. Ann Arbor:
    University of Michigan Press.

Darrach, Halley, Lisa E. Ishii, David Liao, Jason C. Nellis, Kristin Bater,
    Roxana Cobo, Patrick J. Byrne, Kofi D. O. Boahene, Ira D. Papel,
    Theda C. Kontis, and Masaru Ishii. 2019. "Assessment of the Influence
    of 'Other-Race Effect' on Visual Attention and Perception of Attrac-
    tiveness before and after Rhinoplasty." *JAMA Facial Plastic Surgery*
    21 (2):96-102. DOI: 10.1001/jamafacial.2018.1697.

Davila, Arlene. 2001. *Latinos, Inc.: The Marketing and Making of a
    People*. Berkeley: University of California Press.

Davis, Kathy. 1995. *Reshaping the Female Body: The Dilemma of Cos-
    metic Surgery*. New York: Routledge.

———. 1998. "Pygmalions in Plastic Surgery." *Health* 2 (1):23-40.

———. 2003. "Surgical Passing: Or Why Michael Jackson's Nose Makes
    'Us' Uneasy." *Feminist Theory* 4 (1):73-92.

de Boer, Mintsje, Flora E. van Leeuwen, Michael Hauptmann, Lucy I. H.
    Overbeek, Jan Paul de Boer, Nathalie J. Hijmering, Arthur Sernee,
    Caroline A. H. Klazen, Marc B. I. Lobbes, Rene R. W. J. van der Hulst,
    Hinne A. Rakhorst, and Daphne de Jong. 2018. "Breast Implants and
    the Risk of Anaplastic Large-Cell Lymphoma in the Breast." *JAMA
    Oncology* 4 (3):335-41. DOI: 10.1001/jamaoncol.2017.4510.

Delinsky, Sherrie Selwyn. 2005. "Cosmetic Surgery: A Common and
    Accepted Form of Self-Improvement?" *Journal of Applied Psychology*
    35 (10):2012-28.

DiMoia, John. 2013. *Reconstructing Bodies: Biomedicine, Health, and
    Nation-Building in South Korea since 1945*. Stanford, CA: Stanford
    University Press.

Dolnick, Sam. 2011. "Plastic Surgeons in City's Enclaves See
    Beauty Trends Emerge by Culture." *New York Times*, 19 February,
    A17.

Duffy, Brooke Erin. 2017. *(Not) Getting Paid to Do What You Love:
    Gender, Social Media, and Aspirational Work*. New Haven, CT: Yale
    University Press.

Dull, Diana, and Candace West. 1991. "Accounting for Cosmetic Surgery: The Accomplishment of Gender." *Social Problems* 38 (1):54–70.

Dumit, Joseph. 2004. *Picturing Personhood: Brain Scans and Biomedical Identity*. Princeton, NJ: Princeton University Press.

Duster, Troy. 2015. "A Post-Genomic Surprise: The Molecular Reinscription of Race in Science, Law and Medicine." *British Journal of Sociology* 66 (1):1–27.

Dworkin, Shari, and Faye Linda Wachs. 2009. *Body Panic: Gender, Health and the Selling of Fitness*. New York: New York University Press.

Edmonds, Alexander. 2010. *Pretty Modern: Beauty, Sex and Plastic Surgery in Brazil*. Durham, NC: Duke University Press.

Epstein, Steven G. 2007. *Inclusion: The Politics of Difference in Medical Research*. Chicago: University of Chicago Press.

———. 2022. *The Quest for Sexual Health: How an Elusive Ideal Has Transformed Science, Politics, and Everyday Life*. Chicago: University of Chicago Press.

Epstein, Steven, and Stefan Timmermans. 2021. "From Medicine to Health: The Proliferation and Diversification of Cultural Authority." *Journal of Health and Social Behavior* 62 (3):240–54.

Essén, Anna, and Michael Sauder. 2017. "The Evolution of Weak Standards: The Case of the Swedish Rheumatology Quality Registry." *Sociology of Health and Illness* 39 (4):513–31.

Etcoff, Nancy. 2000. *Survival of the Prettiest: The Science of Beauty*. New York: Anchor.

Eyal, Gil. 2013. "For a Sociology of Expertise: The Social Origins of the Autism Epidemic." *American Journal of Sociology* 118 (4): 863–907.

Fabian, Ann. 2010. *The Skull Collectors: Race, Science, and America's Unburied Dead*. Chicago: University of Chicago Press.

Fausto-Sterling, Anne. 2000. *Sexing the Body: Gender Politics and the Construction of Sexuality*. New York: Basic Books.

———. 2008. "The Bare Bones of Race." *Social Studies of Science* 38 (5):657–94.

Fischer, Johan. 2016. "Manufacturing Halal in Malaysia." *Contemporary Islam* 10:35–52.

Fleck, Ludwik. 1981 [1935]. *Genesis and Development of a Scientific Fact*. Chicago: University of Chicago Press.

Foucault, Michel. 1980. *The History of Sexuality, Vol. 1, An Introduction*. New York: Vintage.

Freidson, Eliot. 1970. *Profession of Medicine: A Study of the Sociology of Applied Knowledge*. New York: Dodd, Mead & Co.

Fujimura, Joan, and Ramya Rajagopalan. 2011. "Different Differences: The Use of 'Genetic Ancestry' versus Race in Biomedical Human Genetic Research." *Social Studies of Science* 41 (1):5–30.

Fullwiley, Duana. 2008. "The Biologistical Construction of Race: 'Admixture' Technology and the New Genetic Medicine." *Social Studies of Science* 38 (5):695–735.

Gaines, James R. 1993. "Time Magazine Cover: The New Face of America—Nov. 18, 1993." *Time*. http://content.time.com/time/covers/0,16641,19931118,00.html.

Galdino, Gregory, Dennis DaSilva, and Jack P. Gunter. 2002. "Digital Photography for Rhinoplasty." *Plastic and Reconstructive Surgery* 109 (4):1421–34.

Geltzer, Anna. 2009. "When the Standards Aren't Standard: Evidence-Based Medicine in the Russian Context." *Social Science and Medicine* 68:526–32.

Gilman, Sander. 2000. *Making the Body Beautiful: A Cultural History of Aesthetic Surgery*. Princeton, NJ: Princeton University Press.

Gimlin, Debra. 2002. *Body Work: Beauty and Self-Image in American Culture*. Berkeley: University of California Press.

———. 2013. "'Too Good to Be Real': The Obviously Augmented Breast in Women's Narratives of Cosmetic Surgery." *Gender and Society* 27:913–34.

———. 2014. "Exploring the Glocal Flow of Beauty." In *European Glocalization in Global Context*, edited by R. Robertson, 147–70. New York: Palgrave Macmillan.

Glenn, Evelyn Nakano. 2008. "Yearning for Lightness: Transnational Circuits in the Marketing and Consumption of Skin Lighteners." *Gender and Society* 22 (3):281–302.

Goh, David. 2008. "From Colonial Pluralism to Postcolonial Multiculturalism: Race, State Formation and the Question of Cultural Diversity in Malaysia and Singapore." *Sociology Compass* 2 (1):232–62.

Golan, Tal. 1998. "The Authority of Shadows: The Legal Embrace of the X-Ray." *Historical Reflections* 24 (3):437–58.

Goodwin, Charles. 1994. "Professional Vision." *American Anthropologist* 96 (3):606–33.

Gould, Stephen Jay. 1996. *The Mismeasure of Man*. New York: W. W. Norton.

Gruber, Ronald, Anna Kuang, and David Kahn. 2004. "Asian-American Rhinoplasty." *Aesthetic Surgery Journal* 24:423–30.

Gulbas, Lauren E. 2012. "Embodying Racism: Race, Rhinoplasty, and Self-Esteem in Venezuela." *Qualitative Health Research* 23 (3):326–35.

Haiken, Elizabeth. 1997. *Venus Envy: A History of Cosmetic Surgery.* Baltimore: Johns Hopkins University Press.

Hamilton, Mark M., and Todd Hobgood. 2005. "Emerging Trends and Techniques in Male Aesthetic Surgery." *Facial Plastic Surgery* 21:325.

Haraway, Donna. 1990. *Simians, Cyborgs, and Women: The Reinvention of Nature.* New York: Routledge.

Hargittai, Eszter, and Walejko, Gina. 2008. "The Participation Divide: Content Creation and Sharing in the Digital Age." *Information, Communication and Society* 11 (2):239–56. DOI: 10.1080/13691180801946150.

Henderson, Carol E. 2014. "AKA: Sarah Baartman, The Hottentot Venus, and Black Women's Identity." *Women's Studies* 43 (7):946–59.

Heyes, Cressida J. 2009. "All Cosmetic Surgery Is 'Ethnic': Asian Eyelids, Feminist Indignation, and the Politics of Whiteness." In *Cosmetic Surgery: A Feminist Primer*, edited by C. J. Heyes and M. Jones, 191–208. Burlington, VT: Ashgate.

Hirschman, Charles. 1986. "The Making of Race in Colonial Malaya: Political Economy and Racial Ideology." *Sociological Forum* 1 (2):330–61.

Hoang, Kimberly. 2014. "Competing Technologies of Embodiment: Pan-Asian Modernity and Third World Dependency in Vietnam's Contemporary Sex Industry." *Gender and Society* 28 (4):513–36.

———. 2015. *Dealing in Desire: Asian Ascendancy, Western Decline, and the Hidden Currencies of Global Sex Work.* Oakland: University of California Press.

Hobbs, Allyson. 2014. *A Chosen Exile: A History of Racial Passing in American Life.* Cambridge, MA: Harvard University Press.

Hobson, J. 2005. "The 'Batty' Politic: Towards an Aesthetic of the Black Female Body." *Hypatia* 18 (4): 87–105.

Hoffstaedter, Gerhard. 2011. *Modern Muslim Identities: Negotiating Religion and Ethnicity in Malaysia.* Copenhagen: NIAS Press.

Holliday, Ruth, David Bell, Olive Cheung, and Jihyun Cho. 2017. "Trading Faces: The 'Korean Look' and Medical Nationalism in South Korean Cosmetic Surgery Tourism." *Asia Pacific Viewpoint* 58 (2):190–202.

Holliday, Ruth, David Bell, Olive Cheung, Meredith Jones, and Elspeth Probyn. 2015. "Brief Encounters: Assembling Cosmetic Surgery Tourism." *Social Science and Medicine* 124:298–304.

Holliday, Ruth, and Joanna Elfving-Hwang. 2012. "Gender, Globalization and Aesthetic Surgery in South Korea." *Body and Society* 18:58.

Holliday, Ruth, Meredith Jones, and David Bell. 2019. *Beautyscapes: Mapping Cosmetic Surgery Tourism.* Manchester: Manchester University Press.

hooks, bell. 2015. "Selling Hot Pussy: Representations of Black Female Sexuality in the Cultural Marketplace." In bell hooks, *Black Looks: Race and Representation*, 2nd ed., 61–78. New York: Routledge.

Hunter, Margaret L. 2005. *Race, Gender, and the Politics of Skin Tone.* New York: Routledge.

Immerwahr, Daniel. 2019. *How to Hide an Empire: A History of the Greater United States.* New York: Farrar, Straus and Giroux.

IMCAS. 2014. "Value of Global Aesthetic Medical and Surgical Market from 2012 to 2018, by Region (in Billion Euros)" [Graph]. Statista. https://www-statista-com.yale.idm.oclc.org/statistics/319147/global-aesthetic-medical-and-surgery-market-value-by-region/. Accessed 9 March 2022.

International Society of Aesthetic Plastic Surgery. 2017. "ISAPS International Survey on Aesthetic/Cosmetic Procedures Performed in 2016." https://www.isaps.org/wp-content/uploads/2017/10/2016-ISAPS-Results-1.pdf. Accessed 19 October 2022.

———. 2018. "The International Study of Aesthetic/Cosmetic Procedures Performed in 2017." https://www.isaps.org/wp-content/uploads /2019/03/ISAPS_2017_International_Study_Cosmetic_Procedures_ NEW.pdf. Accessed 19 October 2022.

———. 2019. "ISAPS International Survey on Aesthetic/Cosmetic Procedures Performed in 2018." https://www.isaps.org/wp-content /uploads/2020/10/ISAPS-Global-Survey-Results-2018-1.pdf. Accessed 6 February 2021.

Inter-Society Gluteal Fat Grafting Task Force. 2018. "Gluteal Fat Grafting Advisory." https://www.plasticsurgery.org/for-medical-professionals /advocacy/key-issues/gluteal-fat-grafting-advisory. Accessed 18 June 2021.

Ishii, Clyde H. 2014. "Current Update in Asian Rhinoplasty." *Plastic and Reconstructive Surgery Global Open* 2 (4). https://doi.org/10.1097 /GOX.0000000000000081.

Jang, Yong Ju, and Sung Hee Kim. 2018. "Tip Grafting for the Asian Nose." *Facial Plastic Surgery Clinics of North America* 26 (3):343–56. DOI: 10.1016/j.fsc.2018.03.008.

Jarrín, Alvaro. 2017. *The Biopolitics of Beauty: Cosmetic Citizenship and Affective Capital in Brazil.* Oakland: University of California Press.

Jarvis, Rebecca, Claire Pedersen, Taylor Dunn, and Alexa Valiente. 2016. "This Miami Plastic Surgeon Uses Snapchat to Record His Surgeries Live in the Operating Room." *ABC News*, 29 April. https://abcnews. go.com/Technology/miami-plastic-surgeon-snapchat-record-surgeries-live-operating/story?id = 38745074. Accessed 25 May 2021.

Jena, Anupam B., Seth Seabury, Darius Lakdawalla, and Amitabh Chandra. 2011. "Malpractice Risk According to Physician Specialty." *New England Journal of Medicine* 365 (7):629–36. DOI: 10.1056 /NEJMsa1012370.

Jha, Meeta Rani. 2016. *The Global Beauty Industry: Colorism, Racism, and the National Body.* New York: Routledge.

Jones, Meredith. 2008. *Skintight: An Anatomy of Cosmetic Surgery.* London: Bloomsbury.

Jordan-Young, Rebecca. 2010. *Brain Storm: The Flaws in the Science of Sex Differences.* Cambridge, MA: Harvard University Press.

Kahn, Jonathan. 2013. *Race in a Bottle: The Story of BiDil and Racialized Medicine in a Post-Genomic Age.* New York: Columbia University Press.

Kane, Leslie. 2019. "Medscape Physician Compensation Report," 10 April. Medscape. https://www.medscape.com/slideshow/2019-compensation-overview-6011286#29. Accessed 29 January 2021.

Kang, Miliann. 2010. *The Managed Hand: Race, Gender, and the Body in Beauty Service Work.* Berkeley: University of California Press.

Kaw, Eugenia. 1993. "Medicalization of Racial Features: Asian American Women and Cosmetic Surgery." *Medical Anthropology Quarterly* 7:74–89.

Khoo, Boo-Chai. 1963. "Plastic Construction of the Superior Palpebral Fold," *Plastic and Reconstructive Surgery* 31 (1):73–78.

———. 1964. "Augmentation Rhinoplasty in the Orientals." *Plastic and Reconstructive Surgery* 34 (1):81–89.

———. 1966. "An Ancient Chinese Text on a Cleft Lip." *Plastic and Reconstructive Surgery* 38 (2):89–91.

———. 1969. "Some Aspects of Plastic (Cosmetic) Surgery in Orientals." *British Journal of Plastic Surgery* 22 (1):60–69.

Khoo, Gaik Cheng. 2014. "Introduction: Theorizing Different Forms of Belonging in a Cosmopolitan Malaysia." *Citizenship Studies* 18 (8):791–806.

Korver-Glenn, Elizabeth. 2021. *Race Brokers: Housing Markets and Segregation in 21st Century Urban America*. New York: Oxford University Press.

Kridel, Russell W. H., and Julian Rowe-Jones. 2010. "Ethnicity in Facial Plastic Surgery." *Facial Plastic Surgery* 26 (2):61–62. DOI: 10.1055/s-0030-1253495.

Kuipers, Giselinde. 2011. "Cultural Globalization as the Emergence of a Transnational Cultural Field: Transnational Television and National Media Landscapes in Four European Countries." *American Behavioral Scientist* 55 (5):541–57.

———. 2015. "Beauty and Distinction? The Evaluation of Appearance and Cultural Capital in Five European Countries." *Poetics* 54:38–51.

Kuipers, Giselinde, Yiu Fai Chow, and Elise van der Laan. 2014. "*Vogue* and the Possibility of Cosmopolitics: Race, Health and Cosmopolitan Engagement in the Global Beauty Industry." *Ethnic and Racial Studies* 37 (12):2158–75.

Kwan, Samantha, and Jennifer Graves. 2020. *Under the Knife: Cosmetic Surgery, Boundary Work, and the Pursuit of the Natural Fake*. Philadelphia: Temple University Press.

Lam, Samuel. 2005. "Aesthetic Facial Surgery for the Asian Male." *Facial Plastic Surgery* 29:317–23.

———. 2009. "Asian Rhinoplasty." *Seminars in Plastic Surgery* 23(3): 215–22. https://doi.org/10.1055/s-0029-1224801.

Lamont, Michelle, and Ann Swidler. 2014. "Methodological Pluralism and the Possibilities and Limits of Interviewing." *Qualitative Sociology* 37:153–71.

Latour, Bruno. 2007. *Reassembling the Social: An Introduction to Actor-Network-Theory*. Oxford: Oxford University Press.

Lee, Catherine. 2009. "'Race' and 'Ethnicity' in Biomedical Research: How Do Scientists Construct and Explain Differences in Health?" *Social Science and Medicine* 68:1183–90.

Lee, Jennifer, and Frank D. Bean. 2010. *The Diversity Paradox: Immigration and the Color Line in Twenty-First Century America*. New York: Russell Sage Foundation.

Lee, Myung Ju, and Hyung-Min Song. 2015. "Asian Rhinoplasty with Rib Cartilage." *Seminars in Plastic Surgery* 29 (4):262–68. DOI: 10.1055/s-0035-1564815.

Lee, Michael R., Jacob G. Unger, and Rod J. Rohrich. 2011. "Management of the Nasal Dorsum in Rhinoplasty: A Systematic Review of the Literature regarding Technique, Outcomes, and Complications." *Plastic and Reconstructive Surgery* 128 (5):538e–50e.

Lee, R. L. M. 2004. "The Transformation of Race Relations in Malaysia: From Ethnic Discourse to National Imagery, 1993–2003." *African and Asian Studies* 3 (2): 119–43.

Lee, Sharon Heijin. 2016. "Beauty between Empires: Global Feminism, Plastic Surgery, and the Trouble with Self-Esteem." *Frontiers: A Journal of Women Studies* 37 (1):12–31.

Leem, So Yeon. 2016a. "The Anxious Production of Beauty: Unruly Bodies, Surgical Anxiety and Invisible Care." *Social Studies of Science* 46 (1):34–55.

———. 2016b. "The Dubious Enhancement: Making South Korea a Plastic Surgery Nation." *East Asian Science, Technology and Society* 10 (1):51–71.

Lenehan, Sara. 2011. "Nose Aesthetics: Rhinoplasty and Identity in Tehran." *Anthropology of the Middle East* 6 (1):47–62.

Leong, S. C., and Ronald Eccles. 2010. "Race and Ethnicity in Nasal Plastic Surgery: A Need for Science." *Facial Plastic Surgery* 26 (2):63–68. https://doi.org/10.1055/s-0030-1253505.

Lewis, Reina. 2013. *Modest Fashion: Styling Bodies, Mediating Faith*. London: I. B. Tauris.

Li, Zhangqiang, Jacob G. Unger, Jason Roostaeian, Fadi Constantine, and Rod J. Rohrich. 2014. "Individualized Asian Rhinoplasty: A Systematic Approach to Facial Balance." *Plastic and Reconstructive Surgery* 134 (1):24e–32e.

Lipsitz, George. 2006. *The Possessive Investment in Whiteness: How White People Profit from Identity Politics*. Philadelphia: Temple University Press.

Liu, Jennifer A. 2010. "Making Taiwanese (Stem Cells): Identity, Genetics, and Hybridity." In *Asian Biotech: Ethics and Communities of Fate*, edited by Aihwa Ong and Nancy N. Chen, 239–62. Durham, NC: Duke University Press.

Lohuis, Peter J. F. M., and Frank R. Datema. 2015. "Patient Satisfaction in Caucasian and Mediterranean Open Rhinoplasty Using the Tongue-in-Groove Technique: Prospective Statistical Analysis of Change in Subjective Body Image in Relation to Nasal Appearance following Aesthetic Rhinoplasty." *Laryngoscope* 125 (4):831–36.

Loveman, Mara, and Jeronimo O. Muniz. 2007. "How Puerto Rico Became White: Boundary Dynamics and Intercensus Racial Reclassification," *American Sociological Review* 72:915–39.

Lunt, Neil, R. Smith, M. Exworthy, S. T. Green, D. Horsfall, and R. Mannion. 2011. "Medical Tourism: Treatments, Markets, and Health System Implications: A Scoping Review." Paris: OECD Directorate for Employment, Labour and Social Affairs.

Lynch, Michael, and Steve Woolgar. 2014. "Introduction: Representations in Scientific Practice Revisited." In *Representation in Scientific Practice Revisited*, edited by Catelijne Coopmans, Janet Vertesi, Michael Lynch, and Steve Woolgar, vii–ix. Cambridge, MA: MIT Press.

MacGregor, Frances. 1967. "Social and Cultural Components in the Motivations of Persons Seeking Plastic Surgery of the Nose." *Journal of Health and Social Behavior* 8:125–35.

Mandavilli, Apoorva. 2021. "Editor of JAMA Leaves after Outcry over Colleague's Remarks on Racism." *New York Times*. https://www.nytimes.com/2021/06/01/health/jama-bauchner-racism.html.

M'charek, Amade. 2013. "Beyond Fact or Fiction: On the Materiality of Race in Practice." *Cultural Anthropology* 28 (3):420–42. DOI: 10.1111/cuan.12012.

Mears, Ashley. 2010. "Size Zero High-End Ethnic: Cultural Production and the Reproduction of Culture in Fashion Modeling." *Poetics* 38:21–46.

———. 2011. *Pricing Beauty: The Making of a Fashion Model.* Berkeley: University of California Press.

———. 2020. *Very Important People: Status and Beauty in the Global Party Circuit.* Princeton, NJ: Princeton University Press.

Mehta, Nikhil, and Rakesh K. Srivastava. 2017. "The Indian Nose: An Anthropometric Analysis." *Journal of Plastic, Reconstructive and Aesthetic Surgery* 70 (10):1472–82. https://doi.org/10.1016/j.bjps.2017.05.042.

Menon, Alka V. 2017a. "Do Online Reviews Diminish Physician Authority? The Case of Cosmetic Surgery in the U.S." *Social Science and Medicine* 181:1–8. DOI: 10.1016/j.socscimed.2017.03.046.

———. 2017b. "Reconstructing Race in American Cosmetic Surgery." *Ethnic and Racial Studies* 40:597–616.

———. 2019. "Cultural Gatekeeping in Cosmetic Surgery: Transnational Beauty Ideals in Multicultural Malaysia." *Poetics* 75:1–11.

Millard, J. R. 1955. "Oriental Peregrinations." *Plastic and Reconstructive Surgery* 16 (5):319–36.

Miller, Laura. 2006. *Beauty up: Exploring Contemporary Japanese Body Aesthetics*. Berkeley: University of California Press.

Milner, Anthony. 2008. *The Malays*. Malden, MA: Wiley-Blackwell.

Misra, Joya, and Kyla Walters. 2022. *Walking Mannequins: How Race and Gender Inequalities Shape Retail Clothing Work*. Oakland: University of California Press.

Mittelman, Melissa. 2015. "Sientra Breast Implants Stuck in Limbo after Supplier's Setbacks." *Bloomberg*, 16 October. https://www.bloomberg.com/news/articles/2015-10-16/sientra-breast-implants-stuck-in-limbo-after-supplier-s-setbacks.

Mol, Annemarie. 2002. *The Body Multiple: Ontology in Medical Practice*. Durham, NC: Duke University Press.

Molina-Guzman, Isabel. 2010. *Dangerous Curves: Latina Bodies in the Media*. New York: New York University Press.

Monk, E. P. Jr., 2015. "The Cost of Color: Skin Color, Discrimination, and Health among African-Americans." *American Journal of Sociology*, 121 (2):396–444.

Montoya, Michael. 2011. *Making the Mexican Diabetic: Race, Science and the Genetics of Inequality*. Berkeley: University of California Press.

Mora, G. Christina. 2014. *Making Hispanics: How Activists, Bureaucrats, and Media Constructed a New American*. Chicago: University of Chicago Press.

Morgan, Kathryn Pauly. 1991. "Women and the Knife: Cosmetic Surgery and the Colonization of Women's Bodies." *Hypatia* 6:25–53.

Morning, Ann. 2011. *The Nature of Race: How Scientists Think and Teach about Human Difference*. Berkeley: University of California Press.

Nagarkar, Purushottam, Ronnie A. Pezeshk, and Rod J. Rohrich. 2016. "The Indian Nose." *Plastic and Reconstructive Surgery* 138 (5):836e–43e. https://doi.org/10.1097/PRS.0000000000002687.

Nelson, Alondra. 2008. "Bio Science: Genetic Genealogy Testing and the Pursuit of African Ancestry." *Social Studies of Science* 38 (5): 759–83.

Niechajev, Igor. 2016. "Noses of the Middle East: Variety of Phenotypes and Surgical Approaches." *Journal of Craniofacial Surgery* 27 (7):1700. DOI: 10.1097/SCS.0000000000002927.

Niechajev, Igor, and Per-Olle Haraldsson. 1997. "Ethnic Profile of Patients Undergoing Aesthetic Rhinoplasty in Stockholm." *Aesthetic Plastic Surgery* 21 (3):139–45. https://doi.org/10.1007/s002669900099.

Norris, Michele L. 2013. "Visualizing Race, Identity, and Change." *National Geographic*, 4 May 2021. https://www.nationalgeographic .com/photography/article/visualizing-change.

Office of Chief Statistician Malaysia, Department of Statistics Malaysia. 2016. "Current Population Estimates, 2014–2016." https://www.dosm .gov.my/v1/index.php?r=column/ctheme&menu_id=L0pheU43NWJw RWVSZklWdzQ4TlhUUT09&bul_id=OWlxdEVoYlJCSOhUZzJyRUcv ZEYxZz09. Accessed 14 July 2020.

Ofodile, Ferdinand, Farhat J. Bokhari, and Charlotte Ellis. 1993. "The Black American Nose." *Annals of Plastic Surgery* 31 (3): 209–19.

Omi, Michael, and Howard Winant. 1994. *Racial Formation in the United States: From the 1960s to the 1990s.* New York: Routledge.

———. 2014. *Racial Formation in the United States.* 3rd ed. New York: Routledge. https://doi.org/10.4324/9780203076804.

Ong, Aihwa. 1999. *Flexible Citizenship: The Cultural Logics of Transnationality.* Durham, NC: Duke University Press.

———. 2016. *Fungible Life: Experiment in the Asian City of Life.* Durham, NC: Duke University Press.

Ong, Aihwa, and Nancy N. Chen, eds. 2013. *Asian Biotech: Ethics and Communities of Fate.* Durham, NC: Duke University Press.

Okamoto, Dina, and G. C. Mora. 2014. "Panethnicity." *Annual Review of Sociology* 40:219–39.

Ormond, Meghann. 2013. *Neoliberal Governance and International Medical Travel in Malaysia.* London: Routledge.

Ormond, Meghann, Wong Kee Mun, and Chan Chee Khoon. 2014. "Medical Tourism in Malaysia: How Can We Better Identify and Manage Its Advantages and Disadvantages?" *Global Health Action* 7 (1):2.

Osagie, Obasogie. 2014. *Blinded by Sight: Seeing Race through the Eyes of the Blind.* Stanford, CA: Stanford University Press.

Panofsky, Aaron, and Catherine Bliss. 2017. "Ambiguity and Scientific Authority: Population Classification in Genomic Science." *American Sociological Review* 82 (1):59–87.

Papanicolas, Irene, Liana R. Woskie, and Ashish K. Jha. 2018. "Health Care Spending in the United States and Other High-Income Countries." *JAMA* 319 (10):1024–39.

Parthasarathy, Shobita. 2007. *Building Genetic Medicine: Breast Cancer, Technology, and the Comparative Politics of Health Care.* Cambridge, MA: MIT Press.

Patel, Sejal M., and Rollin K. Daniel. 2012. "Indian American Rhino-
    plasty: An Emerging Ethnic Group." *Plastic and Reconstructive
    Surgery* 129:519e–27e.
Patel, Anand D., and Russell W. H. Kridel. 2010a. "African-American
    Rhinoplasty." *Facial Plastic Surgery* 26 (2):131–41. https://doi.
    org/10.1055/s-0030-1253499.
———. 2010b. "Hispanic-American Rhinoplasty." *Facial Plastic Surgery*
    26:142–53.
Pearl, Sharrona. 2010. *About Faces: Physiognomy in Nineteenth-Century
    Britain*. Cambridge, MA: Harvard University Press.
———. 2017. *Face/On: Face Transplants and the Ethics of the Other*.
    Chicago: University of Chicago Press.
Peiss, Kathy. 1998. *Hope in a Jar*. Philadelphia: University of Pennsylva-
    nia Press.
Pitts-Taylor, Victoria. 2007. *Surgery Junkies: Wellness and Pathology in
    Cosmetic Culture*. New Brunswick, NJ: Rutgers University Press.
Plemons, Eric. 2017. *The Look of a Woman: Facial Feminization
    Surgery and the Aims of Trans-Medicine*. Durham, NC: Duke
    University Press.
Pollock, Anne. 2012. *Medicating Race: Heart Disease and Durable Preoc-
    cupation with Difference*. Durham, NC: Duke University Press.
Pope, Catherine. 2002. "Contingency in Everyday Surgical Work." *Sociol-
    ogy of Health and Illness* 24 (4):369–84.
Porter, Jennifer Parker, and Janet I. Lee. 2002. "Facial Analysis: Main-
    taining Ethnic Balance." *Facial Plastic Surgery Clinics of North Amer-
    ica* 10 (4):343–49. https://doi.org/10.1016/S1064–7406(02)00030-5.
Porter, Jennifer Parker, and Krista L. Olson. 2001. "Anthropometric
    Facial Analysis of the African American Woman." *Archives of Facial
    Plastic Surgery* 3 (3):191–97.
———. 2003. "Analysis of the African American Female Nose." *Plas-
    tic and Reconstructive Surgery* 111 (2):620–26. DOI: 10.1097/01.
    PRS.0000042176.18118.99.
Rajanala, Susruthi, Mayra B. C. Maymone, and Neelam A. Vashi. 2018.
    "Selfies: Living in the Era of Filtered Photographs." *JAMA Facial
    Plastic Surgery* 20 (6):443–44.
Rana, Junaid. 2011. *Terrifying Muslims: Race and Labor in the South
    Asian Diaspora*. Durham, NC: Duke University Press.
Reardon, Jenny. 2004. *Race to the Finish: Identity and Governance in an
    Age of Genomics*. Princeton, NJ: Princeton University Press.

Richardson, Sarah S. 2013. *Sex Itself: The Search for Male and Female in the Human Genome*. Chicago: University of Chicago Press.

Richtel, Matt. 2020. "Don't Like What You See on Zoom? Get a Face-Lift and Join the Crowd." *New York Times*, 13 August. https://www.nytimes.com/2020/08/13/health/coronavirus-cosmetic-surgery.html.

Roberts, Dorothy. 2011. *Fatal Invention: How Science, Politics, and Big Business Re-Create Race in the Twenty-First Century*. New York: The New Press.

Rodríguez-Muñiz, Michael. 2021. *Figures of the Future: Latino Civil Rights and the Politics of Demographic Change*. Princeton, NJ: Princeton University Press.

Rohrich, Rod J., and Ashkan Ghavami. 2009. "Rhinoplasty for Middle Eastern Noses." *Plastic and Reconstructive Surgery* 123 (3):1343–54.

Rohrich, Rod J., and Arshad R. Muzaffar. 2003. "Rhinoplasty in the African-American Patient." *Plastic and Reconstructive Surgery* 111:1322–39.

Romo, Thomas III, and Manoj T. Abraham. 2003. "The Ethnic Nose." *Facial Plastic Surgery* 19 (3):269–77.

Rondilla, Joanne, and Paul Spickard. 2007. *Is Lighter Better? Skin-Tone Discrimination among Asian Americans*. Lanham, MD: Rowman & Littlefield.

Roth, Lorna. 2009. "Looking at Shirley, the Ultimate Norm: Colour Balance, Image Technologies, and Cognitive Equity." *Canadian Journal of Communication* 34 (1):111–36.

Roth, Wendy D. 2016. "The Multiple Dimensions of Race." *Ethnic and Racial Studies* 39(8): 1310–38.

Rowe-Jones, Julian, and Frederik Carl van Wyk. 2010. "Special Considerations in Northern European Primary Aesthetic Rhinoplasty." *Facial Plastic Surgery* 26 (2):75–85. DOI: 10.1055/s-0030-1253506.

Salas-Rodriguez, Israel, and Tanyel Mustafa. 2020. "Mama West: Who Was Kanye West's Mom Donda and How Did She Die?" https://www.thesun.co.uk/news/12177537/kanye-west-donda-mom-death/. Accessed 21 May 2021.

Sarmiento, Samuel, Charles Wen, Michael A. Cheah, Stacey Lee, and Gedge D. Rosson. 2020. "Malpractice Litigation in Plastic Surgery: Can We Identify Patterns?" *Aesthetic Surgery Journal* 40 (6):NP394–401. DOI: 10.1093/asj/sjz258.

Schwartz, Joseph S., Meredith Young, Ana M. Velly, and Lily H. P. Nguyen. 2013. "The Evolution of Racial, Ethnic, and Gender Diversity in US Otolaryngology Residency Programs." *Otolaryngology—Head and Neck Surgery* 149 (1):71–76.

Schweik, Susan M. 2010. *The Ugly Laws: Disability in Public*. New York: New York University Press.

Scott, Joan. 1986. "Gender: A Useful Category of Historical Analysis." *American Historical Review* 91 (5):1053–75.

Serlin, David. 2004. *Replaceable You: Engineering the Body in Postwar America*. Chicago: University of Chicago Press.

Sexton, Jared. 2008. *Amalgamation Schemes: Antiblackness and the Critique of Multiracialism*. Minneapolis: University of Minnesota Press.

Shamsul, A. B. 2001. "A History of an Identity, an Identity of a History: The Idea and Practice of 'Malayness' in Malaysia Reconsidered." *Journal of Southeast Asian Studies* 32 (3):355–66.

Shankar, Shalini. 2015. *Advertising Diversity: Ad Agencies and the Creation of Asian American Consumers*. Durham, NC: Duke University Press.

——. 2020. "Nothing Sells Like Whiteness: Race, Ontology, and American Advertising." *American Anthropologist* 122 (1):112–19. DOI: 10.1111/aman.13354.

Shaw, Susan J., and Julie Armin. 2011. "The Ethical Self-Fashioning of Physicians and Health Care Systems in Culturally Appropriate Health Care." *Cultural Medical Psychiatry* 35:236–61.

Shea, Molly. 2019. "The Shocking Rise of Dangerous and Illegal Black-Market Butt Lifts." *New York Post*, 26 February. https://nypost.com /2019/02/16/the-shocking-rise-of-dangerous-and-illegal-black-market-butt-lifts/. Accessed 25 May 2021.

Shuster, Stef. 2016. "Uncertain Expertise and the Limitations of Clinical Guidelines in Transgender Healthcare." *Journal of Health and Social Behavior* 57 (3):319–32.

——. 2021. *Trans Medicine: The Emergence and Practice of Treating Gender*. New York: New York University Press.

Silvestre, Jason, Joseph M. Serletti, and Benjamin Chang. 2016. "Racial and Ethnic Diversity of U.S. Plastic Surgery Trainees." *Journal of Surgical Education* 74:117–23.

Smart, Andrew, Richard Tutton, Paul Martin, George T. H. Ellison, and Richard Ashcroft. 2008. "The Standardization of Race and Ethnicity in Biomedical Science Editorials and UK Biobanks." *Social Studies of Science* 38 (3):407–23.

Star, Susan Leigh, and James R. Griesemer. 1989. "Institutional Ecology, 'Translations' and Boundary Objects: Amateurs and Professionals in

Berkeley's Museum of Vertebrate Zoology, 1907–39." *Social Studies of Science* 19 (3):387–420.

Stevens, Wesley E. 2021. "Blackfishing on Instagram: Influencing and the Commodification of Black Urban Aesthetics." *Social Media + Society* 7 (3). https://doi.org/10.1177/20563051211038.

Stocking, George. 1990. *Bones, Bodies, Behavior: Essays on Biological Anthropology.* Madison: University of Wisconsin Press.

Strings, Sabrina. 2019. *Fearing the Black Body: The Racial Origins of Fat Phobia.* New York: New York University.

Stuart, Forrest. 2020. *Ballad of the Bullet: Gangs, Drill Music and the Power of Online Infamy.* Princeton, NJ: Princeton University Press.

Sullivan, Deborah. 2001. *Cosmetic Surgery: The Cutting Edge of Commercial Medicine in America.* New Brunswick, NJ: Rutgers University Press.

Sun, Shirley. 2016. *Socio-economics of Personalized Medicine in Asia.* New York: Routledge.

Sunder Rajan, Karthik. 2006. *Biocapital: The Constitution of Post-Genomic Life.* Durham, NC: Duke University Press.

Swami, Viren, and Martin J. Tovee. 2005. "Female Physical Attractiveness in Britain and Malaysia: A Cross-Cultural Study." *Body Image* 2 (20):115–28.

Tait, Sue. 2007. "Television and the Domestication of Cosmetic Surgery." *Feminist Media Studies* 7 (2):119–35.

TallBear, Kim. 2013. *Native American DNA: Tribal Belonging and the False Promise of Genetic Science.* Minneapolis: University of Minnesota Press.

Talley, Heather Laine. 2014. *Saving Face: Disfigurement and the Politics of Appearance.* New York: New York University Press.

Tapper, Melbourne. 1999. *In the Blood: Sickle Cell Anemia and the Politics of Race.* Philadelphia: University of Pennsylvania Press.

Tardy, M. Eugene, and Robert Brown. 1992. *Principles of Photography in Facial Plastic Surgery.* New York: Thieme.

Tate, Shirley. 2007. "Black Beauty: Shade, Hair and Anti-racist Aesthetics." *Ethnic and Racial Studies* 30 (2):300–19.

———. 2015. *Black Women's Bodies and the Nation: Race, Gender and Culture.* New York: Palgrave Macmillan.

Taussig, Michael. 2012. *Beauty and the Beast.* Chicago: University of Chicago Press.

Thompson, Charis. 2006. "Race Science." *Theory, Culture and Society* 23 (2–3):547–49.

Timmermans, Stefan, and Rene Almeling. 2009. "Objectification, Standardization, and Commodification in Health Care: A Conceptual Readjustment." *Social Science and Medicine* 69:21–27.

Timmermans, Stefan, and Alison Angell. 2001. "Evidence-Based Medicine, Clinical Uncertainty, and Learning to Doctor." *Journal of Health and Social Behavior* 42 (4):342–59. https://doi.org/10.2307/3090183.

Timmermans, Stefan, and Marc Berg. 1997. "Standardization in Action: Achieving Local Universality through Medical Protocols." *Social Studies of Science* 27:273–305.

———. 2003. *The Gold Standard: The Challenge of Evidence-Based Medicine*. Philadelphia: Temple University Press.

Timmermans, Stefan, and Steven Epstein. 2010. "A World of Standards but not a Standard World: Toward a Sociology of Standards and Standardization." *Annual Review of Sociology* 36:69–89.

Tolentino, Jia. 2019. "The Age of Instagram Face." *New Yorker*, 12 December. https://www.newyorker.com/culture/decade-in-review/the-age-of-instagram-face. Accessed 1 January 2021.

Tomes, Nancy. 2016. *Remaking the American Patient: How Madison Avenue and Modern Medicine Turned Patients into Consumers*. Chapel Hill: University of North Carolina Press.

Treichler, Paula A., Lisa Cartwright, and Constance Penley. 1998. "Introduction: Paradoxes of Visibility." In *The Visible Woman: Imaging Technologies, Gender, and Science*, edited by Paula A. Treichler, Lisa Cartwright, and Constance Penley, 1–20. New York: New York University Press.

U.S. Food and Drug Administration. 2011. "FDA Update on the Safety of Silicone Gel-Filled Breast Implants." Center for Devices and Radiological Health, U.S. Food and Drug Administration. https://www.fda.gov/media/80685/download.

———. 2019. "FDA Safety Communication: The FDA Requests Allergan Voluntarily Recall Natrelle BIOCELL Textured Breast Implants and Tissue Expanders from the Market to Protect Patients: FDA Safety Communication." https://www.fda.gov/medical-devices/safety-communications/fda-requests-allergan-voluntarily-recall-natrelle-biocell-textured-breast-implants-and-tissue.

Wacquant, Loic. 2006. *Body and Soul: Notebooks of an Apprentice Boxer*. New York: Oxford University Press.

Wade, Peter, Carlos López-Beltrán, Eduardo Restrepo, and Ricardo Ventura Santos. 2014. *Mestizo Genomics: Race Mixture, Nation, and Science in Latin America*. Durham, NC: Duke University Press.

Waldby, Cathy, and Robert Mitchell. 2006. *Tissue Economies: Blood, Organs, and Cell Lines in Late Capitalism*. Durham, NC: Duke University Press.

Wang, Tom D. 2003. "Non-Caucasian Rhinoplasty." *Facial Plastic Surgery* 19:247–56.

Wen, Hua. 2013. *Buying Beauty: Cosmetic Surgery in China*. Hong Kong: Hong Kong University Press.

Wilson, Ara. 2010. "Medical Tourism in Thailand." In *Asian Biotech: Ethics and Communities of Fate*, edited by Aihwa Ong and Nancy N. Chen, 118–43. Durham, NC: Duke University Press.

———. 2011. "Foreign Bodies and National Scales: Medical Tourism in Thailand." *Body and Society* 17 (2 and 3):121–37.

Wimalawansa, Sunishka, Aisha McKnight, and Jamal M. Bullocks. 2009. "Socioeconomic Impact of Ethnic Cosmetic Surgery: Trends and Potential Financial Impact the African American, Asian American, Latin American, and Middle Eastern Communities Have on Cosmetic Surgery." *Seminars in Plastic Surgery* 23:159–62.

World Tourism Organization and European Travel Commission. 2018. "Exploring Health Tourism." Madrid: UNWTO. https://www.e-unwto .org/doi/pdf/10.18111/9789284420209.

Yellin, Seth. 1997. "Aesthetics for the Next Millennium." *Facial Plastic Surgery* 13 (4):231–39.

Zane, Kathleen. 1998. "Reflections on a Yellow Eye: Asian I(Eye)Cons and Cosmetic Surgery." In *Talking Visions: Multicultural Feminism in a Transnational Age*, edited by Ella Shohat, 161–86. Cambridge, MA: MIT Press.

Zelken, Jonathan A., Chun-Shin Chang, Shiow-Shuh Chuang, Jui-Yung Yang, and Yen-Chang Hsiao. 2016. "An Economical Approach to Ethnic Asian Rhinoplasty." *Facial Plastic Surgery* 32:95–104.

Zelken, Jonathan A., Joon Pio Hong, Chun-Shin Chang, and Yen-Chang Hsaio. 2017. "Silicone-Polytetrafluoroethylene Composite Implants for Asian Rhinoplasty," *Annals of Plastic Surgery* 78 (2):131–37.

Index

clinical consultations, images used in
(continued)
photographs presented to support the
surgeon's vision, 169, 172, 177–79,
237nn14–15; camera equipment, inherent bias in representation of patients of
color, 179–80, 190; communication
with the patient via, vs. verbal communication, 165–66, 172, 174–75, 188, 199–
200; flash of the camera as diagnostic
tool, 166, 168, 169; mirror image vs.
photographic image, 168; narration by
the surgeon of what they see in the
images, 169, 172–73, 189; patient's negative reactions to their own image, 166,
168; patient's push-back on surgeon's
narrative, 169; photographs taken by
the patient (selfies), 236n174; photographs taken of the patient by the surgeon, 166, 168, 173–74, 236n10;
simulated changes with image-editing
software ("morphed" images), 168, 174–
76, 176n11, 189; simulated changes,
waiver indicating no implied guaran-
tees, 176; surgeon coaching patients on
their own image, 168–69, 171, 173–76,
177, 236n10; surgeon coaching the
patient's gaze on best outcome, 172; 3D
imaging technologies, 176, 189. See also
clinical judgment, and refusal to grant
patient requests
clinical judgment: aesthetic judgment as
selling point, 132; Asian cosmetic surgery results as dependent on clinical
experience, 73–74; brand marketing
and, 97; and the craft of medicine, 13,
97; definition of, 8; as foil for evidence-based standards, 8; natural
looks as dependent on, 95–96, 125–
26. See also clinical judgment, and
ambiguity in racial categories; clinical
judgment, and evaluation of patient
requests; clinical judgment, and
refusal to grant patient requests
clinical judgment, and ambiguity in racial
categories: overview, 12–13, 196, 200;
and Asian cosmetic surgery, definition
of "Asian," 25, 91; brand identities as
served by, 13, 91, 143, 145, 147, 159–

62; in consultations, 170–71, 196; conventional norms of appearance
generally adhered to, 28, 196; and
racialized looks (U.S. brand identities), 143, 145, 147, 162; standardization of the use of categories, 3, 192
clinical judgment, and evaluation of patient
requests: overview, 28, 97–98, 125–28;
ability to satisfy the expectations of
patients as factor in (psychosocial
meaning), 98, 104, 106–7, 175, 231n9;
aesthetic judgment and expertise in
racialized looks (U.S. brand identities),
132, 146, 234n19; aesthetics as factor in,
95–96, 98, 107, 113, 121, 175–76;
assessed for their conformity to racial,
gender, and class boundaries, 28,
53–54, 173, 176–77, 193, 198; celebrity
models, 182; commonsense ideas about
race as factor in, 97, 99; generally
agreed upon principles, 97, 231n4; as
moral judgment, 28, 98, 99, 107, 113,
121; the narratives of change as important in, 53–54, 98, 103–6, 114–15, 121,
124, 126–28, 176–77, 198; simulated
changes in digital images, 174–76;
standards as tailored to the body of each
patient, 12–13, 26, 97. See also clinical
consultations; clinical judgment, and
refusal to grant patient requests; ethnic
preservation norm; expertise; natural
looks as preferred ideal
clinical judgment, and refusal to grant
patient requests: as assertion of
authority and expertise, 28, 106; vs.
assumption that all requests are
granted, 28; brand identity not compatible, 129–30, 139–40, 175; "ethnic
enhancement" procedures and racialized stigma, 139–40; and fear of malpractice suits, 106–7, 231n9; and fear
of unhappy patients, 106–7; psychiatric problems of patient, 53, 104, 107;
screening for body dysmorphic disorder, 53, 182; screening for "surgery
junkies," 53; screening male patients'
motivations, as heightened, 53–54;
simulated changes ("morphed"
images) allowing graceful rejection,

174–75; wish pics, criticizing or disqualifying, 172–73, 182, 189
clinics: languages used in (English and code-switching into other languages), 150, 154–55, 216; methodology of observation in, 23–24, 213–14
clinic staff: code-switching by cosmetic surgeons with, 216; multiracial, and culturally sensitive care (Malaysian brand identity), 155–56
Cobo, Roxana, 39, 40–41
Colombia: cosmopolitan science as decentering the West, 66; and "Latin" as racial category presented at professional conferences, 88
colonialism: British, in Malaysia, 17–18, 148–49, 150, 154, 159, 221n81, 222n87, 234n22; medical tourism and friction due to history of, 159; the racial structure of the U.S. and, 18, 222n91
colorblindness norm (U.S.): definition of, 10; and "diversity" as watchword, 10–11; and racial references in U.S. brand identities, 131, 141, 160; seeing color despite norm of, 201, 202–3. See also racial justice activism
colorism, 122–23
complications (including death): buttocks augmentation and risk of, 139, 233n7; of celebrities, 184; in nonmedical settings, 139, 184, 233n7; obligation to discuss possible complications with prospective patients, 179. See also malpractice lawsuits
Confucius, 68
constructionist grounded theory, 214
consultations. See clinical consultations; clinical consultations, images used in
consumerism: and biomedicalization, cosmetic surgery as case of, 15–16; racial identity and appearance of the body in, 9–10, 11–12, 202–3. See also advertising; brand identity of cosmetic surgeons; media; popular culture and cosmetic surgery; social media
cosmetic dermatology, classification based on physical morphology in, 56
cosmetic surgeons: as amateur sociologists, 1–2, 191; defined for the purposes of this study, 240n9; demographics of, 19, 210–12, 222nn94–95, 240n10–12; expertise of, 2–3, 217–18n6; as "gurus of the face," 173; the many hats worn by, 191–92; salaries of (U.S.), 16; stereotypes of, 201–2; subspecialties vs. general practitioners, 19; surgical anxiety of, 81, 201. See also brand identity of cosmetic surgeons; clinical consultations; clinical judgment; craft of cosmetic surgery; gatekeeper role of cosmetic surgeons; racial identity of cosmetic surgeons; risk, differences in cosmetic surgeons' attitudes toward
cosmetic surgery: as a form of body work, 6–7; as body capital, 6–7, 219nn26,28; and the cyborg metaphor (Haraway), 11, 192, 220n54; defined as term, 2, 217n2; as elective and non-acute, 15; institutional oversight as weaker for, 15; as luxury service, 7; new looks created by, as focus of this book, 7; prices for, 21–22, 223nn105–106; statistics on procedures, 6, 19–20, 221–23nn96,98, 233n5; as stigmatized (viewed as morally fraught and ethically marginal), 9, 27, 181, 220n43. See also craft of cosmetic surgery; health insurance, and coverage of cosmetic surgery under some circumstances; natural looks as preferred ideal; plastic surgery; popular culture and cosmetic surgery; racial project(s)
cosmopolitan science, 66
craft of cosmetic surgery: as analytic category, 64, 200, 228n4; Asian cosmetic surgery as, 64, 73–74, 87, 90–92; Asian cosmetic surgery as, uniqueness of, 87–90; Asian/Western difference in implant preferences and, 78; clinical experience and, 73–74; clinical judgment as central to, 13, 97; defined as the negotiated outcomes of the art/science tension, 8; state interests and, 91–92. See also brand identity; clinical judgment; race-specific standards (in medical journal articles)

152–53; visa policies and, 21, 223n110. *See also* culturally sensitive care (Malaysian brand identity)

Malaysian patients: and culturally sensitive care (Malaysian brand identity), 150–51, 154–56, 160; deferring to cosmetic surgeons' preference for natural "Asian" beauty, 113–14; narratives of change in requests by, 114–15, 121, 124, 126–28. *See also* Malaysian Chinese patients

male patients: gender norms and rhinoplasties for men of color, 51–54; as percentage of rhinoplasties, 51, 226n68; psychological screening as prospective patients (SIMON criteria), 53–54

malpractice lawsuits: Asian system as relatively weak, 84; and choice of synthetic implants by U.S. surgeons, 84–85; fear of, and refusals by U.S. surgeons, 106–7, 231n9

MAPACS (Malaysian Association of Plastic, Aesthetic and Craniomaxillofacial Surgeons), membership of, 222n94

marketing. *See* advertising; brand identity of cosmetic surgeons

Mears, Ashley, 218n7

media: cosmetic surgeons appearing in, 181; cultural appropriation covered in, 233n10; on "Hiroshima Maidens" traveling to the U.S. for reparative surgeries, 228n14; information on cosmetic surgery in, 131, 233n3; on the mixed-race future, 231–32n12; pop culture and cosmetic surgery covered in, 1, 183–84; reality television, 7, 131, 142, 145, 181, 182, 183–84; and subconscious desire for whitening, 105. *See also* popular culture; social media

medical devices: direct-to-consumer advertising allowed by the U.S., 20, 131; FDA (U.S.) regulation of, 20–21, 81–82, 223n100, 230n36. *See also* implants

medical journals: Asian cosmetic surgery articles in, 67, 68, 69, 75, 87; before-and-after photos, standards for, 237n15; as expert discourse, 33; on the eyes as "ethnically sensitive," 164;

and the macro (global) dimension, 33; methodology of choice and content analysis of articles, 23, 36–37, 51, 208, 225n20, 226nn67–68, 239nn2–4; reputation of authors writing for, 33, 59, 224n9; special issues on race-specific themes, 32–33, 239n4; transnational audience of, 33; on visualization technology, 174; warning on color-balance bias inherent to camera equipment, 180. *See also* expertise; race-specific standards (in medical journal articles)

medical nationalism, 14, 65, 86

medical tourism: colonial history of Southeast Asia and, 159; healthcare affordability and access in developing countries as hampered by, 230n44; lack of state investment in, 89; for plastic surgery, the "Hiroshima Maidens" and, 228n14; state investment in, 16, 86; the U.S. as largest global market for, 21. *See also* medical tourism (cosmetic surgery)

medical tourism (cosmetic surgery): overview, 15; cultural gaps and friction in, 153, 157–59; estimates of economic value of, 85; and expansion of cosmetic surgery to U.S. communities of color, 42; and implicitly racialized place-name looks (U.S. brand identities), 142, 143, 145, 147, 233–34n13; intermediary organizations to bridge gaps of understanding in, 158; Korean package deals, 124; malpractice lawsuit systems and price differentials in, 84; racial category labels and legibility to patients in, 91; regional networks for, 85; socioeconomic status of patients as issue in, 158; state investment in, 16, 21, 68, 86; statistics for the U.S., 233–34n17; visa policies and, 21, 223n110. *See also* Malaysian medical tourism

medical travel agencies, 158

"Mediterranean" noses, 46

"mesorrhine" nose, 38

"mestizo" as racial category: cosmopolitan science as decentering the West, 66; diversity within categories, 49; origin story for, 39–40. *See also* "Latin"/"Hispanic," as racial category

looks used explicitly to construct U.S. brand identities, 134, *135*; and racialized looks used implicitly to construct U.S. brand identities, 142, 143, *144*, 145, 147; and skin lightening/bleaching, 122–23; and subconscious desire for whitening, 105; wish pics taken from, 167, 182, 189, 190; worst-case scenario cases, 182. *See also* consumerism; media; online discussion boards; public opinion; social media; stereotypes and stereotyping

professional judgment. *See* clinical judgment

professional medical conferences: overview, 25, 64–65, 195; Asian cosmetic surgery and, 64–65, 69–70, 75, 76–78, 87, 91, 229n31; before-and-after photos, lack of rigorousness of, 237n15; Black patients either excluded or presented as spectacle, 87–88, 230n51; Latin Americans recognized at, 88; methodology and, 23, 209–10, 239n5, 240nn7–8. *See also* Asian cosmetic surgery

professional societies: false or deceptive advertising prohibited by, 131, 233n2; membership requirements, 239n5; statistics on procedures and demographics of patients, 19–20, 222–23nn96,98, 233n5. *See also* professional medical conferences

professional vision, 164–65, 173, 236n3

prototypical whiteness, 180

psychological and psychiatric issues: racial transformation requests from patients viewed as evidence of, 104, 107; screening for body dysmorphic disorder, 53, 182; screening for, suggested for prospective patients, 53–54; screening for "surgery junkies," 53; view of mixed-race people as source of, 108–9

public opinion: cosmetic surgeons as driven primarily by financial motives, 15–16; cosmetic surgery as morally fraught, 9, 27, 220n43; increasing acceptance of cosmetic surgery, 7. *See also* popular culture and cosmetic surgery

Puerto Rico, 18

race: biomedicine's racist legacy of locating on the body, 9, 35, 37, 38, 57, 59, 220n47; essentialist perspective, 3, 218n8; malleability of, 4; as multidimensional, 4, 218n13; as naturalized on the body, while erasing the historical forces behind, 11–12; "pure" racial types, logic of, 39, 225n29; social constructivist perspective of social hierarchy and ranking by, 3–4, 199, 218n8; use of term by the author, 218n10. *See also* racial categories; racial identity; racial project(s)

race brokers. *See* gatekeeper role of cosmetic surgeons

race-specific standards (in medical journal articles): overview, 32–33, 200–201; alternate strategies proposed, for classification based in physical morphology vs. "race," 48–49, 54–56, 195; ambiguity and subjectivity in, 34, 35, 47, 57; as assertion of surgeons' authority over racial categorization, 57; balance between customization and, 3, 5, 12, 34, 56, 162, 196; and cultural stereotypes, 47, 49–51, 59; ethnic preservation goal and proliferation of distinct standards, 46–47; as niche specialty, 55, 56; racial categories as context dependent, 55; racial categories as limited in utility for surgeons, 48–49, 54–55; racial categories defined using both physical and cultural criteria, 47; surgical anxiety produced by, 201; as weapon of exclusion, 57; the white norm as underlying, 43–45, 46, 47–48, 57, 58. *See also* race-specific standards for noses (in medical journal articles)

race-specific standards for noses (in medical journal articles): overview, 25, 195–96; alternate strategies proposed, for classification based in physical morphology vs. "race," 48–49, 54–56, 195; ambiguity and subjectivity in, 34, 35, 47; anthropometry referenced in, 37, 220n47; the Asian nose as referent, 44–45; and assumptions about intersecting social identities, 36; and balance between customization and

(Haraway), 11, 192, 220n54; "ethnic enhancement" procedures as affirmation of historically marginalized, 136; of the patient, as not aligning with their physical features, 171; racial categories as recuperating valorized identities, 65. *See also* Black identity; Latina identity; racial identity of cosmetic surgeons; racial pride

racial identity of cosmetic surgeons: and culturally sensitive care (Malaysian brand identity), 149, 153, 154–55, 156, 160; demographics, 19, 211, 222n95, 240n11; and "ethnic" marketing in the U.S., 130–31; and explicitly racialized looks (U.S. brand identities), 133, 140; methodology and, 210–11, 212, 240n10; methodology of notation in the text, 231n2; and patient requests for ethnic preservation, 102; and racial category of patients, perception of, 55; and racial category origin stories, 40

racialized looks used explicitly (U.S. brand identities): overview, 26, 131; aesthetic judgment and expertise advertised for, 132; as affirmation of historically marginalized racial identities, 136; as artificial looks, 131, 137, 138, 141–42; the colorblindness norm and, 131, 141, 160; cultural appropriation not raised as issue in, 140, 187–88, 233n10, 238n33; "ethnic enhancement" marketing and procedures, 134–40, *135*, 197, 198, 233nn5,7,9–10; "ethnic" looks as marketing tool, 132–34, 160; and gender conformity, 142; patient requests for, 136–37; patient requests for, refusals by surgeons, 139–40; patients as "walking billboards" for, 129–30, 138; popular culture and, 134, *135*; racial or ethnic identification of the surgeon and, 133, 140, 160; stereotypes in, reinforcing the otherness of Black and Latina women, 131, 137–38, 139–40, 141, 233n9; white norms of beauty as challenged by, 141; white patients and, 137–38, 139, 140; white patients, and worry of tainting the brand for, 139–41, 147–48, 160, 161. *See also* racialized looks used

implicitly as place-based names of looks (U.S. brand identities)

racialized looks used implicitly as place-based names of looks (U.S. brand identities): overview, 131, 142; aesthetic judgment and expertise advertised for, 146, 234n19; as artificial looks, 142–143, 145, 146; the colorblindness norm and, 131, 141, 160; cultural associations as differing for various looks, 143, 145–147; inventiveness of surgeons and, 161; medical tourism and, 142, 143, 145, 147, 233–234n13; as niche strategy, 147–148; popular culture and, 142, 143, *144*, 145, 147; and race as invoked or elided as value dictates, 147, 162; racialized connotations as ambiguous, 143, 145, 147, 162; socioeconomic status and, 146–147; white femininity, regional identities as standing in for specific versions of, 145–146. *See also* racialized looks used explicitly (U.S. brand identities)

racial justice activism: biomedical assertion of authority over race as mobilized in support of, 57; biomedical institutions in the U.S. as engaging with, 205–6; cosmetic surgeons adjusting behavior in response to, 28

racially sensitive products and services. *See* Asian cosmetic surgery; culturally sensitive care (Malaysian brand identity); ethnic cosmetic surgery

racial pride: and cosmetic surgeons' role as racial gatekeepers, 128; "ethnic enhancement" procedures and (U.S.), 134, 136; and reenvisioning of beauty ideals, 10. *See also* Black identity; Latina identity; racial identity

racial project(s): cosmetic surgery as, 7, 159–60; definition of, 3–4, 218n11; as multiscalar (macro, meso, and micro), 4, 218n14; the slenderness beauty ideal as, 7; and space, methodology for analyzing across, 194; as typically documented within a single society, 193. *See also* methodology; racial categories; racial project, cosmetic surgery as transnational and multiscalar (macro, meso, and micro)

Founded in 1893,
UNIVERSITY OF CALIFORNIA PRESS
publishes bold, progressive books and journals
on topics in the arts, humanities, social sciences,
and natural sciences—with a focus on social
justice issues—that inspire thought and action
among readers worldwide.

The UC PRESS FOUNDATION
raises funds to uphold the press's vital role
as an independent, nonprofit publisher, and
receives philanthropic support from a wide
range of individuals and institutions—and from
committed readers like you. To learn more, visit
ucpress.edu/supportus.